Digital Platforms
and the Press

Digital Platforms and the Press

James Meese

Bristol, UK / Chicago, USA

First published in the UK in 2023 by
Intellect, The Mill, Parnall Road, Fishponds, Bristol, BS16 3JG, UK

First published in the USA in 2023 by
Intellect, The University of Chicago Press, 1427 E. 60th Street,
Chicago, IL 60637, USA

The publication of this book was made possible through the generous
support of the Australian Research Council, through a Discovery
Early Career Researcher Award (DE190100458).

A catalogue record for this book is available from
the British Library.

Copy editor: MPS Limited
Cover designer: Holly Rose
Production manager: Sophia Munyengeterwa
Typesetter: MPS Limited

Hardback ISBN 978-1-78938-833-6
Paerback ISBN 978-1-78938-879-4
ePDF ISBN 978-1-78938-834-3
ePUB ISBN 978-1-78938-835-0

To find out about all our publications, please visit our website.
There you can subscribe to our e-newsletter, browse or download our current
catalogue and buy any titles that are in print.

www.intellectbooks.com

This is a peer-reviewed publication.

Contents

Figures

Table

Acknowledgements

Every researcher incurs significant debts as they conduct their work, and I am no different. I am grateful to the Australian Research Council for the provision of a Discovery Early Career Researcher Award (2019–21). The fellowship gave me time to collect data and develop the arguments that ultimately found their way into this book.

I am particularly thankful to three incredibly capable early-career researchers who provided valuable research assistance and advice over the life of this project: Edward Hurcombe, Kate Mannell, and Cheyne Anderson. I also want to acknowledge Mike Riethmuller who prototyped some early data collection efforts.

I am grateful to everyone from the news media and technology industries who were willing to speak to me on and off the record at a challenging time for both sectors.

I started to plan the book as the world came to grips with a global pandemic, which meant that much of this initial structuring work was done in lockdown. Thankfully, regular discussions with Amanda Moon, from Moon & Company, kept me on track. Her valuable advice helped me frame the overall project and kept the book going while I was trapped in my house.

The argument emerged gradually, and I was able to draw on the advice and expertise of generous friends and colleagues as I started to write. Thanks to Jean Burgess, Andrea Carson, Suneel Jethani, Sam Kininmonth, Tama Leaver, Ramon Lobato, Merja Myllylahti, Theresa Seipp, and Emily van der Nagel. I especially want to thank Jenny Kennedy and Rowan Wilken for regular encouragement, Elizabeth Humphrys for the Shut Up and Write sessions, and Julian Thomas for his support and guidance.

I was also lucky enough to work with several wonderful scholars on related articles, edited collections, conference papers, panels, and submissions. This work and the adjacent conversations (and disagreements) all influenced how I approached the book. Thanks to Daniel Angus, Francesco Bailo, Belinda Barnet, Sara Bannerman, Diana Bossio, Axel Bruns, Andrea Carson, Terry Flew, Peter Fray, Chrisanthi Giotis, Edward Hurcombe, Tama Leaver, David Lindsay, Sacha Molitorisz, Kate Mannell, Merja Myllylahti, Abdul Obeid, and Derek Wilding.

I benefited from supportive intellectual homes at the Technology Policy and Communication Lab, based at the School of Communication at RMIT University and more recently, working as part of the RMIT Node of the Australian Research Council Centre of Excellence for Automated Decision-Making and Society.

As the book was nearing completion, I was able to rely on the brilliant Andrew Schrock from Indelible Voice who helped refine my arguments and edited a document that could very loosely be called the final draft.

The book has found a fantastic home at Intellect, and I am grateful to Julia Brockley for seeing potential in the project and for her support throughout the publishing process.

The greatest thanks are due to my partner Caitlin, who generously allowed the book to live with us in a very small apartment during one of the longest lockdowns in the world.

The book is dedicated to John Schwartz, who first opened my eyes to the power of the news media during a one-off lecture at my high school, and then introduced me to political economy and media policy at university.

Despite all this help and assistance, any errors in the text are mine alone.

Introduction

A journalist working at a successful digital news outlet posts a story on the company's Facebook Page. The business has cultivated a large audience of young people and generally expects to get a hundred to a thousand likes per post. The story gets three likes in a matter of minutes, but then the numbers stop rising. "It might be a slow starter," the journalist thinks, and they decide to check back in a few hours. When they return, to their shock, the post is stuck on three likes. In the meantime, their senior editor has noticed that overall traffic to their website is also down. By mid-afternoon, it's clear to everyone that there is a problem: the algorithmic systems that structure Facebook's News Feed have been adjusted.

The next week is a blur of crisis meetings, brainstorming sessions, and chaotic Slack channel discussions as the entire newsroom tries to work out what happened. Did the algorithm change? Can they make a post go viral? The latter option is a quick fix. The likes and comments generated from a popular post tell the News Feed that they are generating what Facebook calls "engagement." This works as a signal to Facebook telling the platform that their content is interesting. Facebook's algorithmic systems recognize the popularity of the viral post and start to prioritize *all* their content in the News Feed, revealing it once again to their audience. They don't know why this fix works. A collapse in Facebook performance happens a few times each year. When it does, the entire company must run experiments, informed only by their accumulated folk knowledge, to restore a core distribution channel for news.

A young regional reporter is working at a small, under-resourced local news outlet. They occasionally receive valuable mentorship from the editor and lone senior reporter, but they mainly learn by doing—especially when it comes to online news. The paper now has a digital presence—which sits alongside its still-popular printed editions—but the website is functional and not particularly flashy. Senior staff can post stories and tag content, but the reporter feels they probably could do more with their online presence. One day, the reporter looks through their e-mail inbox and comes across an invitation from their editor to something called a "Digital News Academy." The programme, funded by Google and News Corp, promises to teach them "digital journalism, video and audio production, data journalism, audience measurement, reader revenue, digital business models and marketing" (Shepherd, 2021). The reporter signs up, along with other colleagues working in regional and remote newsrooms. By the end of the programme, the reporter has improved their short video skills, can visualize various data sets, and knows about the "Subscribe with Google" programme, which could help their small outlet improve subscription conversions.

Elsewhere, a large news organization secures a deal with Meta and Google and receives millions of dollars. These companies have finally agreed to pay newsrooms to use their content in Google News Showcase and Facebook News Tab. Revenues on the company's publishing balance sheets rise and they can afford to hire more reporters and editors, as an editor of a smaller media organization watches on in frustration. Their outlet has secured a much smaller amount of money from Google and is unable to secure a deal with Meta or even get a meeting with representatives. They are used to running a "lean" operation and have a small and unassuming online presence. The editor will continue to wonder why Meta didn't make a phone call.

The previous vignettes offer a glimpse into the complex relationship between platforms and news media organizations, two sectors that have become increasingly connected over the last decade. Digital platforms have become an important distribution channel for news media outlets, who use search engines and social media to reach fragmented audiences, some of whom rarely access a news website directly. Two in particular—Meta and Google—have also become a vital source of revenue for the struggling news sector. In addition to directly paying news organizations for content, these companies have also made significant investments in journalism training and local news provision. Other platform companies have also started to dabble in this space. Apple operates its news aggregator product Apple News and billionaire Amazon owner Jeff Bezos now owns *The Washington Post*. While the commitment of individual platforms to news can be erratic, there is no denying the fact that technology companies are now central actors in the sector.

This book is focused on the relationship between news media companies and platforms. I discuss how platforms have gradually intensified their engagement with news over the last decade, examine their interactions with news media businesses, and assess the impact of this transformation on the entire sector. I do so by focusing on how power imbalances manifest throughout this relationship—an analysis that rests on the concept of platform dependence (van Dijck et al., 2019; Poell et al., 2022). Thomas Poell et al. (2022, p. 13) explain the concept of platform dependence and make a distinction between platform-dependent and platform-independent cultural producers. While platform-dependent producers "rely on platforms in the 'creation, distribution, marketing and monetization of content and services,' independent producers can engage in these activities separately"

(Poell et al., 2022, p. 13). They go on to explain that "many cultural producers are positioned somewhere on the spectrum between platform-dependence and independence" (Poell et al., 2022, p. 13).

The central argument of the book is that the news media are becoming increasingly dependent on digital platforms. I make this case through a careful study of the relationship between platform companies and news media organizations, placing particular focus on the legal and economic ties between these sectors (Nielsen, 2019). I do so from a neo-institutionalist perspective, a widely used paradigm from social science that views "the market as an institution composed of norms and rules" (Mansell and Steinmueller, 2020, p. 46). This approach accounts for formal arrangements and legislation while recognizing that "common beliefs, mutual expectations and cognitive frameworks" (Katzenbach, 2012, p. 122) also play a key role. It also accounts for the public interest, recognizing "collective interests that may be understood as plural" (Mansell and Steinmueller, 2020, p. 52), allowing this book to address the impacts of these commercial developments on democracy more generally.

I show that these intensifying legal and commercial arrangements present significant challenges to normative goals associated with journalism's proper function in democratic societies. Journalism, and so necessarily the wider news media industry, plays an important role in liberal democracies. It relays important information to publics, functions as a "watchdog" for government and corporations, offers visions of alternative futures, and provides a space for cities, towns, communities, and countries to deliberate about decisions and tell stories (Christians et al., 2010). In adopting this description, I recognize that the democratic function of journalism allows the news media industry to account for deliberation towards the common good while also facilitating disagreement between parties and interest groups (Baker, 2002). To maintain these functions, the news media requires autonomy and independence from the government and the market, an audience that can meaningfully access and trust the news, and the organizational capacity to effectively function.

Of course, journalism has struggled to live up to these ideals. The news media has long been accused of being captured by powerful interests, with the critical political economy tradition clearly showing that the commercial media sector struggles to produce these democratic outcomes (McChesney, 2008; Pickard, 2020). The structural independence of the news media has also always been qualified. Many European countries have actively intervened in the news media sector by providing subsidies and tax exemptions to media companies. Intervention is largely welcomed across the region and justified as a wider public good (Allern and Pollack, 2019). While the United States adopts a more negative approach, construing media independence as freedom from the government

(Kenyon, 2021; Tambini, 2021), the government's presence has often been subtly felt in the breach. To note one example, government advertising spending has propped up struggling newspapers (Picard, 1982; Pickard, 2011).

Considering this long history, platform dependence does not represent a fall from grace for the news media. However, it is worth studying because many of the threats that emerge from this situation are new. The press is now part of a complex and fast-moving sociotechnical environment full of new actors, from algorithmic systems to obscure ad-tech companies (Ananny, 2018; Diakopolous, 2019). These all challenge the core democratic role assigned to the news media industry and should be explored in the same way that scholars examined similar threats in the eras of print and broadcast. The goal of this book is to identify and map these novel challenges and offer possible solutions. As part of this process, I argue that we must think about platform dependence as a multi-faceted phenomenon, one that affects the news media sector in a variety of ways and in turn avoid reductive understandings of platform power. While acknowledging these contrasting experiences, I go on to argue that there is a macro trend pointing towards a greater systemic reliance on platforms.

My argument rests on José van Dijck et al.'s (2019) reframing of platform power. Their broad approach aims to move the analytical lens of researchers from markets to "societal infrastructures, in which platforms introduce new hierarchies and dependencies" (van Dijck et al., 2019). As part of this process, they argue that we need "untangle patterns of dependence that tie platforms, end-users, and complementors together," patterns that may encompass multiple sectors and markets (van Dijck et al., 2019). Adjacent work has explored how platform dependence and cultural production manifests across markets, infrastructures, and forms of governance (Poell et al., 2022). In contributing to this area of work, I focus on the news media industry and provide a granular account of how platform dependence affects this sector. In the sections that follow, I explain platform dependence in more detail and discuss how it manifests across the news media economy.

Before doing so, it is worth briefly demarcating the scope of this study. Considering the global reach of US-based platforms, my argument may resonate in many countries. However, my analysis is necessarily limited to anglophone nations and Europe. This confined scope is due to the limitations of my own expertise and language. Simply put, other scholars are better placed to examine how the relationship between platforms and news media outlets unfolds in other regions or nations. However, this geographical framing is not absolute, and at points, I will refer to other countries. Another reason for my confined geographic focus is because many platforms focus their attention on political battles and policy discussions across the North Atlantic region, partially due to the region's longstanding history as a site of global power (Meese and Hurcombe, 2022).

The study is also focused on two specific platforms. When it comes to the news media industry, policy-makers, scholars, and industry figures have largely been concerned with Meta and Alphabet, the companies that own Facebook, Instagram, and Google.[1] This is because these two companies have been at the forefront of the platformization of news (Nielsen and Ganter, 2022). As such, most of the book is similarly concerned with these actors, meaning when I use the term "platforms," I will be predominantly referring to them. However, as noted earlier, Apple and Amazon also have engaged in the news business, and I mention these companies occasionally. When it comes to news organizations, I take an inclusive approach and focus on major and minor players from a variety of countries to provide an overarching survey of media markets and identify broad sectoral trends. This deliberate choice means that I will not attempt to offer a deep contextual analysis of specific markets or countries.

Dominance and dependence

From the mid-to-late 2000s onwards, a select group of technology companies from the United States—often referred to as GAFA (Google, Amazon, Facebook, Apple) or FAANG (Facebook, Amazon, Apple, Netflix, Google)—strategically expanded their operations in an attempt to establish global dominance. These firms have been successful and many of them now sit at the top of NASDAQ, the tech-oriented US stock exchange. As a result, these companies now function as critical online infrastructure for ordinary people and other businesses, mainly because they have invented and perfected the platform business model. It is necessary to discuss the model to see how it allows few dominant intermediaries to emerge in specific markets. From this, platform dependence commonly occurs, due to the growing importance of these intermediaries and the lack of competition surrounding them.

Defining what a platform actually is starts to offer some insight into this overall business model. I follow van Dijck et al. and view platforms as "(re-)programmable architectures designed to organize interactions among heterogeneous users that are geared toward the systematic collection, algorithmic processing, circulation, and monetization of data" (van Dijck et al., 2018, p. 4). The first part of the definition above points to one of the central features of platforms: they operate as central intermediaries and connect different consumers on their sites. Markets in which a firm interacts with "more than one set of customers" are referred to as *multi-sided* markets (Shelanski, 2013, p. 1677). The term describes a common situation, where "different groups of consumers are all users of the platform's services and in turn relate to each other vertically as buyers and sellers" (Shelanski, 2013, p. 1677). Multi-sided market structures aren't unique to the platform economy. Indeed, the news media industry (encompassing press and broadcast) was one of the original proponents, providing a space to connect advertisers with readers and viewers (who they on-sold to advertisers as audiences). However, platforms have not only supplanted many of these earlier models but have improved upon them. While some platforms make money through product sales and cloud services (Apple and Amazon), Google and Meta predominantly connect advertisers with audiences.

The second part of the above definition points to the importance that the combination of market dominance and strategic data collection plays in the overall business model. Platforms operate in "winner takes all" markets, which generally see one (or two) platforms succeed as the preferred leader in specific markets, such as search or social networking. One core reason for this market dominance is because of the network effects associated with platform businesses. Platforms offer various incentives for consumers to join. While these processes are familiar to most platforms, let's take Facebook as a quick example. People can do various activities on the platform easily and for free, from setting up an event and inviting their social network to finding an old high school friend. These benefits entice other consumers to join, growing the platform in a manner akin to a self-reinforcing feedback loop (Mansell and Steinmueller 2020, p. 38). In addition, not using the platform starts to appear more inefficient for people. Why search for everyone's e-mail addresses for a birthday invitation when everyone is already connected on Facebook?

Network effects offer additional benefits to platforms. As more and more people join a platform, the technology firm collects data on who these users are and how they use their products. Data can be used to improve their products and services, further setting the platform apart from the competition and increasing their dominance. For advertising-supported platforms like Facebook and Google, data is also of benefit when working with the other side of the market. The main revenue source for these companies comes from targeted advertising and as such, the reserves of data they collect are particularly valuable. As a result, advertisers are also caught up in this network effect. They believe that the platform's significant data stores about a vast audience base and dominant platforms are likely to provide accurate customer information. Therefore, advertisers also become invested in the platform, as it supports their goal of delivering advertisements to targeted audiences and converting online attention to purchases.

However, network effects aren't everything and viable competitors can still emerge on the horizon. This takes us to the other reason why platforms are so dominant: their aggressive and expansive business strategy. Most of these firms began by focusing on one market in their infancy. Apple sold computer hardware and software, Amazon sold books online, Facebook ran a popular social network, and Google ran a search engine. Over time these companies gradually entered new markets and offered additional products and services. In addition to relying on the ingenuity of their own employees, tech firms also acquired small promising start-ups doing interesting things. They would then task these newly purchased employees to keep innovating and just produce their products and services under the platform's name. A prominent example is when Google bought YouTube for USD 1.65 billion in the mid 2000s (Associated Press, 2006). More controversially, platforms have also been accused of buying companies that pose a future threat to their dominance. Meta's purchase of Instagram for USD 1 billion in 2012 has been an example of note, with the company (then called Facebook) accused of buying the popular photo-sharing social network to neutralize a future challenger in the social network market (Rusli, 2012).

Platform dependence

As the above description makes clear, market dominance has been a long-term goal of many US technology companies, which has been largely realized, thanks to the strategic deployment of the platform business model (Moore and Tambini, 2018). While this is excellent news for founders and shareholders, it is a less-than-ideal situation for the public. It produces a situation where a variety of consumers are forced to engage with dominant intermediaries to achieve their goals. While new markets enabled by platforms offer some new opportunities, as we will go on to see, these very same markets are also defined by power imbalances and economic asymmetries between actors (Poell et al., 2022; Mansell and Steinmuller, 2020). It is these latter two elements that sit at the heart of platform dependence.

Platform dependence is what happens when a particular business (or sector) relies on platforms for its long-term survival. The phenomenon occurs when businesses either choose or are forced to align with platform goals and priorities. The above definition is similar to existing accounts of platform dependence (van Dijck et al., 2019; Poell et al., 2022). Thomas Poell et al.'s (2022, p. 13) definition, noted earlier in this introduction, argues that platform dependence occurs when producers become dependent on platforms for "creation, distribution, marketing, monetization." As a result, most cultural producers are not completely platform-dependent and generally retain at least some independence in one or more of the above areas. This is true of the news industry as we will see throughout the book. However, I go on to suggest that the sector is a special case due to its important democratic role. Therefore, a reliance on platforms, even at one part of the supply chain should be of particular concern.

From the above definition, we can start to discuss what platform dependence looks like in the news media sector. The process often happens *on-platform* through *distribution* with news media organizations working to ensure content is picked up by algorithmic systems. These dependencies are *dynamic* because distribution channels change regularly and both institutions retain some agency. For example, news media organizations can decide to preference other distribution channels over platforms or decide to not distribute content on platforms at all. Platforms can also make decisions about how their algorithmic systems will treat certain types of news, or whether they will carry news at all. On-platform dependence can also emerge through engaging with a platform's *online advertising* systems. The latter dependency is more *static* because news media organizations have no other choice. In both cases, platforms can make momentous and largely independent decisions about their role and are usually guided by their own corporate goals. They rarely consider or consult with the wider ecosystem of content producers and businesses they support. As a result, these decisions usually have significant downstream impacts on a variety of sectors including the news industry.

Platform dependence also has an *off-platform* component, which is less discussed. Off-platform dependence similarly varies between dynamic and static dependencies. Technology companies encourage certain types of corporate alignment and engage in *public relations* efforts to manage relationships. Some of these processes involve subtle forms of engagement, such as training workers in certain industries to better orient them to platform tools. These are *dynamic* interpersonal processes, and while they can assist in generating dependencies, news organizations often have a choice about whether to engage and can manage the scope of their involvement. Other attempts are more overt, with platforms providing money to news businesses on a one-time or ongoing basis, often in exchange for news content. Meta is unsure about whether it will keep paying for news content, but Google seems to be more invested. The core risk here is from *ongoing payments*, which can establish static dependencies across a longer timeframe. While they too are changeable, enabling legislation in various jurisdictions is trying to entrench these arrangements. As the vignettes that opened this introduction show, both strategies are particularly prevalent in the news media industry.

These latter examples emphasize the organizational aspects of platform dependence (Caplan and boyd, 2018). Workers and management may learn about platform tools through training initiatives and start to gradually rely on them, in turn pulling their wider business operations into the platform's orbit. Alternatively, management may start to expect payments from platforms, and continue to engage with technology companies to maintain their revenue streams. Below, I will provide some context for these general descriptions by discussing how platform dependence manifests in the news industry with reference to recent literature. Doing so will also provide additional detail about the book's overarching argument.

Platform dependence in the news media industry

Platform dependence occurs primarily because news organizations need audiences (Napoli, 2003, 2010). Frustratingly for the entire sector, some audiences now find news content through platforms. There has been a global decline in audiences directly accessing online news websites, with the 2021 Digital News Report (Newman, 2021, p. 23) revealing that only 28 per cent of people did so. The majority stated that their main way of finding news was through aggregators, search engines, or social media platforms. As a result, platforms have become a crucial *distribution channel* for the news media industry. Most newsrooms are trying to lessen their reliance on platforms and working to avoid platform dependence (Meese and Hurcombe, 2021; Wang, 2021). Part of this process involves changing their business model. Instead of selling large audiences to advertisers, many news media organizations are targeting a specific cohort of readers who will pay for subscriptions. However, these companies still need to distribute content through platforms to find readers who they can turn into paying subscribers.

Consequently, news media organizations also come to rely on platforms for valuable data (Caplan and boyd, 2018). Once a news media business distributes content through social media, it will need metrics offered by platform companies. Most news organizations are no longer solely focused on the number of Facebook likes or retweets they receive (Christin, 2020; Hurcombe, 2022; Meese and Hurcombe, 2021; Petre, 2021). However, their reliance on platforms for audience access means that news organizations still depend on other forms of platform data. Platforms are also careful to follow news industry trends to maintain relevance and as a result, now people can subscribe to news organizations through various platforms. These changes ensure that platform data will continue to be of import for companies, regardless of the business models adopted by the news media industry.

The organizing power of algorithmic systems on platforms can also generate dependencies (Diakopolous, 2019; Napoli, 2015, 2019). They can determine the visibility of content in social media news feeds (Bucher, 2012; Bell and Owen, 2017), the placement of content, and its ranking within Google searches (Meese and Hurcombe, 2021). The news media sector can view the internal workings of algorithmic systems as opaque, and as we saw in the opening vignette, notice is rarely given when significant adjustments are made. An infamous example explored later in the Introduction is the 2018 adjustment to the Facebook News Feed that devalued content from Public Pages in favour of posts from "friends and family" (Mosseri, 2018). Another form of platform dependence can occur when editors orient their newsrooms towards platform distribution channels and their algorithmic systems. As we will see, many newsrooms have attempted to reverse-engineer these systems to ensure that their content is revealed to platform audiences, going so far as to radically change their content production to maximize visibility. Of course, not every newsroom attempts to "game" algorithmic systems and orient their content production around what these computational models favour. However, even these more cautious outlets become subjected to these algorithmic systems whenever they want to distribute content on platforms.

Additional dependencies also emerge around revenue. Despite the move towards subscription models, a significant number of companies still rely on advertising for revenue (Bakke and Barland, 2022). With most advertising revenue moving online, this requires them to engage in an online advertising market dominated by Google and Facebook (Pickard, 2020). Google and Meta have built a large audience of habitual users who access their products to manage their lives, look for information, and consume content such as news. Most of these products are free. In exchange for their use, people allow their online activity to be tracked. Their behaviour produces a trove of data that platforms use to generate granular audience categories and on-sell to advertisers through byzantine online auctions. When it comes to platform dependence, the biggest issue is that Google owns a significant portion of the online advertising supply chain. Google's advertising business spreads across the web, whereas Meta's dominance is limited to social media. This means that to generate revenue, most of the news media industry ultimately depends on Google to manage its online advertising inventory. Even if the news industry stopped putting content on social media and decided to block Google News from aggregating its content, many organizations would still rely on Google to secure advertising revenue.

Technology companies are also starting to offer financial support for news media companies. The most prominent example sees payments offered to certain organizations for news content. In many cases, payments have been voluntary, but a growing number of jurisdictions are forcing Google and Meta to pay up to millions of dollars across several years for news content. While this additional revenue is clearly beneficial for the news media industry, it can also function as an additional form of dependence. Many news organizations will come to expect these payments from platforms and structure their budgets accordingly. Google and Meta also function as news patrons. They both offered ad hoc payments to news organizations as a form of immediate relief following the COVID-19 pandemic. Their preferred approach is to provide support for business development, offering programmes on online business model structures and how to work with their various products. It would be the rare news media company that becomes totally reliant on payments and patronage, and it is also unclear whether platforms (in particular, Meta) are willing to continue handing over money to newsrooms.

Notably, Meta has warned US news publishers that they will no longer pay for news that features on their News Tab (Fischer, 2022). However, efforts to secure ongoing platform payments have the potential to further entrench the link between platforms and news media.

These examples demonstrate the power imbalances and economic asymmetries that contribute to a state of platform dependence (Poell et al., 2022; Mansell and Steinmuller, 2020). Leaders of news organizations have made their feelings clear, with research revealing that "large, digitally developed news media organizations [feel] that they have very little leverage with digital intermediaries" (Nielsen and Ganter, 2018, p. 1612). Adjacent work has found that platforms have been exerting pressure on journalism, and in a similar fashion to the above research notes that journalism has a comparatively weak institutional position when compared to platforms (Vos and Russell, 2019). This scholarship goes on to signal that news organizations may feel pressured to maintain strong relationships with platforms and that the algorithmic systems that structure platform recommender systems could influence "decisions by journalists or news organizations about what stories to pursue" (Vos and Russell, 2019, p. 2343).

This overview also provides strong evidence that platform dependence is an ongoing problem for the news media industry. The purpose of this book is to outline the phenomenon, highlight its complexities, and produce a set of proposals to combat it. I do not propose a reductive account of platform power that suggests that the news media is dependent on platforms in just one way. As we have already seen, there is a variable aspect to dependence that is worth taking seriously, one that is heavily influenced by the strategic decisions of both platforms and the news media sector. Adopting an approach that can account for dynamic (often short-term) dependencies and more static (or long-term) institutional dependence is particularly useful, as it allows us to consider variance across the sector.

The model shown in Figure I.1 adopts this approach and proposes a model of platform dependence that will be used throughout the book. I identify four key dependencies, show how they emerge, and assess their likely impact on the news sector. *Distribution* and *training and patronage* are relatively changeable. We see evidence of news organizations carefully weighing up engagements with platforms across all these areas, and they often choose another direction. Conversely, *platform payments* and *advertising* are more pernicious, as news organizations struggle to break away from Google's advertising systems or, alternatively, refuse payments from platforms. Broadly speaking, distribution is best viewed as a weak form of dependence in comparison to advertising, but I have avoided introducing a hierarchical element to the model, as dependence is always contextual. As we will see, some outlets are heavily dependent on a platform's algorithmic systems. Conversely, well-resourced news companies can develop their own advertising platforms to compete against Google or have enough money coming in from alternative streams, which means that payments from platforms are welcome contributions but may not form a significant percentage of revenue. Platforms also play a critical role in this relationship and make decisions that influence dependencies, from reducing training budgets to refusing to pay for news content.

The above makes it clear that digital platforms are becoming an integral element of the wider sociotechnical infrastructure that we call "the press" (Ananny, 2018). However, the above model allows us to understand these interactions with some nuance. Platform dependence does not just mean that news organizations are desperately following Facebook's algorithm and orienting their entire business around it. Instead, it means that the ties between the news media and a range of platforms are being strengthened across a range of areas. The notion that much of the news media industry is unable to operate without platform systems and infrastructure has been referred to as "infrastructural capture" (Nechushtai, 2018). In the chapters that follow, it becomes clear that such a description may be best given to the pervasiveness of Google's advertising platforms, rather than anything associated with distribution. Along with providing further insights into platform dependence, these developments also represent a significant change for journalism as an industry and as an institution that plays a core role in democratic societies. In the next section, I explain how these developments threaten the ability of journalism to perform its democratic role by introducing normative concepts that will be discussed in the chapters that follow.

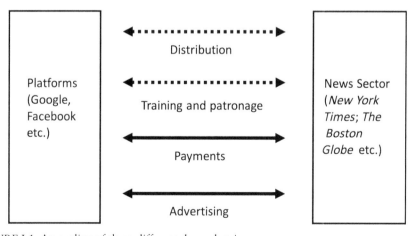

FIGURE I.1: An outline of these different dependencies.

Dependence and democracy

In democratic societies, there are several important roles assigned to the institution of journalism. These are best introduced through the work of Clifford G. Christians et al. (2010). The "least controversial" is the *monitorial* role, which "refers to all aspects of the collection, processing, and dissemination of information of all kinds about current and recent events, plus warnings about future developments" (Christians et al., 2010, p. 125). This role covers everything from the passive recording of events to active watchdog journalism. Most news organizations engage in a combination of both. The *facilitative* role sees the press function as a public sphere, offering the foundational conditions for deliberative democracy and providing space for people to talk about substantive issues (Habermas, 1992). This role also has a cultural component, which sees the press provide a broad pluralist space that seeks to fully represent a democratic society (Napoli, 1999). A less prominent role in liberal democratic societies is the *radical* role, which sees the press engage based on a set of clearly stated values that outweigh professional norms and market considerations (Christians et al., 2010). The final role is a *collaborative* role, which sees the media work with the State during moments of crisis such as war, natural disasters, or a global pandemic.

The institution of journalism can only perform these roles meaningfully if they retain sufficient independence and autonomy from the State and other influential institutional actors. As noted earlier, these normative principles do not completely exclude governments from intervening in media systems but require some level of separation between the two. In a similar fashion, the news media are often influenced by commercial imperatives, and these can and do inform and shape coverage. Despite these qualifications, media independence, and autonomy (or media freedom; see Tambini, 2021), are central normative principles that support the above roles. These normative theories and principles inform general media policy settings and regulatory frameworks in liberal democratic countries (Ogbebor, 2020).

I argue that platform dependence presents new challenges to these core normative theories and principles. In making this claim, I focus on three areas that I see as particularly at risk due to the intensification of the relationship between platforms and the press. The first area of concern is around journalism's need to support an informed citizenry, which encompasses its monitorial, facilitative, and collaborative roles. The second area relates to the maintenance of a diverse media environment, which addresses the facilitative and radical role of journalism, as well as wider normative goals associated with a rich vein of media policy scholarship that explores the importance of a diverse media for a democratic society (Karppinen, 2013; Napoli, 1999; Helberger, 2019; Dwyer and Wilding, 2022). The third area is media independence and autonomy. These categories provide an introductory explanation, but as we will see below, also overlap and naturally reinforce each other. They do in service of an overarching goal: aligning the production, distribution, and consumption of news media with positive democratic outcomes. Of course, as should be evident from the explanations above, platforms are not the sole threat to journalism, but they offer a new set of problems that are worthy of further exploration. I will now discuss how platforms specifically affect these areas.

An informed citizenry

Democracies rely on informed citizens to function effectively, and elements of this task are entrusted to journalism. In theory, the press operates as infrastructure, allowing citizens to follow political, social, economic, and cultural developments as well as providing a space for citizens to debate and discuss current issues (Ananny, 2018). In practice, this relationship between citizens, the press, and the wider political system is changing because of how platforms handle news distribution. News media organizations now must navigate the opaque algorithmic systems that assess and present content. These developments raise genuine concerns about whether the press can continue to effectively inform citizens. Initial worries centred around recommender systems and the algorithmic systems that serve content to people. Commentators argued that people would be stuck in algorithmically generated "filter bubbles" (Pariser, 2011) or "echo chambers" (O'Hara and Stevens, 2015). These fears have since been disproven, with early research showing that these systems often recommend a diverse range of content and do not engage in deep personalization (Bruns, 2019b; Haim et al., 2018; Möller et al., 2018; Nechushtai and Lewis, 2019). However, early positive findings do not necessarily mean that the companies that own and run these algorithmic systems are actively working to support an informed citizenry.

This charge is possible to make because platforms have long been clear that the careful curation of information on platforms is often secondary to profit imperatives (Pickard, 2020). Algorithmic systems on platforms are also not yet invested with enduring principles aligned with the wider public interest (Napoli, 2015; Helberger et al., 2018; Helberger, 2019). Moreover, platforms can make largely autonomous decisions about how news is presented to their audiences. They also play an important (but not determining) role in how online advertising is placed on websites. These developments mean that platforms are now news distributors, and in some cases, also funders. However, these actors do not always accept the charge that they are contributing to the broader democratic goal of maintaining an informed citizenry (Napoli and Caplan, 2017). We also know too little about the impacts of these new intermediaries. What does it mean now that platforms form part of the wider news media ecosystem? To take one example, while propaganda and misinformation have long been a part of journalism, the velocity and speed of distribution on these platforms have seen policy-makers, politicians, and scholars raise concerns about misinformation and polarization (Ong and Cabañes, 2019; Carson and Fallon, 2021). As we will see throughout this book, as news organizations continue to engage with platforms, ensuring that people receive accurate news of sufficient quality emerges as an enduring problem that has not yet been sufficiently addressed.

A diverse media

As the above discussion already implies, democracies rely on a diverse media environment. The neutral identification of heterogeneity in the media environment is commonly referred to as "media diversity," whereas the positive adoption of this view as a democratic value is defined as "media pluralism" (Karppinen, 2013). Until recently, scholars have been mainly concerned with who owned the media (ownership diversity) and what was on the media (content diversity) (Napoli, 1997). Both areas were seen as critical to democratic health. A lack of ownership diversity means missing alternative voices in the public sphere (McQuail and Van Cuilenburg, 1983). A lack of content diversity could mean that too few people are represented in the media, that a limited spectrum of ideas is presented in programmes, or that there is too much of one genre of programming and not enough of another (Napoli, 1999).

The growing importance of platforms and algorithmic distribution has raised the profile of what scholars call exposure diversity, simply defined as the media people see (Helberger et al., 2018). In the context of an increasingly complex and disaggregated media environment, we cannot turn to television ratings or newspaper circulation figures to get a good grasp on what people are consuming. The problem of exposure diversity becomes even more challenging once we consider the impacts of algorithmic selection and personalization. This issue is currently one of the most pressing areas of concern in media policy studies. The above discussion about keeping citizens informed has already gestured to exposure diversity, raising the important issues of how algorithmic systems select and present news to audiences (Diakopolous, 2019; Helberger, 2019). This is a central focus for those currently researching exposure diversity and links media pluralism with positive democratic outcomes. In the early chapters of this book, I discuss how the intensifying relationship between platforms and the news media industry can lead to a greater reliance on these opaque algorithmic systems.

I also show how the involvement of platforms in the news media industry and governmental responses carry downstream impacts on media pluralism. This turns our attention from the increasingly popular issue of exposure diversity to the "structural hierarchies of power that influence and shape our media environment" (Karppinen, 2013, p. 80). Throughout the book, we see large media organizations adapting to the long-term platformization of news better than smaller ones, opaque advertising systems unfairly harming alternative news organizations, and platforms selecting winners, both through independent patronage and in response to government-mandated demands to pay for news content. These examples show one of the more onerous issues associated with this intensification of platform dependence in the news sector: the market-shaping role that platforms play. In so doing, the book explores the important role that power relations have when it comes to realizing media diversity. Immediate outcomes from initial interventions suggest that platform dependence does not align with the long-term maintenance of a diverse (and therefore healthy) news media system. As I go on to discuss below, they also raise important (and as yet unanswered) questions about media independence.

An independent media

The growing involvement of platforms in the news media sector and the concept of platform dependence raises genuine concerns about whether news media can remain independent from platforms. As noted earlier, the independence of media is a core normative principle that requires media organizations to have "operational autonomy from other interests" (Tambini, 2021, p. 138). It is unlikely that the institutional ethics of journalism will decline to such an extent that Google or Meta will direct stories, meaning editorial independence will remain secure. However, more subtle forms of influence may well impact the independence of the news media industry. As already outlined above, platforms are providing additional revenue and one-off financial gifts to selected news organizations with little transparency around this generosity. Worryingly, the variability of payments is also found when it comes to payments made in response to government mandates. Australia currently requires platforms to pay media companies for any news content they use, and other countries are considering adopting similar models. However, payment mechanisms have been implemented in a relatively haphazard fashion, with little consistency around which media companies can expect to receive money from participating platforms or the size of each individual payment. In extreme examples, profits from the success of platforms are even sustaining entire newspapers, as seen through Amazon owner Jeff Bezos's USD 250 million purchase of *The Washington Post* in 2013.

Meta and Google also offer grants targeting relevant industry issues like newsroom innovation and training sessions. These efforts can subtly orient newsrooms in a manner that aligns with the broader goals of these two platforms. Encouraging newsrooms to embrace automation or data-processing functions enriches the wider sociotechnical milieu in which Google and Meta thrive. As we will see, these efforts also function as public relations, encouraging journalists to work *with* Google and Meta and no longer see them as the source of all their industry's ills. In addition to these examples of direct payments and grants, the algorithmic systems of these companies also raise issues around editorial independence (Diakopolous, 2019; van Drunen, 2021). The critical intermediary role that Google and Meta play means that these companies set news agendas on their products and collect meaningful data about how individuals interact with content posted on these platforms. With news organizations unable to meaningfully engage with these decisions and under pressure to improve the technical capacity of their staff, the ideal of an autonomous and independent news media seems to be genuinely under threat.

On method and structure

Digital Platforms and the Press emerges from a multi-year study of the relationship between platforms and the news media sector in Australia. I have conducted interviews, fieldwork (Meese and Hurcombe, 2021), analyzed social media data (Bailo et al., 2021), and studied policy frameworks (Bossio et al., 2021; Meese, 2020; Meese and Hurcombe, 2022a) to establish a strong understanding of the relationship between these two institutions at a national level. When devising this project, I had grand plans about comparing these findings to trends in other countries, but then COVID-19 hit. As a result, the international analysis involved more sedentary (and much less glamorous) online fieldwork and desk research. This included a multi-year membership with the International News Media Association (INMA), which provided access to industry reports, annual conferences, plenaries, and slide decks. The INMA offered ongoing insights into the news media sector at an international, regional, and local level. Along with the collection of other grey literature and contemporaneous reporting, it forms the basis of my industry analysis. I also conducted policy analysis through desk research and accounted for international developments in competition law and privacy law, as well as more targeted reforms focused on the relationship between platforms and the news media sector.

The above research supports this book's analysis of the relationship between platforms and news media. In the following chapters, we will see how the news media is starting to rely on platforms for core operations and explore how these developments can lead to negative impacts on liberal democracies. While the book identifies this macro-trend, chapters also contextualize these dependencies, pointing out moments of change and variance. As part of this process, the book also aims to emphasize the importance of economic dependencies, namely those tied to advertising and payments, which have often been ignored in favour of a focus on traffic and distribution channels. We also come to see that well-resourced news companies are best situated to challenge all levels of dependence. In contrast, smaller news organizations are at the mercy of platform decision-making and may be unwillingly influenced by patronage and payments (or even ignored entirely). However, the divide between large and small news media organizations does not offer complete protection and major news media companies may struggle to fully extricate themselves from platform relationships.

The book approaches the above argument by providing a brief history of the relationship between the two institutions, before focusing on specific problem areas. We begin with a chronological orientation that maps the initial interactions between platforms and the news media industry from the mid 2010s to the present day (Chapters 1 and 2). The analysis then tracks the rise of social news (Hurcombe, 2022) and follows Facebook's decision to change its algorithmic systems in early 2018 to no longer favour news content (Bailo et al., 2018). As part of this analysis, I also show how the role of platforms in news distribution is much more dynamic than is often presumed.

In Chapter 3, we turn to online advertising and see that the news media sector still deeply relies on these flawed and unequal systems. We start at the birth of the cookie in the mid 1990s, discuss Google's growing dominance over the supply chain across the early years of the twenty-first century, and end up discussing what a cookie-less future might mean for the news media sector. The chapter highlights the sector's ongoing dependence on Google for advertising revenue and the subsequent efforts of major media companies to reduce their dependence by changing their business model. Chapter 4 addresses the growing policy consensus around forcing platforms to pay for news content, starting with the controversy around news aggregators in the mid 2000s. We see how various European countries, and then the European Parliament, unsuccessfully attempted to force Google to pay for content. It takes until the early 2020s for Australia to successfully introduce a reform that secures payments from Google and Meta. I suggest that as currently designed, reforms that legislate payments simply support existing interactions between platforms and the news sector and may not reduce dependence.

Chapter 5 focuses on the late 2010s and early 2020s and examines the patronage activity of Google and Meta across the news sector. I argue that platforms are engaging in this sort of activity to avoid regulation. The trend is most obvious in the provision of voluntary payments to news organizations so that countries will not be inspired to adopt Australian regulation that forces mandatory payments. The chapter also discusses other patronage efforts and shows how these initiatives often encourage dependence on platform products and services. The final two chapters look towards the future. Chapter 6 discusses possible solutions that could address or ameliorate some of these problems. I suggest that regulating the online advertising sector and establishing platform observatories are more likely to help reduce dependence and ensure that there are no negative downstream impacts on democracy. These areas are contrasted with the current regulatory clamour over platform payments. In the conclusion, as well as restating the central arguments of the book, I move from practical to scholarly considerations and discuss new perspectives for the field to consider in future research on platforms and the news media sector.

In closing this introduction, I feel it is necessary to briefly address the growing criticism of digital platforms that have become increasingly prevalent inside and outside of the academy. The goal of this book is to provide the first full-length critical account of platform dependence in the news media industry. In so doing, I offer a sustained critique of the contemporary news media environment and identify clear areas where platforms have contributed to an unhealthy state of affairs. However, I do not want to solely blame platforms for the situation we are in. Rather, I will show that decisions made by news organizations, wider sectoral trends across the news industry, and regulatory interventions by the government have also contributed to this problem. While Google and Meta are the centres of much attention and concern, dependence is a multi-faceted problem. I will critique these actors fairly but won't lay every problem at the doorstep of corporate Goliaths. Indeed, I want to move beyond blaming Big Tech to consider the more pressing question, what do we need to do next?

NOTE

1. Facebook has recently changed their name to Meta, to better represent the various social platforms that they own and their growing interest in the metaverse. I will use Meta when referring to the company and Facebook when referring to the platform.

1

When News Went Social

Our goal is to build the perfect personalised newspaper for every person in the world.

(Mark Zuckerberg, cited in Kim, 2014)

It is September 2014 and *Vice* has completed another successful funding round, selling 10 per cent of the company to the multinational broadcasting company A&E Networks for USD 250 million. Now worth USD 2.5 billion dollars, the company has almost doubled in value from 2013, when 21st Century Fox valued it at USD 1.4 billion and handed over USD 70 million for a 5 per cent stake (Ha, 2013; Quinn, 2013). These are heady times for *Vice*, who pivoted from their punk origins to become one of the leading publishers of the digital news revolution. The company regularly produces a free magazine covering edgy topics like drugs, sex, and rock & roll from the perspective of an early 2000s hipster. It's available at record stores, cafes, and anywhere else frequented by skinny-jeans-wearing millennials. However, in response to the digital revolution, *Vice* moves online. In addition to producing the ironic and sometimes shocking content the magazine is famed for, they started producing investigative journalism. Some efforts are still at best "gonzo" and at worse gratuitous, like sending Dennis Rodman to North Korea. However, they also cover often-ignored beats like internet culture and offer alternative perspectives on international political developments.

Investors rushed to be part of this transition. They put money into *Vice* for two reasons. First, the company created compelling online content and resonated with a difficult-to-reach youth demographic rarely interested in news (Gobry, 2014). Second, *Vice* was already generating revenue. They earned more than USD 100 million in 2011 (Lincoln, 2012) and had estimated revenues of USD 175 million in 2012 (Gobry, 2014). Revenue growth was largely attributable to *Vice*'s ability to seamlessly align its content with the needs of advertisers. These were strong numbers for a media sector struggling to ensure regular and consistent revenue amidst a global economy still recovering from the 2008 financial crisis. CEO

Shane Smith sought growth and told the annual *TechCrunch Disrupt* conference that "We won't be the next CNN or ESPN or MTV, we will be 10 times that size" (Ha, 2014).

The future is now! The birth of social news

Vice perfectly encapsulates the chaos and optimism surrounding news media in the mid 2010s. Several new digital-first media companies emerged to produce news that aligned with the logics of social media (Hurcombe, 2022; Usher and Kammer, 2019). Alongside these new entrants, completely different businesses also started to produce news. Lucy Küng (2014, p. 4) calls these companies "reverse entrants" because they did not set out to become news providers. *Vice* was a hipster magazine, *BuzzFeed* focused on pop culture, and Australian news website *Junkee* emerged from a dance music website. In a surprising turn of events, these digitally oriented news companies quickly found success by building large online audiences around their content and receiving venture capital funding (Carlson and Usher, 2016; Kosterich and Weber, 2018).

They were also able to find success because they ruthlessly optimized content for social media platforms and their algorithmic systems, especially Facebook. Companies were focused on brand awareness and growth, and most of them tried to use Facebook to build audiences (Meese and Hurcombe, 2021; Ganter and Nielsen, 2022). Building an online audience through social media was an exciting opportunity for these smaller news businesses, who historically may have been stuck fighting established incumbents for a purely national audience. Now they could use Facebook Pages to extend their reach internationally and potentially become global news brands. People could also click through their social media posts and get directed to the news website, forming an audience that these companies could then sell advertising against (Napoli, 2010). Print media outlets and even well-established digital news publications were only taking tentative steps into the world of social media. They had mainly focused on securing advertising income and only recently turned to Google Search and Facebook for distribution (Bossio, 2017).

The decision of these new companies to rely on Facebook also influenced the type of content they produced. They preferred a breezy, informal style that referenced the novel discursive cultures emerging across the internet. They weren't afraid to put "LOL" in a headline, use emojis, and report on controversial or under-reported beats (Hurcombe, 2022). Content was also often delivered in lists or through "explainers", allowing information to be delivered quickly. As a result, readers could scan articles rather than read them closely. Scannability was partly a generational trait, and many of these outlets directly targeted a younger and presumably more tech-savvy demographic. As Edward Hurcombe et al. have noted (2021), these features defined an emerging news genre that operated differently than existing approaches to journalism.

Hurcombe et al. (2021) called this genre "social news" and identified its features. First, these companies deliberately produced content to be shared across social networks to achieve the ambitious growth targets discussed above (Harcup and O'Neill, 2017; Martin and Dwyer, 2019). As a result, social news content was aligned "with the logics of social media platforms" and featured GIFs and tweets, with a playful attitude that made content "*fun* to share among peers" (Hurcombe et al., 2021, p. 386, original emphasis). Second, social news companies were clear about their politics and explicitly advocated for social causes. Their political engagement starkly contrasted with the studied journalistic objectivity that was a central feature of "high modern" journalism during the mid-to-late-twentieth century (Hallin, 1992). Finally, and most importantly, Hurcombe et al. argued that social news was still news. While their tone might have been different, these outlets were investigating, reporting, and commenting on "traditionally newsworthy events and public issues" (Hurcombe et al., 2021, p. 380). Indeed, as this space matured, many of these outlets ended up producing reportage and investigations with a more familiar journalistic tone, in addition to emoji-stuffed, news-oriented listicles.

The alignment of news companies with the logics of social media helps explain the early success of social news outlets. The genre-specific orientation towards social media contrasted with how older news outlets approached these new distribution platforms. Legacy news media were struggling to respond to a dramatic decline in online advertising revenue, which reached a high point in 2006 (Lotz, 2021; Giblin and Doctorow, 2022). Google and Facebook were quickly becoming the preferred business partners for advertisers, forcing news outlets to rethink their business models. Rather than seeking out new revenue streams, many companies tried to maximize their audience numbers through "clickbait" strategies (Anderson, 2011). Diana Bossio's (2017, p. 76) research reveals that in the Australian context, "the commercial imperatives for 'hits'" even influenced the practices of journalists at once-esteemed Australian broadsheet *The Age*. Journalists faced "expectations that they will write what potential audiences might click on, rather than what is needed for the public record" (Bossio, 2017, p. 77), a problem present in newsrooms worldwide (Fürst, 2020).

Doubling down on advertising meant that the metrics-driven culture of legacy outlets was most attentive to the number of times people viewed a story or navigated to the home page after reading it (Petre, 2015; Ferrucci and Tandoc, 2014; Bossio, 2017; Tandoc, 2019). They only tentatively engaged with social media, and experimentation with these technologies was mostly conducted by junior- or mid-level employees (Meese and Hurcombe, 2021). The *New York Times* 2014 innovation report noted that even though their home page traffic was declining significantly, the newsroom was paying "less attention" to Twitter and Facebook "even though they offer our main, and sometimes only, channels to tens of millions of readers" (*NYT*, 2014, p. 24). In this environment of financial uncertainty, social news outlets were often seen as the future of journalism. Industry commentators went so far as to suggest that these newer entrants may outpace more esteemed newspaper businesses befuddled by social media (Willens, 2018b).

The growing connections between of social media and news did not just emerge from a combination of audience demand and industry "disruption." Digital platforms actively encouraged news publishers to use them for distribution. In 2015, platforms released formats that allowed news media companies to directly post on their websites. Facebook released Instant Articles, Snapchat launched Discover—a news feed product that surfaces content from news partners (McCormick, 2015)—and Google introduced Accelerated Mobile Pages (AMP). In certain cases, these products gave readers an improved user experience through faster load times, cleaner formatting, or greater visibility, further cementing the connections between news and platforms. Around the same time, Facebook was reporting astronomical viewing numbers back to advertisers and news outlets from its Facebook videos. These statistics encouraged news sectors to sink even more of their money into producing content for platforms. Perhaps unsurprisingly, these statistics were later revealed to be false (Fischer, 2016; Welch, 2018).

The scholarly community and industry commentators watched closely as new institutional relationships formed and people started to express concerns about what it meant for the press. As we saw in the introduction, platform dependence was one of the major concerns raised during this period (Poell et al., 2022; van Dijck et al., 2019). There were worries that news organizations would make too many concessions, wholly orient their production towards platforms, and eventually rely on their algorithmic systems for audience traffic, visibility, and revenue. This chapter makes the case that while some news businesses became partly dependent on platforms for traffic during this period, others could keep a careful distance while experimenting with these new methods of distribution. However, as we will see later on in the book, even these partial engagements set the stage for a subsequent intensification of platform dependence through other means.

Riding the algorithmic lightning

When considering which companies jumped on platforms or steered clear, a distinction can be drawn between social news outlets and more traditional news organizations. While legacy news outlets experimented with these new players, companies producing social news built their businesses around platforms and their algorithmic systems (Meese and Hurcombe, 2021). Indeed, in the early 2010s, many new outlets "effectively subsumed their organisational practices to the logics of Facebook's algorithms" (Caplan and boyd, 2018, p. 5). As a result, discussions of news during this period largely focused on Facebook. Companies were able to game these algorithmic systems because Facebook had a relatively "hands off" attitude when it came to news during this period. One plausible argument for the laissez-faire approach was that Facebook was still developing an advertising revenue stream (Olsen, 2008). Presenting itself as a viable location for advertisers required the company to attract more users who would stay on Facebook for longer. One way to ensure time on-site was to become a hub for information including news (Carlson, 2018). The company publicly boasted about their role in the news ecosystem, stating in 2013 that "referral traffic from Facebook to media sites [...] increased by over 170 per cent throughout the past year" (Constine, 2013).

The news companies that formed during this period largely based their business model around working out Facebook's algorithmic systems. Once their story was visible, their stories would hopefully get shared across the network and drive clicks (or "referrals") to their websites. The most notable of these referral-based companies was *UpWorthy*, which created and curated positive stories, delivered to readers through social media with a special feature: a "curiosity gap" headline (Meyer, 2013). These headlines presented basic information about a story in a compelling fashion while withholding the substantive explanation (e.g., the headline "Semicolon tattoo: Here's what it means and why it matters") (Willard, 2015). For another example, *Mic* would repeat the construction of a headline "relentlessly" if it did well on Facebook (Stachan, 2019). Facebook welcomed all kinds of news on its platform during this time and ensured that the recommender systems powering its News Feed surfaced news. As a result, news publishers across the board started to see a growth in Facebook referrals starting in late 2013 (Kacholia and Ji, 2013; Meyer, 2013).

Noting the success of referral companies is important because Facebook gradually tried to improve the quality of news while limiting publishers' ability to game their algorithmic systems. Facebook restricted what they termed "clickbait" and "engagement bait," which generally refers to publishers that encouraged people to click or "react" to posts. Curtailing "clickbait" limited the reach of the more blatant offenders, including websites like *UpWorthy* and its successors *Elite Daily*, *Distractify*, and *Little Things* (Stein, 2016). Facebook also limited the ability of news stories to spread across the whole platform. As former *Upworthy* employee Gabriel Stein noted, while news stories used to compete "against every other piece of content on the platform," Facebook started to group similar stories (Stein, 2016). Story grouping meant that every published article faced a zero-sum battle to be featured as *the story* on an individual's News Feed about a particular topic.

For example, if there were ten stories about a recent house fire, only one would win out. These publishers had to adjust their strategies accordingly and focus on producing quality content on social issues rather than just sharable, feel-good stories that were easily repeatable (Carlson, 2015; Bilton, 2016). However, some social news companies were not as heavily impacted, revealing variance within this broad cohort of publishers. Other new entrants including *BuzzFeed*, *Mic*, and *Vice* continued to find success on Facebook and grow their audience.

There are several reasons why some social news companies endured while others failed. First, and most importantly, success stories produced news. Legacy media organizations often tarred emerging news businesses with the same brush. They unfairly treated the entire sector like they were producing vacuous listicles for millennials with short attention spans (Hurcombe, 2022). However, it soon became clear that these newer outlets were building news teams and producing journalism (Tandoc, 2018). *Vice* had produced their own form of "gonzo journalism" since the mid 2000s (Bødker, 2017). *BuzzFeed*, *Mic*, and other companies soon got in on the act by the mid 2010s and started to build news teams. While their journalists were often younger than those in legacy newsrooms, they reported on traditional beats by using the classic "inverted pyramid" writing style and producing serious investigations (Stringer, 2020; Tandoc, 2018). As a result, these outlets were not impacted by Facebook's attempt to limit the visibility of posts from companies asking people to "like" videos of two animals becoming friends (Carlson, 2015).

The second way these companies differentiated themselves from the competition was by obtaining funding; they were backed by a significant amount of venture capital, a phenomenon that peaked in the mid 2010s (Carlson and Usher, 2016; Kosterich and Weber, 2018). Entrants like *UpWorthy* were only able to secure a reported USD 12 million (Crunchbase, n.d.a), but as the opening vignette of this chapter showed, other companies were far more successful. *Mic* raised USD 97.5 million (Crunchbase, n.d.b), *BuzzFeed* received over USD 490 million (Crunchbase, n.d.c) and *Vice* secured USD 1.5 billion (Crunchbase, n.d.d). The story of venture capital in journalism was a very American experience, yet other countries also felt the aftershocks of these funding rounds as some of these companies set up offices across the world (Meade, 2019). Local social news outlets in other countries were also backed by private funds or legacy media seeking to diversify their offerings (Hurcombe, 2022; Hayes, 2016; Christensen, 2015). As a result, these companies had the funds to pay a growing coterie of journalists and digital media specialists to manage their relationship with platforms.

An influx of labour into the news ecosystem also determined which companies would survive this algorithmic cull. Well-staffed companies were able to use their growing staff numbers to ride out algorithmic changes and decide how to adjust their online distribution strategy (LaFrance, 2014). Edward Hurcombe and

I spoke with several journalists and editors who were working or had worked at social news outlets across Australia (Meese and Hurcombe, 2021). Organizations continually re-oriented themselves towards Facebook's algorithmic systems. When these systems changed, editors and senior journalists often spent a whole week test posting content to see what it preferred and discussing results. In one company, a more subtle example of influence emerged: the performance of algorithm was regularly raised as a point of discussion in meetings. Another example of wider sectoral dependence on Facebook was when these companies suddenly purchased video cameras to record video content in the infamous international "pivot to video" phenomenon (Willens, 2018a; Tandoc and Maitra, 2018). In the space of what felt like a few months, news outlets (many of whom had never owned a video camera) decided to invest in and produce video content. Decisions to move to video were fuelled by Facebook's sudden decision to prioritize video in the mid 2010s and the positive metrics they released (Honan, 2016). Facebook explained that people were not just skipping past videos but actually stopping to watch them. As *Slate* explains, this was "catnip to online advertisers" and publishers understandably followed the advertising budgets (Oremus, 2018b).

Facebook did more than just establish a positive narrative around video. They also paid publishers to upload pre-recorded videos and broadcast live videos for their live-streaming service Facebook Live. The platform secured deals with over one hundred publishers and celebrities in mid 2016 including the *New York Times* (USD 3 million), *Buzzfeed* (USD 3.1 million), and *CNN* (USD 2.5 million) (Patel, 2017; Perlberg, 2016). These funds allowed news outlets to hire staff who could focus solely on producing video content for Facebook. The payments gave material support to news organizations and essentially subsidized these content producers, encouraging them to fall in line with Facebook's wider corporate strategy. However, the pivot to video was short lived and the numbers Facebook circulated with the format proved to be inflated (Oremus, 2018b). Still, in retrospect, it serves as a compelling example of how Facebook oriented the news media sector towards their goals.

Alongside investing in video, major players like *Vice* and *Buzzfeed* used their additional funding to orient their content towards Facebook's algorithmic systems (Hurcombe, 2022). However, these companies had also learned from *Up Worthy* and also turned to other platforms for distribution. *Vice* was a Snapchat Discover launch partner in 2015 (Crook, 2015), and *BuzzFeed* also circulated content on Twitter (Wang, 2017). Many of these companies also used Search Engine Optimization (SEO) (Dick, 2011; Meese and Hurcombe, 2021) to ensure their content was ranked highly on Google search. SEO involves writing carefully constructed headlines, creating better target search keywords, and ensuring that websites are structured logically and loaded quickly (Dick, 2011; Giomelakis and

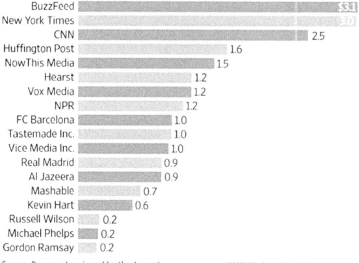

Now Playing, Live on Facebook

A selection of companies and individuals paid by Facebook to provide live video content. **Amount of contracts, in millions of dollars**

BuzzFeed	$3.1
New York Times	3.0
CNN	2.5
Huffington Post	1.6
NowThis Media	1.5
Hearst	1.2
Vox Media	1.2
NPR	1.2
FC Barcelona	1.0
Tastemade Inc.	1.0
Vice Media Inc.	1.0
Real Madrid	0.9
Al Jazeera	0.9
Mashable	0.7
Kevin Hart	0.6
Russell Wilson	0.2
Michael Phelps	0.2
Gordon Ramsay	0.2

Source: Document reviewed by the Journal

THE WALL STREET JOURNAL.

FIGURE 1.1: Live video deals made between Facebook and content creators in 2016 (Pelberg, 2016).

Veglis, 2016). As a result of these factors, a wider set of dependencies emerged around this subset of social news outlets. These outlets clearly still relied on Facebook's algorithmic systems, however they also reflected a more general level of platform dependence across the social news genre. For example, Australian social news site *Junkee* noted that almost 75 per cent of their traffic was "driven through search and social" (Junkee Media, 2021). In the next chapter, we will see that this diversification intensified after Facebook's algorithm change in January 2018.

Companies also started to make decisions about distribution by considering younger demographics. Australian social news outlet *Junkee* made younger audiences a cornerstone of their business model, running an annual youth survey that helped to position them as the voice of Australian youth among advertisers (*Junkee*, 2017; OMA, 2019). One of the reasons that *Mic* found early success was because their young founders successfully targeted the 18–34 demographic (Strachan, 2019). Vice Media was essentially funded off the back of founder Shane Smith's bombastic claims "that only he could connect them with the oh-so-coveted millennial viewers" (Cohan, 2020). These companies were able to generate such impressive venture capital funding because they promised to deliver news and other content to a famously news-shy millennial audience.

These details help us nuance the claim that these emerging social news outlets were completely dependent on Facebook's algorithmic systems (Caplan and boyd, 2018). While there is no doubt that these outlets were oriented to distribute content on Facebook, they were also turning to other platforms. In addition, they also had captured a youth demographic that in some cases, helped companies secure millions of dollars in funding. Their efforts were just as likely to be driven by demographic trends and media consumption as the whims of Mark Zuckerberg and his News Feed programmers.

A cautious press: The internet and institutional legacies

If you only looked at the media industry headlines and scholarly and industry commentary during the 2010s, you would think that every media outlet was rushing to put their content on Facebook. Of course, there was an element of truth to these narratives. Legacy media were watching these new entrants build large audiences on social media and were keen to get in on the action. Chris Ledlin, the former head of content strategy for Nine Entertainment—one of Australia's largest media companies—made his company's goals clear in a series of public reflections after Facebook's January 2018 algorithm change. He recalled that "[p]hrases like the 'Social Strategy' at conferences I attended even started to be spoken of less and less, it quickly became 'The Facebook Strategy'" (Ledlin, 2018). He also noted that in his old role for Twitter Australia, he faced an "uphill battle" when reaching out to news outlets and advertisers because Twitter was constantly being compared to Facebook's "ability to reach and engage anyone" (Ledlin, 2018). As noted earlier, native consumption formed part of a broader push from legacy media outlets to expand their audience through the new distributive possibilities of social media. Our Australian-based research found that the bulk of the country's major news outlets set up Facebook pages in the early 2010s (Meese and Hurcombe, 2020). Around the same time, journalists started to experiment with Twitter and contribute to new online reporting cultures (Bruns, 2012; Bossio and Bebawi, 2016).

However, legacy media was nowhere near as enmeshed with the logics of social media. Nikki Usher (2014) offered a useful reminder of the resilience of existing institutional practices in her study of the *New York Times* in 2010. While social media was on the radar of employees, it was clearly not their primary focus. There were stories of editors struggling to use TweetDeck (a Twitter client) and journalists who rejected these new tools. The social media strategy was also "likely to change" and staff were "uncertain about whether any of it would work" (Usher, 2014,

p. 190). Overlapping work conducted by Caitlin Petre (2021, p. 15) also noted that metrics had a strange position in the *New York Times* newsroom; access to them was restricted to "editors and select digital staffers." Moreover, there was still a clear divide between print and online products during her research. While a reporter received a plaque when they wrote a story that "appeared on page one of the print edition" for the first time, there was no equivalent fanfare for the digital equivalent (Petre, 2021, p. 149).

The *New York Times* is admittedly an extreme case study. The esteemed institution is seen as a bellwether for journalism across the Anglosphere. Other newsrooms already had a more inclusive approach to metrics and social data. The available literature describes a scenario in which web analytics had infiltrated—and in some cases completely taken over—newsrooms (Blanchett, 2018; Hanusch, 2016; Bunce, 2015). The *New York Times* stood in stark contrast to *The Washington Post*, which displayed "detailed web metrics [...] on a television screen for the entire newsroom" in a manner reminiscent of a digital news start-up (Vu, 2014, p. 1094). A similar scenario could also be found at *The Daily Telegraph* in London from the early 2010s, which installed "screens constantly updating lists of telegraph.co.uk's most popular stories" dominating their "newsroom of the future" (Media, Entertainment and Arts Alliance, 2010, p. 32). However, even in many of these data-rich environments, editors still performed a critical function, operating as a "intermediary between audience data and the newsroom" (Ferrer-Conill and Tandoc, 2018, p. 438).

As social media became news distributors, media companies used these platforms to break stories, promote their brand and boost underperforming stories. These practices required editors and journalists to pay attention to how stories performed on social media platforms, and so platform metrics rose in importance (Petre, 2021). However, newsrooms remained focused on the performance of their website, whether that was measured through pageviews (Zamith, 2018) or more complex analyses that attempted to represent audience attention (Neheli, 2018; Christin and Petre, 2020). Numbers from social media poured into an ever-growing pool of metrics, yet in legacy newsrooms, they did not shape editorial decisions to the same extent as we saw in social news.

Industry literature during the mid 2010s supports a narrative of legacy newsrooms approaching social media cautiously. While there was a lot of hype about social media, documents reveal that newsrooms were still in a state of organizational change and generational transformation. As noted earlier, most native forms of social media news distribution had only launched in 2015, meaning news media were just starting to post content on platforms in a planned fashion, rather than as a "hodgepodge activity" (Wilkinson, 2016). News media leaders were recognizing that platforms were no longer "geeky novelties in media houses" and the sole responsibility of the "young social media editor" (Piechota, 2016, p. 19). There has been a common belief that media companies were hopelessly naïve and misread their ability to negotiate their relationship with digital platforms. However, industry reports reveal a cautious institutional stance in which publishers recognized the awkward dance they were playing with these new distributors. Executives and leaders were told at the outset that "throwing news content on platforms without an end game […] is not a strategy" (Piechota, 2016, p. 19), and industry literature continued to note careful strategizing with respect to their "love–hate" relationship with platforms as the years continued (Whitehead, 2019, p. 5).

The audiences of legacy news outlets were also less entangled with platforms. Indeed, we heard from Australian editors and journalists that their homepages still got a reasonable amount of traffic (Meese and Hurcombe, 2021). This may come as a shock to people who witnessed the decline of the *New York Times* homepage (*NYT*, 2014) and our social news interviewee who explained that the home page of his company became effectively worthless across the 2010s (Meese and Hurcombe, 2021). However, other interviewees who worked for established multi-platform news outlets noted that they had a diverse audience base. Home pages still held value, particularly for legacy media outlets that often had been part of a familiar and habitual routine for older online news consumers since the turn of the millennium. We collected independent data to confirm this point and traffic data showed that from October 2017 to March 2018, around 50 per cent of traffic to print websites in Australia came from direct traffic (Bailo et al., 2021).

International comparisons point to similar trends. Internal data is difficult to find, but a leaked *Wall Street Journal* report revealed that in 2020, 26 per cent of website visits came from search and 25 per cent from social media (*WSJ*, 2020, p. 62). Publicly available online metrics are opaque but can also offer insight into how leading international publications were approaching this problem. Data collected from April 2020 to April 2021 from selected leading news outlets tells a similar story. Direct traffic was the most prominent audience source for the *New York Times*, *The Washington Post*, *The Globe and Mail*, *The Guardian*, the *Daily Mail*, *Die Welt*, and *Le Monde*, with search traffic a close second. *Dagbladet* (Norway) benefitted from direct traffic but it was an outlier and likely tied to a strong culture of newspaper readership and paying for news (Newman et al., 2018, 2020). *The Hindu* (India) also was an outlier, as it received 59 per cent of its traffic from Google. This could be attributed to a "platform dominated" news market (Newman et al., 2019), and the fact that this data only referred to desktop consumption, which excluded people using smartphones to access news (see Newman et al., 2019).

Our analysis reveals a more nuanced story of gradual transition and adaptation across legacy media. While newsroom decision makers engaged with social media early on, new distribution platforms were not their central concern during the early 2010s. Legacy outlets did get caught up in the digital hype later in the decade, leading them to post content on multiple platforms (Bell and Owen, 2017) and directing staff to produce videos (Shaw, 2017). Some of their owners spent millions of dollars on promising digital properties like *Vice*. However, these outlets were not as dependent on platforms for traffic. While cognizant of changes, they were also, in many cases, not desperately following algorithmic systems in the same way that completely socially oriented outlets were. News media companies became even more cautious of platforms following Facebook's algorithm change in January 2018. Of course, they had to balance this restraint with an audience that was increasingly turning to platforms to access news and we will see how this played out in the chapters that follow.

The end of news on Facebook?

Editors and journalists should have been shaking their fists at Russian cyber-operatives as they watched their Facebook metrics collapse across the first quarter of 2018. In a now infamous story, Russian-backed actors attempted to spread disinformation across Facebook in the leadup to the 2016 USA election. Mark Zuckerberg originally rejected suggestions that disinformation circulating on Facebook could influence voters, calling the idea "crazy" (Weinberger, 2016; Newton, 2016; Weiss, 2017). However, it soon became clear that there was evidence of coordinated Russians regularly publishing inaccurate news stories on Facebook Pages (BBC, 2017; Lee, 2017; Warrell et al., 2020). Already facing growing regulatory attention (Flew, 2021; Flew and Wilding, 2021), the platform was now at the centre of an electoral integrity matter, and quickly became entangled in an investigation headed by Robert Mueller.

From this point on, news became a serious problem for Facebook. The company inaccurately viewed itself as a neutral facilitator that simply allowed content to circulate freely (Gillespie, 2010; Napoli and Caplan, 2017). Regulators and legislators across the globe were no longer buying this argument, especially once it became clear that Russian-backed actors were able to propagate disinformation through the platform so easily. Facebook was being asked to take a more hands-on role when it came to news and content, which it was uncomfortable with (Gillespie, 2010; Napoli and Caplan, 2017). The platform was also struggling with its growing importance to the USA commercial news ecosystem. It started to face accusations of political bias, as conservative commentators argued that the now-defunct Facebook Trending algorithms had favoured progressive stories (Herrman and Isaac, 2016). With the circulation of disinformation on Facebook now an international and domestic political flashpoint, the company simply decided to start favouring content from other sources when constructing News Feeds for users (Mosseri, 2018).

The obvious upshot of Facebook's shift towards friend-driven posts was that news would appear less regularly on people's News Feed. Unsurprisingly, the news media sector was worried. While they had to deal with uncertain algorithmic systems, most companies had broadly met with success when publishing their content on Facebook. Now the sector faced an uncertain future. Facebook's decision presented a genuine threat to social news outlets that based their entire business on their ability to target a crucial demographic through social media. While other news companies were not as reliant on the Facebook algorithm, they still welcomed traffic that was generated through their Facebook page. It became clear that Facebook's change in policy would soon mercilessly expose any media company that was solely making strategic decisions in response to Facebook's algorithmic systems.

Of course, this chapter has already shown that while some publications needed their content to perform well on Facebook's News Feed to achieve their goals, this wasn't the case for every publication in the mid 2010s. News companies' engagement with social media platforms and search engines varied. Considering such a finding, we should approach the comparatively brief period when publishers turned to social media to distribute news content with a critical eye. Matthew Carlson and Seth Lewis note that it is important to consider "whether some phenomenon is indeed a break from what came before, a continuation of what has existed, or some middle-ground mutation" (Carlson and Lewis, 2019). We may well be closer to the latter phenomenon, in which long-standing institutional histories and orientations influenced how platform dependence manifested across the news media sector.

Indeed, the reaction to these changes to Facebook's algorithmic systems in 2018 tells a complicated tale about how news organizations came to rely on platforms for traffic. Some media companies—particularly social news companies discussed above—struggled with the changes. It was clear that many were oriented towards platform algorithms and dependent on the Facebook platform for an ongoing audience (which media organizations could sell advertising against). However, other organizations were not punished by the change because they could turn to other business strategies. Of course, in many cases, these strategies involved turning alternative platforms. This suggests that while dependence on Facebook's News Feed for audience traffic may well have been overstated, even legacy news organizations were becoming dependent on wider platform ecosystem. Their dependence might not have manifested in an ongoing reliance on platforms for traffic (as argued in this chapter) but points to a deeper set of dependencies, which the book will go on to explore.

2

After the Algorithm

We are not interested in talking to you about your traffic and referrals anymore. That is the old world and there is no going back.
(Rumoured comments made by Campbell
Brown, Facebook's head of news partnerships,
in a 2018 meeting with Australian
publishers [Solon, 2018])

News companies were not completely sidelined by the January 2018 change as the "glory days" of Facebook were already over. The platform had been clear about no longer wanting to be a major player in the news sector. Of course, Meta also recognized that news would continue to be posted on its platform and so it worked to improve the quality of news that was being served to its global audience (Meese and Hurcombe, 2021; Mediapoint, 2018). Their efforts around promoting high-quality news intensified following the chaos around the 2016 election campaign. Facebook even prioritized friends and family over publishers during an earlier change in 2016 (Wagner, 2016). As a result, many publishers were already diversifying their online distribution, intensifying engagements with Google, Snapchat, Twitter, and a more recent player, Apple News (Moses, 2017a). Facebook also pre-warned people across the news sector in the lead-up to the algorithm change. A week or two beforehand, a group of publishers knew that Facebook was, if not turning off the audience traffic tap completely, at least slowing it to a trickle. However, it was still something of a shock when an innocuously titled post on the Facebook Newsroom blog entitled "Bringing People Closer Together" declared that the platform would now be "showing more posts from friends and family and updates that spark conversation" (Mosseri, 2018).

The update was appended with a post from Chief Executive Officer, Mark Zuckerberg. He explained that:

> Video and other public content have exploded on Facebook in the past couple of years. Since there's more public content than posts from your friends and family,

the balance of what's in News Feed has shifted away from the most important thing
Facebook can do—help us connect with each other.

(Mosseri, 2018)

Zuckerberg went on to argue that social media was beneficial so long as people
were using it to connect with other people. The company was going to focus
on encouraging "meaningful interactions between people" because "too often
today, watching video, reading news or getting a page update is just a passive
experience" (Mosseri, 2018). This repositioning had much to do with mitigating
growing public concern about Facebook's influence on society. Executives were
evidently trying to frame the platform as a place to catch up with family and friends
rather than a hub of misinformation, political polarization, and the mindless
consumption of content. In a sign of naivety or blind optimism, it is notable that
executives viewed these outcomes as diametrically opposed rather than horribly
enmeshed. Perhaps Facebook's leaders had carefully pruned their friends list and
were not dodging multi-level marketing offers from high school friends in their
direct messages, seeing misinformation from distant elderly relatives appearing
on their News Feed, or "doomscrolling" in the middle of the night when they
couldn't sleep.

I begin this chapter by discussing the immediate impacts of this change by
tracking the immediate decline in traffic witnessed by many editors and journalists, and noting early responses to the change. I then explore the 2019 digital journalism crisis, which saw several social news outlets lay off staff, and in
some cases, shut down. While some of this decline was due to the companies'
reliance on the Facebook algorithm, we also see how the sky-high venture
capital valuations (discussed in the previous chapter) also determined the fate
of social news companies. Finally, I consider how media companies navigated
the post-Facebook environment. While they were focused on generating revenue from readers to avoid platform dependence, they remained enmeshed in
platform infrastructure, turning to newer Facebook-owned properties (like
Instagram) or familiar platforms like Google. As part of this process, I start to
identify moments of democratic harm, which have emerged because of these
changes. I go on to discuss how platform dependence has downstream impacts
on revenue models for news media, in turn raising significant concerns about
media pluralism. We also see more worrying threats to an informed citizenry,
with much of the news media sector focusing less on Facebook only to be
replaced on News Feed with more populist content. These outcomes start to
shed some light on the democratic harms associated with algorithmic systems
and underline how hard it is for the sector as a whole to escape platform
dependence.

From scoops to socializing

It is hard to emphasize how much of a change downplaying news on Facebook was for the entire news sector. The *New York Times* described it as "the most significant overhaul in years to Facebook's News Feed" (Isaac, 2018). A platform that had successfully become a central intermediary for news was now walking away (*à la* the early 2000s star Craig David). Publishers had dealt with News Feed changes for some time and were comfortable with amending practices, like changing the construction of headlines. By way of contrast, this was a macro-level decision that appeared to affect news *in general* and the impact of the change was soon felt across the industry. Most publishers kept their traffic data close to their chest, but the online publication *Slate Magazine* was remarkably transparent.

Slate revealed that their "traffic from Facebook plummeted a staggering 87 percent, from a January 2017 peak of 28 million to less than 4 million in May 2018" (Oremus, 2018a). The same article noted that "sources at several major publications" were "now seeing less than half the referral traffic from Facebook that they were receiving in the first half of 2017" (Oremus, 2018a). *Talking Points Memo*, an independent online political news site in the United States, supported this interpretation of events, noting that their own internal data had revealed a similar decline in Facebook referrals (see Figure 2.1). Additional evidence came from financial reports or companies folding. For example, the UK's *Daily Mail* reported a 10 per cent reduction in the overall audience soon after the algorithm change (Sweney, 2018) and *LittleThings* shut down in March 2018 after the algorithm change made their traffic drop significantly (Ha, 2018; Mullin, 2018).

These stories of dramatic falls in Facebook referrals and publisher closures didn't tell the whole story. As already foreshadowed in the previous chapter, not every outlet was getting significant amounts of audience traffic from Facebook. For example, the editor of *Talking Points Memo* Josh Marshall (2018) explained that while the graph looked bad, "in page view terms all social traffic never accounted […] for more than 10% of total traffic." Facebook traffic was also modest for many older news outlets, which got traffic directly from people accessing the home page (Meese and Hurcombe, 2021). In contrast, the change presented a genuine challenge to social news outlets, many of which had oriented themselves towards specific platform vernaculars (Gibbs et al., 2015) and algorithmic logics (Hurcombe, 2022). In other words, Facebook referrals were always part of a broader picture. While everyone was disappointed with a collapse in referrals, the real impact depended on exactly how much that metric meant to you and your business model.

Social news editors may have just been putting on a brave face, but many appeared to be nonplussed by the change. Jonah Perretti at *BuzzFeed* optimistically

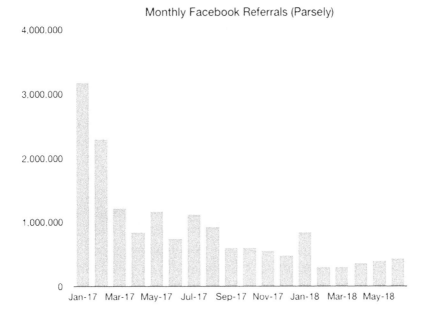

FIGURE 2.1: *Talking Points Memos'* referral traffic from Facebook, January 2017–June 2018 (Marshall, 2018).

argued that the changes played "to our sweet spot, which is making social content that is about bringing people together" (Ingram, 2018). Tim Duggan at the Australian social news site *Junkee* was not worried, explaining that "The Facebook algorithm changes all the time, so we're pretty used to riding the waves of it" (Samios, 2018). Other Australian social news employees offered more detailed responses, attempting to explain how this change from Facebook fit into their wider social strategy. Chris Wirasinha, the co-founder of *Pedestrian*, one of Australia's more popular social news outlets (Hurcombe, 2022), explained that while they had seen "a 9% decline in users from Facebook when compared to the corresponding period (October–January)," the audience that was coming from Facebook to their site was "more engaged than in the past" (Samios, 2018). Sarvesh Jasuja from *Vice Australia* also offered a similarly nuanced story, explaining that while they were not getting lots of likes and shares across the board, they were "still seeing plenty of posts with good engagement getting big reach though, and at times better than before" (Samios, 2018).

These attempts by social news editors to minimize the impact of the Facebook algorithm change align neatly with existing scholarly understandings of how journalists and editors engage with metrics. Journalism researchers have tracked the growing importance of metrics and stories of everyone being able to track the "most viewed" articles or the amount of "quality clicks" are now commonplace (Zamith, 2018; Moyo et al., 2019; Bunce, 2019; Christin and Petre, 2020).[1]

However, "an 'engagement' metric may be operationalized differently across systems even as they use the same label" (Zamith, 2018, p. 422). The above varied reactions to the Facebook algorithm change show how business models and existing newsroom cultures directly influence the valuing and interpretation of metrics (Bunce, 2019; Christin and Petre, 2020). It also reinforces what Dumisani Moyo et al. refer to as "the strategic and managerial deployment of editorial analytics" (2019, p. 495).

Two social news outlets, *Pedestrian* and *Vice Australia*, provide a salutary example of how metrics can be strategically mobilized to support different corporate goals. While *Pedestrian* was largely concerned with what happened once people got on their site from Facebook, *Vice Australia* was still focusing on likes, shares, and audience reach that they got from within the Facebook ecosystem. At a functional level, these point to the variability around metric adoption and use discussed by the scholars above. However, they also suggest a "managerial" slippage around metrics (Moyo et al., 2019) in which alternative performance data are drawn on when existing ones decline. Indeed, while the above Australian social news outlets were reasonably positive about the change, many of these companies also had a long history of platform dependence, relying heavily on Facebook's algorithm as part of their business model (Meese and Hurcombe, 2021; Hurcombe, 2022; Hurcombe et al., 2021). As a result, it is worth considering whether the metrics they claimed were always more important than Facebook referrals were always front of mind, or did they grab hold of new data points to mollify themselves, other executives, and investors as Facebook moved in a different direction?

These questions came to the fore as I conducted longitudinal research with a team, to explore the subsequent impact of the algorithm change on the Australian news media sector (Bailo et al., 2021). Using data from CrowdTangle, we were able to see how much on-platform engagement publications and news genres were getting from 2014 to 2020. While this data couldn't tell us how many people on Facebook saw news stories, it did give us a good insight into engagement—how many people liked, commented, or shared each post. Results further supported our understanding of how Facebook's changes to its algorithmic systems had impacted Australian news businesses. Engagement declined for online news websites (like *The Guardian Australia*) and print publications over time, but these outlets did not receive lots of engagement to begin with. Perhaps surprisingly, engagement rose for public service media outlets, but this made sense considering that Facebook's attempt to improve quality news on its site coincided with domestic and international crises, which usually see Australians turn to public service news in droves (Bailo et al., 2021).

However, what was particularly noticeable in our results was the complete crash in engagement across Australian social news websites. We compared our data set against baseline periods of January–April 2017. During the mid 2010s, the social news genre generated over six times the number of shares. These shares fell below our baseline in mid 2017 and never recovered. It was a similar story for comments and shares, suggesting that the clear loser in terms of on-platform engagement was social news sites. These findings challenge the above social news editors, who claimed that they were managing to ride out the algorithm change. There was a general presumption that apart from a few notable closures like *Little-Things*, other social news outlets would be able to muddle through. However, it soon became evident that all was not right in the world. From late 2018 onwards, a series of mostly US-based social news outlets either collapsed or underwent major restructures in a last-ditch attempt to stop haemorrhaging money. Naturally, questions arose. Were all these outlets dependent on Facebook? Was this perhaps just a delayed reaction, or was something else at play? And why did so many non-US outlets survive?

The end of social news?

The seriousness of the crisis hit home when previously the feted digital media company *Mic* collapsed overnight. The outlet, seen as a crucial part of the vanguard for millennial news and digital journalism, laid off most of its staff (Chokshi, 2018). It was subsequently sold to the Bustle Digital Group for around USD 5 million in November 2018 (Spangler, 2018). This was a dramatic drop in its valuation, which was sitting in the mid-hundreds-of-millions only a few years earlier (Shields, 2017b). More bad news came in the new year as other digital media companies started to fire journalists. *BuzzFeed* sacked 43 journalists from its US news team and set a company-wide goal of reducing its employees by 15 per cent in late January (Peiser, 2019). As part of this process, the company closed their Australian newsroom (Wolfe, 2019) and gradually started to reduce operations across Australia, the United Kingdom, and Canada over the next few years (Samios, 2020). To round off the social news collapse, the formerly high-flying Vice Media announced plans to lay off around ten per cent of its staff in early February (Jarvey, 2019; Spangler, 2019b). The decision came about after Disney wrote off the value of its stake in *Vice* to zero (they inherited this from Rupert Murdoch after the company bought 21st Century Fox). As William Cohan explains, this "doesn't mean Vice is worth nothing, only that Disney and its accountants probably don't expect there to be a payback anytime soon—if ever" (Cohan, 2020).

In perhaps an even worse outcome for the industry, redundancies were not restricted to social news outlets that could have been accused of a certain amount of hubris. Longstanding digital news outlets, who were slower to use social media as a distribution source, were also struggling. Telecommunications company Verizon fired about 800 employees from their AOL and Yahoo groups, which included several recognizable media brands including *HuffPost* and *TechCrunch* (Spangler, 2019a). These redundancies were all publicized over a matter of weeks, leading several outlets to declare this the moment digital journalism died (Helmore, 2019; Israely, 2019). The sector had declined previously, most notably in late 2017, when *BuzzFeed* and *Vice* missed their revenue targets and digital news company Mashable was sold at a fifth of its previous valuation (Sharma and Alpert, 2017; Pallotta, 2017). However, early 2019 felt like a watershed moment, when the entire sector finally realized how difficult it was going to be to get a digital media company to be financially stable (Moses, 2017b).

LittleThings was an obvious example of a company that was dangerously aligned with the Facebook NewsFeed, shutting its doors soon after the January 2018 algorithm change. *Mic* was another failure that could have also been at least partially attributed to the Facebook News Feed. As *Mic* investor Jeremy Liew tweeted: "If you live by the sword you die by the sword. @facebook drove our ascent, when they started to prioritize outside links and later video, and also our decline, when they changed their feed algorithms" (Willens, 2018). While *Mic* attempted to move on from the Facebook News Feed and commit to "premium video" in early 2018, it was too late for a business that had largely been oriented around Facebook, and the business started to fall apart (Willens, 2018).

However, the reliance of social news companies on venture capital means that we cannot place its collapse entirely at the feet of the Facebook algorithm. We also must attend to the political economy of social news. As we saw in the previous chapter, *BuzzFeed* and *Vice* raised a significant amount of income from multinational media companies and private investors (Lewis, 2019). The problem for these social news outlets was that at some point, they needed to provide a return on investment. As we've already seen, both companies regularly missed revenue targets and their plan was no different to legacy media companies (Hurcombe, 2022). The goal was to build a large audience through social media and then sell enough advertising against it to generate profits (Napoli, 2010). Of course, Google and Facebook were already starting to dominate the online advertising market.

While it might seem crazy to try and take on these giants, in the mid 2010s there was still a "prevailing assumption [...] within the industry that if media companies could just reach the right scale, then they could overcome the harsh economics of internet advertising and start clawing back market share" (Owens, 2018b). The wider industry context provides an additional explanation for the significant amount of venture capital flowing to these social news companies. While multinational media companies investing in these companies desperately wanted access to millennial audiences, investors also had a vague plan. For the above companies, this meant building scale through social media distribution and then advertising to this (hopefully global) audience. Of course, with the benefit of hindsight, the plan was always doomed to fail. With younger audiences stubbornly accessing content through Facebook during this period (see Newman et al., 2020), these outlets remained reliant on the platform. As a result, the news media, but social news outlets in particular, fought a losing battle against Facebook and Google for market share.

With these outlets desperate to reduce expenditure and boost revenue, layoffs formed part of a cost-cutting effort to reach profitability across numerous digital media companies (Hurcombe, 2022; Alpert, 2020; Spangler, 2019b). Australian-based social news outlets *Junkee* and *Pedestrian* provide a useful contrast. While these antipodean companies adopted similar business models, they were not funded by venture capital. Instead, they were bought out by larger organizations—a legacy multi-platform media outlet (*Pedestrian* by Nine Entertainment) and an outdoor advertising company (*Junkee* by oOh!media) (Hurcombe, 2022)—and were now subsidiaries. These social news outlets were already valued internally for their "millennial reach, and their marketing prowess" (Hurcombe, 2022, p. 141) providing a stable base for these companies as they rode out these changes. As Hurcombe explains, the regional nature of these outlets also helped. They did not have to produce a global media brand to pacify funders. Instead, they just had to continue to successfully target Australian youth, which was relatively easy because "once they had become recognisable brands early on (for both audiences and advertisers) [...] that status could be more easily perpetuated" (Hurcombe, 2022, p. 142). While *Junkee* has started to struggle financially in recent times, Facebook's changes are only part of this story with alleged mismanagement and a decline in advertising reveue also playing a central role (Wilson, 2022).

The analysis provides an important wrinkle in the tale of platform dependence. There has been increasing concern about the growth of metrics in the newsroom, the crucial role that social media plays in tracking and quantifying attention (Myllylahti, 2020), and the extent to which news outlets engage with algorithmic logics (Caplan and boyd, 2018). However, the above story reminds us that many of these issues associated with the news media sector are also based on a long institutional history, one that sees news outlets (including social news) struggle to establish revenue models not based on advertising (Meese, 2022). During this period, media companies were arguably more impacted by platforms capturing online advertising profits than the adjustments to weightings driving Facebook's core recommender system. That being said, outlets also needed to respond to these changes and media companies started to adopt new business models and distribution strategies.

Distribution after Facebook

As we saw in the previous chapter, at the height of the social media boom in the mid 2010s, Facebook was the central distribution mechanism for many media companies. While these companies posted content across several different platforms (Bell and Owen, 2017), Facebook was the preferred location to distribute content online. Not every media company was dependent on the Facebook News Feed algorithm, but Facebook played a central role in every company's business strategy. Therefore, once Facebook distanced itself from the news, everyone started to look for alternative options. The problem was, as we will see below, that despite companies showing some agency by deprioritizing Facebook, they remained entangled in platform infrastructures.

A popular response saw news media companies turn to a platform they already knew. Some companies replaced Facebook with Google and refocused their digital strategy on search engine optimization (SEO) (Dick, 2011; Bossio, 2017). A return to SEO involved framing and constructing a web page strategically to ensure that it would appear on the first page of Google's search results when relevant keywords were searched (Dick, 2011; Usher, 2013; Lopezosa et al., 2019). To attain more favourable placement in search results, the news worker must place certain keywords in headlines and the article text, ensure that other web pages link back to the story (this is often done through promotions) and check that accurate and appropriate meta descriptions are placed in the HTML of the web page (Moz, n.d.). In our interviews with Australian journalists and editors, some noted that their companies were either returning to SEO strategies or adopting them for the first time (Meese and Hurcombe, 2021). Judging from international reportage and industry data it appears that other publishers followed suit.

Parse.ly is a major data analytics company. Their customer base includes *The Wall Street Journal*, *Spiegel Online*, and *Slate*. One of the public services they offer is a referral graph, which shows where their clients are getting most of their traffic from (Parse.ly, n.d.) and it provides a useful industry weathervane. Therefore, it was notable when Google overtook Facebook in mid 2017 as a dominant referrer for publishers, including news outlets (Molla, 2017). As noted earlier, publishers were diversifying their distribution strategies from the 2016 US election onwards as Facebook started to move away from the news. However, this moment of crossover in mid 2017 represents an inflection point that only intensified following the subsequent algorithm changes in early 2018 (Molla, 2017). Chartbeat data across 2017 and 2018 (including the *New York Times*, *CNN*, *The Washington Post*, and *ESPN* as clients amongst others) also shows a similar inflection point, in which Google was well ahead of Facebook in both mobile and desktop traffic (Molla, 2018; Saroff, 2018).

As you might have already gathered, the above transition from Facebook to Google was in no way a radical rejection of platforms and the algorithmic logics that drive their distribution. Many news organizations simply started to focus on the algorithmic systems that drove Google's search engine instead of Facebook. Indeed, such a change may have represented an intensification of platform dependence. As noted in the previous chapter, not every news organization was slavishly following the Facebook algorithm. By way of contrast, the sector had a long-standing relationship with Google and most news organizations, even established ones, were already thinking about SEO. As one Australian respondent working at a legacy news outlet mentioned in an interview, "you certainly always thought in the headline what would be best for SEO." Therefore, what the above change represented was a greater intensity of focus on SEO across the news sector, encompassing not just the headline but links, site structure, and so on.

Media companies (particularly youth-oriented publishers) also started to post on Instagram (Vázquez-Herrero, 2019). This photo-oriented platform showed immediate promise but was still maturing as a company when Facebook purchased it for USD 1 billion in 2012 (Leaver et al., 2020). While this was seen as a potentially anti-competitive acquisition, it was a smart play by Facebook because the app soon was popular with young people (Leaver et al., 2020; Meese and Hurcombe, 2021). While many "older millennials" (born in the late 1980s or earlier) had lived their young adult lives on Facebook (Singal, 2017), younger people preferred to use a combination of Instagram, Snapchat and TikTok, with Facebook solely used for the maintenance of a wider social network (Bishop, 2020). As a result, many social news outlets were interested in strategic repositioning that allowed them to follow their core demographic: young people.

In a digital marketing seminar, a strategist from *Pedestrian* revealed that they started to invest more in Instagram because their audience was using that platform (Meese and Hurcombe, 2021). Other publishers were making similar decisions (Moses, 2017c). BBC News grew its Instagram audience significantly in the months following the Facebook algorithm change (Eyears, 2019). Many publishers had already been engaging with Snapchat, either through their partnered Discover section or their own independent accounts. However, Snapchat intensified its relationship-building efforts with news outlets following Facebook's decision, clearly trying to capture the interest of publishers leaving behind Facebook

(Moses, 2018). This diversification and search for youth markets continue apace today, with outlets making Tik Tok accounts to reach young people (Vázquez-Herrero et al., 2020).

Apple provided an additional source of audience diversification through Apple News, an app-based service that offered consumers a one-stop shop for news. The app was launched in 2015 and became increasingly popular (Kastrenakes, 2018). It threatened to become a gatekeeper for news alongside Google in mid 2018, around the time Facebook was stepping away from the news. An article in the *New York Times* revealed that their top stories, notably selected by human editors (rather than algorithms), "regularly receive[d] more than a million visits each" (Nicas, 2018). However, while the Apple News platform could drive referral traffic, media organizations also found it difficult to sell advertising against Apple News content. It was hard because people read their stories in Apple's app, which does not collect data on them (Willens, 2019). However, the same story and other reportage revealed a chastened media sector, burnt by their previous interactions with Facebook and Google. Many publishers questioned whether they wanted to get into bed with another technology company.

Across the news media sector, an anti-platform attitude was prominent in the wake of Facebook's algorithm change. However, as the above makes clear, outlets still needed platforms for distribution, branding, and accessing hard-to-reach young consumers who would never visit a web page. Therefore, while many news outlets no longer prioritized Facebook, they were not able to detach from platforms entirely. This points to the pervasiveness of the platform environment and the extent to which this overarching infrastructure is baked into news distribution. It also suggests a more inclusive perspective with respect to platform dependence. As argued in the previous chapter, most of the news media sector was not dependent on Facebook's algorithmic systems for the success of their business. However, they have become dependent on *platforms* in the plural, from Google and Snapchat to Instagram (owned by Meta), as well as Facebook itself. Below, we see how this platform infrastructure works to surround the news media industry, even when it attempts to move beyond revenue models dependent on platforms.

From audiences to readers

The combined impact of Facebook's algorithm change, and Facebook and Google's growing dominance in the online advertising market, forced news media companies to search for new revenue streams. The industry moved from the focus on growth that defined the social media era and returned to an older strategy: asking people to pay for news. In the era of print, advertising paid the bills and reader revenue from subscriptions was not a significant income generator (Pickard, 2019). A longstanding advertising-based business model, along with the fact that many editors saw websites as less important than their print newspapers during the mid 1990s (Boczkowski, 2005), meant that online news tended to be free to access in the early years of the internet. While some outlets introduced "paywalls" blocking non-subscribers during this period, it was not a common approach. However, as print advertising revenues declined and online advertisers moved away from websites and towards platforms, paywalls returned in the early 2010s (Myllylahti, 2014, 2016, 2017; Carson, 2015; Pickard and Williams, 2014). Merja Myllylahti (2014) identified "a rapid proliferation of newspaper paywalls since 2012" but went on to find that "digital-only subscriptions" only represented "10 per cent" of "news companies total circulation/publication revenues" around this period.

A central issue was that news outlets were facing a tension between growing audiences and limiting access. While they were keen to build out this new revenue source, many paywalls were "soft"—outlets regularly removed the wall and offered content to entice new readers (Myllylahti, 2014; Tandoc, 2015). As Andrea Carson (2015, p. 1025) explains, "paywalls were in an experimental phase with [the] initial price [often] lowering and, in some cases, switching models from hard to soft to stem the significant decline in website traffic." These paywalls also did not sufficiently replace "past lucrative print advertising revenues" (Carson, 2015, p. 1038), which meant that outlets did not see paywalls as an instant solution. Many continued to focus on generating clicks and page-views to satisfy their remaining advertisers (Bossio, 2017; Blanchett, 2018) and turned to social media to grow their audience. So, while these earlier paywalls brought in some revenue, management planning, business model structures, and newsroom practices were often oriented around advertising revenue (Meese, 2022).

Reliance on advertising gradually changed as news media companies engaged with social media. As we have seen, the news industry came to recognize that popularity on social media and associated traffic increases did not necessarily lead to new revenue streams. So, the sector returned to subscriptions and paywalls in the early 2020s, but this time media companies did not hedge their bets. Instead, they retooled their marketing strategies and internal practices and focused on securing digital subscriptions. In some cases, a move towards digital subscriptions meant tightening their paywall. Nieman Lab reported that the *New York Times* went from offering twenty free stories a month to only five before the reader was asked to pay (Owen, 2019a). However, the paywall was not deployed as a blunt tool.

Publishers that had the capacity to do so, drew on their own data to establish a dynamic system (Owen, 2018a) that could grant access to a certain number of articles, based on a reader's "propensity to pay," or move popular articles behind the paywall once it reached a certain amount of traffic (Turvill, 2020b; Southern, 2019). Other businesses changed targets and adjusted metrics. Fieldwork across Australian and international in-person and remote industry conferences saw a consistent focus on subscription conversion when it came to editorial strategy, with many companies trying to slow down their publication rate and carefully assess whether *active subscribers* engaged with the content. This had a subsequent impact on metrics as outlets moved away from pageviews to track metrics like "returning visitors," "lifetime reader engagement" (Part, 2020), and conversion rate (whether a click on a published story led to a subscription) (Willens, 2020).

New metrics radically changed the business outlook across newsrooms. Media companies now wanted to sell *to* their audience, rather than sell their audience to advertisers (Logsdon, 2021; Cooper, 2021). The *New York Times* has established a solid revenue base from subscriptions, with about 62 per cent of their fourth-quarter revenues coming from subscriptions against 27 per cent from advertising (Tracy, 2021). The international paper of record also has a significant subscriber base, with over six million subscribers (Usher, 2021). Outlets oriented towards the financial markets have also had success in this area with the *Financial Times* and the *Australian Financial Review* both reporting a growing digital subscriber base that forms an increasingly central part of their overall revenues (Tobitt, 2019; Mason, 2020). However, this transformation is still ongoing. Other major titles are well behind the "Grey Lady." *The Washington Post* and *The Wall Street Journal* are sitting at around three million and 2.4 million subscribers, respectively, and are still in the process of changing their internal structures and systems (Turvill, 2020c). Indeed, it's notable that one of the largest multinational news companies, News Corp, only recently employed consultants to help their Australian holdings build their digital subscription base (Consultancy.com.au, 2020). A contrasting approach is taken by *The Guardian,* which does not implement a paywall and instead relies on a donation model based on memberships, which helped the transnational media organization break even in 2019 (Waterson, 2019).

Platforms have responded to this new strategy which points to their ability to maintain a presence, regardless of what the news sector does. Google launched 'Subscribe with Google' in 2018, which allowed people to subscribe to news outlets by using their Google account (Albrecht, 2018). Many publishers started to integrate the feature into their subscription strategies. The reported terms appear to be generous, with publishers expected to keep 85–95 per cent of generated revenue (AdAge, 2018). In a more surprising move, considering their efforts to limit the appearance of news in their NewsFeed, Facebook has also offered new tools. In 2019 they allowed companies using Instant Articles to embed a subscription button in their content and use various paywall strategies (FJP, 2020). Like with Google, all the collected revenue will go to publishers (Salari, 2019). Additional features include "account linking," which allows someone already paying for a publication to be identified as a subscriber on Facebook and access paywalled content there (Lyons, 2020; Koetsier, 2020). In contrast, Apple takes a 15 per cent cut from any subscriptions sold through News Apps downloaded from their App Store, which is a reduction from their previous rate of 30 per cent (Benton, 2020). The deal for Apple News Plus is arguably worse as Apple requests a 50 per cent cut of profits, with the rest distributed based on how long readers spend on a particular story (Sherman, 2019).

The above response appears to be broadly positive for news outlets since most platforms have avoided the temptation to claim subscription revenue. The main reason for this change is that while platforms can appear to make unfair decisions without consultation (like changing algorithmic systems without notice), at other times decisions about news are made with public relations in mind. Google and Facebook are conscious that their dominance of the online advertising sector has impacted news revenues and have acted accordingly. Apple does not need to be as sensitive about these issues and so has no issues about clipping the ticket. However, regardless of the decision made on this front, these examples also show how platforms can enclose sectors even as those businesses try to chart new trajectories. These new platform options are not necessarily financially deleterious for the sector, but they encourage ongoing reliance on platform tools and audiences.

More worryingly, the transition also presents challenges for media pluralism and points to inequities within the wider news industry with regard to platform dependence. The outlets discussed above give a good indication of the types of outlets that can successfully adopt this approach. They are often internationally respected newspapers that can generate significant subscriber numbers across different markets, popular national papers that can rely on a national audience, or comparatively niche publications focused on a specific topic like finance. In contrast, other outlets struggle to build a sufficient audience to ensure a steady stream of paying customers. Nikki Usher (2021, p. 11) calls these outlets "Goldilocks" publications—papers that are too small to scale but large enough to be "an authoritative voice of a city or region." The move to subscriptions has established "winner takes all dynamics" (Newman et al., 2019, p. 10) and research reveals that a group of global subscription "winners" claims the bulk of reader revenue (Myllylahiti, 2016).

These trends reveal some important variance within the platform dependence phenomenon. Larger players can transition to subscription revenue, and while still relying on platforms for distribution and subscription tools can at least reduce their dependence somewhat in terms of revenue. They no longer compete with Google and Facebook for online advertising, and while they still need to distribute on platforms to reach subscribers, they do not need platforms to deliver them significant audience numbers. Conversely, smaller outlets will struggle to move away from an advertising model. Adopting a subscription model is a complex process and so partly, this is down to capacity issues. Larger organizations have the resources to restructure internal processes, performance targets, internal metrics, and editorial strategies. It is also down to the market dynamics that subscription economies encourage. As a result, remote, regional, and even some larger city papers that are online will all remain dependent on platforms for audiences and will struggle to capture online advertising market share from Facebook and Google.

These likely outcomes naturally raise concerns about the long-term survival of certain outlets and the extent to which these market dynamics, which have emerged due to platformization, are aligned with democratic outcomes. What becomes evident from the above analysis is that attempts to reduce platform dependence likely contribute to a more concentrated media environment. While securing the future of the *New York Times* is helpful, the decline of "Goldilocks" publications will contribute to a diminishing of journalism's role in towns and cities (Usher, 2021, p. 11). We will also see a lack of diversity across markets, which will also impact efforts to ensure a plural media and support the informational and cultural democratic role that journalism provides.

Algorithms and populism

The narrative of this chapter has focused on how news media companies responded to Facebook's decision to move away from the news. This helped us understand the extent to which platform dependence existed across the sector and identify the companies that had the organizational and financial capacity to manage how it impacted their bottom line. However, as we already know, dependence is a dynamic phenomenon and so we must not presume that the relationship between Facebook and the news media was completely dormant. Indeed, the story of what happened *after* Facebook's algorithmic systems changed is illuminating as it reveals the difficulties involved in restructuring relationships between platforms and the news media. It also points to the seductive nature of platforms and some of the ongoing challenges posed by algorithmic distribution.

Apart from the inescapability of platforms discussed above, it is also hard to give up on them because the rewards can be so great for news organizations. If you *can* work out how to align your content with these algorithmic systems and build an audience, you generate significant brand awareness, even if fickle readers never click through to your website. Therefore, while most of the industry diversified, a smaller grouping of populist outlets continued to experiment with the Facebook algorithm and, strangely enough, found success. Most of these companies were generating populist right-wing content, and Facebook's algorithmic systems seemed to love it. A year after the algorithm change, a NewsWhip report cited by *Nieman Lab* showed that Fox News had the most engagements on Facebook, with the angry reaction (a red frowning face) dominating many pages (Owen, 2019b). Notably, Fox News had the angriest reactions of any studied outlet. Other reportage also pointed to the success of Fox, revealing that the outlet had "80 percent more reactions, comments, and shares than CNN," and an "engagement rate [...] higher than any major news organization" (Uberti, 2019). Similar rates of success were cited by other populist media such as Ben Shapiro's *The Daily Wire*, and some left-leaning pages (Owen, 2019).

A move towards populism meant that some media companies started to invest more time and energy on Facebook distribution. Australian journalist Cameron Wilson tracked the digital growth of Sky News Australia, an antipodean cousin to Fox News. His analysis revealed a broadcasting company that gradually turned itself into a populist digital brand. They even reportedly took advice from Facebook and YouTube to identify video content that would "perform" online, which involved a shift towards longer "editorials or panel interviews" (Wilson, 2020). The approach involved prioritizing the more inflammatory opinions often held by the network "talking heads" over the straight news that Sky News had previously favoured. Success quickly followed, with the network featuring an "interaction rate" that was "off the charts" (Wilson, 2020). The interaction rate metric shows "how engaging a post is by dividing the number of interactions an average post gets by the account's follower count" (Wilson, 2020). Sky News had garnered 0.19 per cent with their new strategy compared to an earlier average of 0.04–0.05 per cent interaction rate.

Sky News changed its distribution strategy, which no doubt had some effect on its subsequent success, but there was some suspicion that like Fox News, their success was at least partially due to how Facebook's algorithmic systems were adjusted following the January 2018 change. It took until 2021 for these suspicions to be substantiated through a series of leaks from Facebook whistle-blower Frances Haugen that were published in *The Wall Street Journal*. The leaks revealed that Facebook "treated emoji reactions as five times more valuable than 'likes'" (Merrill and Oremus, 2021) because these reactions seemed to provide a better signal about a person's engagement. While the angry emoji was subsequently "downgraded" in 2018 to "four times the value of a like," it still represented a significant boost. It was also revealed that the January changes to Facebook's algorithmic systems prioritized "comments, replies to comments and replies to re-shares" (Merrill and Oremus, 2021) and heavily weighted "reshared material" (Hagey and Horwitz, 2021). These new weightings contributed to a growing climate of political polarization.

Researchers at the company noted that: "[P]ublishers and political parties were reorienting their posts toward outrage and sensationalism. That tactic produced high levels of comments and reactions that translated into success on Facebook" (Hagey and Horwitz, 2021).

These revelations offered an explanation about why populist content on Facebook continued to be successful and also explained why certain companies were investing in the platform while others were turning away. Those that invested in Facebook distribution were rapidly building an online audience, thanks to a set of favourable algorithms that continued to surface their content. Ironically, while Facebook made these changes with the goal of limiting the presence of news on its platform, populist news content ended up filling the gap. Some publishers even circulated conspiracy theories, particularly following the outbreak of COVID-19. As these concerns about polarization and misinformation increased, changes were made later to "cut the weight of all the reactions to one and a half times that of a like" (Merrill and Oresmus, 2021).

These new algorithmic logics were supporting the circulation of divisive content and misinformation and the threat to democracy should be evident. While Facebook didn't set out to have misinformation circulate on its site, the outcome immediately calls into question the common defence from platforms, that they are merely neutral facilitators of content (Napoli and Caplan, 2017). Of course, Facebook is not the only actor in this scenario. These negative outcomes can only occur if news outlets are drawn to publish content on Facebook. As such, this situation also reveals the *persistence* of platform dependence and the ongoing appeal of platforms for the news sector. Despite Facebook's attempt to distance itself from news, its history of inconsistency, and the public rejection of the site by numerous outlets, other publications were available to fill in the breach. These outlets then became engaged in a similar process of orienting themselves around social metrics and building significant audiences. Of course, the business models of Sky News and Fox News are different to the likes of *Mic* or *Little Things*. They are not solely reliant on Facebook for revenue. However, the platform became a core plank of the overall distribution strategy of these companies and others like them who actively pursue a populist, and at times quite divisive, reporting narrative.

An unavoidable partnership?

This chapter explored the changing relationships between the news industry and platforms, following Facebook's decision to deprioritize news content in 2021. A series of examples helped to articulate an inclusive account of platform dependence, which acknowledged the independence of news organizations while also accounting for the encompassing nature of platform infrastructures. While several news organizations tried to limit their engagement with Facebook, most of them ended up turning to other platforms. Many larger outlets have also started to focus on subscriptions to lessen their reliance on advertising revenue and the need to generate mass audiences through social media. However, platforms quickly followed and set up new tools and mechanisms aligned with subscription models. News outlets will still need to engage with these tools and platforms to some extent, to seek out and convert potential readers. Therefore, while many large news organizations are not utterly reliant on a specific platform and are establishing independent revenue sources, they are reliant more generally on platform infrastructures that continue to develop alongside the sector.

It also became clear later in the chapter that we could not embrace a simple story of news leaving Facebook. While a lot of mainstream news outlets reduced their reliance on this product, populist news outlets not only replaced these departing companies on people's News Feed but also found that the platform appeared to be rewarding content that generated emotive responses and additional comments. These outcomes emphasize the ongoing appeal of algorithmic visibility and suggest that there will always be a group of news companies seeking to secure a prime position in various feeds supported by algorithmic systems.

These developments also reveal new issues that have emerged around media pluralism. We saw that the news media sector's strategic decisions were framed by institutional scale and prestige. Renowned and well-resourced news media companies had the capacity to carefully dabble in social media, and when things went south, immediately turn to subscriptions. Conversely, smaller outlets not only have less ability to invest in subscription business models but are also forced to fight with these large outlets for customers. These latter outlets are likely to remain more dependent on platforms and the long-term sustainability of these outlets looks questionable. These dynamics suggest that the platformization of news will have downstream impacts on the maintenance of a vibrant and diverse media environment. This is of genuine concern because as we have seen earlier, ensuring such pluralism is a central element of journalism's overall democratic role.

Of course, more obvious harms were evident in the example of populist outlets actively adopting Facebook distribution strategies. These point to the genuine democratic risks associated with algorithmic distribution and emphasize the power that platforms like Facebook have when they function as an intermediary. Even if the company didn't expect populist publishers to become prominent on their platform, changes to their algorithmic systems had consequences for the wider audience. Therefore, Facebook and other platforms play a dual role when it comes to media pluralism. While the wider dynamics of platformization influence the survival of specific companies, these platforms play a critical role in facilitating and enabling media pluralism. They set the terms of success and failure on their platforms, which necessarily defines the type of content that people are likely to see. Consequently, platforms play a critical role in delivering information to citizens. For better or worse, they can make decisions that will go on to inform the type of information environment that emerges on their platform. The fact that Facebook's algorithmic changes contributed to the formation of a populist and polarizing media environment, raises concerns about whether platforms can perform this vital democratic role, particularly in the absence of industry frameworks and at a time of nascent regulatory intervention.

These developments also help explain why platform dependence is a democratic concern. Journalism struggles to perform a series of critical roles without platforms, from establishing a plural and democratic space for debate and discussion to informing the general citizenry. These are now complex processes that involve the news media sector *and* the platform economy, and in many cases, news organizations are dependent on platforms to achieve these aims. In the next chapter, we continue to identify these emergent democratic risks through a consideration of online advertising. We see that many news companies depend on Google's opaque advertising technology to sell space to interested buyers. Major media companies are only just now starting to think about building out internal advertising platforms, with smaller outlets once again unable to extract themselves from these asymmetric relationships.

NOTE

1.   The definition of a "quality click" depends on the news organization but it generally means that after a reader clicked through to the article page, they spent at least fifteen seconds of time actually reading the content.

3

Digital Advertising and Democratic Harms

Google has used its vertically integrated position to operate its ad tech services in a way that has, over time, led to a less competitive ad tech industry. This conduct has helped Google to establish and entrench its dominant position in the ad tech supply chain.

(Rod Sims, Former Chairman of the Australian Competition and Consumer Commission, September 28, 2021)

At the start of 2020, news media executives were feeling cautiously optimistic. Their positive attitude made perfect sense. It was a very "new year, new me" scenario. As we saw, many major news companies had decided that their complicated relationship with Facebook was no longer worth it. These outlets started to focus on transitioning their revenue model from advertising to subscription and looked ahead to a more commercially viable future. However, this optimism was short-lived. COVID-19 was gradually spreading around the world and by March 2020, it was clear we were facing a global pandemic. Businesses across every sector faced significantly reduced revenues and in response, they decreased their advertising spending. Platforms that captured most of the online advertising market could weather this storm, but news companies had little room to move. Revenue streams collapsed and news media in the United States faced declines in revenue of up to 50 per cent (Radcliffe, 2020). Companies in other countries faced similar challenges (Mayhew, 2020).

Poynter, a journalism research and education organization, provided a sobering regular update on the crisis. Major publishers like the *Los Angeles Times* were barely keeping afloat and journalists had to reduce their hours to stay employed (Tracy, 2020a, 2020b; L.A.T. Guild, 2020). Other large news organizations responded in a similar fashion. Local newspapers were grappling with difficult circumstances, shrinking their already small newsrooms through layoffs.

Some papers stopped printing on weekends, and in the most dramatic cases, stopped printing altogether (James, 2020). The revenue crisis spread outside the United States as well. News organizations in the United Kingdom retrenched staff (Mayhew and Tobitt, 2020) and some regional newspapers in Australia paused printing or completely shut down (Meade, 2020).

The economic crisis sparked by COVID-19 reveals an important fact about the news media industry: it still relies heavily on advertising revenue. News executives knew the bottom had fallen out of the print advertising market and that they had lost the online advertising battle to Facebook and Google. In response, they had been trying to establish new revenue sources for years. We have already seen that they started to refocus on subscription revenue, realizing that Google and Facebook dominated the online advertising market. "Innovation" is a constant slogan in the industry, and judging by how frequently it was heard, one might think that publishers had solved their revenue crisis (McChesney, 2013; Hardy, 2017). However, the pandemic revealed that innovation was easy to talk about but hard to implement. Alternate revenue sources had not matured sufficiently, and it soon became clear that the discussion around business model innovation was more talk than action.

Advertising revenues remain important to the news sector, even as the entire advertising market moves online and away from news (Zenith, 2019; Seale, 2020a; IAB, 2020). What this means in practice is that most news organizations are reliant on Google's products and services across the advertising supply chain. I argue that these relationships not only contribute to the overarching phenomenon of platform dependence in the news media industry but are the most prominent example of such a dependence. While we often focus on the algorithmic selection and presentation of news in news feeds, most news media business models are deeply reliant on Google, which dominates the online advertising industry. The sector also has to engage with an unregulated online advertising system. These relationships are even harder to map and, more importantly for the news media sector, control. The online advertising market is chaotic and under-regulated and as such presents a genuine threat to many news media outlets (Braun and Eklund, 2019).

I go on to show how these dependencies cause democratic harms. Some harms are specific to the sector. Advertisers can automatically de-fund content, threatening diverse and alternative media sources, a phenomenon I call *algorithmic defunding*. The very same environment also allows suspect intermediaries to capture some of the money advertisers spend, meaning that news publishers can often end up with only 50 per cent of the initial cost of the ad placement (ISBA, 2020). Other harms are more structural and point to the wider problems associated with platform dependence. In what must be a familiar story, we also see a growing divide between larger and smaller news outlets. Larger news outlets can build independent advertising networks, potentially limit their exposure to platforms and even benefit from such an under-regulated sector. In contrast, smaller outlets are stuck relying on platform services or larger competitors to generate advertising revenue and must keep navigating an anarchic sector with limited support.

To get a better handle on the online advertising world, we'll need to examine how programmatic advertising works. The best way to do this is to return to the early years of the internet and follow the birth of online advertising. Two small, scrappy start-ups called DoubleClick and Google, with a lot of help from the "serial entrepreneur" Bill Gross and his now-forgotten search engine Go-To (Oremus, 2013), developed the underlying technical system that supports today's programmatic advertising landscape.

Impressions, clicks, and auctions

In the mid 1990s, online advertising was a relatively simple affair and essentially mimicked the analogue world. Websites worked with advertising agencies to sell space to clients in the same way that they sold space in newspapers and minutes on television (Edelman, 2020c). The model matured quickly, and new start-ups appeared that offered advertising networks. This innovation meant that companies no longer had to deal with websites on an individual basis. Instead, they dealt with intermediaries that would ensure that a company's advertisements were posted across a network of websites (Kelly, 2017). These ads were originally called "banner ads" because they were posted at the top of web pages, and eventually came to be known as "display ads." An enterprising New York company called DoubleClick soon realized that online ads could use advertisements to collect additional information about website visitors. Instead of distributing an advertisement to an undifferentiated mass of newspaper readers without knowing who was viewing the advertisement, you could place an online ad on a website. Double-Click would then tell you how many people clicked on the ad and even find out the websites people visited after viewing the ad. This leap in customization was all thanks to the "cookie," a technology that was developed in the mid 1990s.

Cookies worked by collecting information about what people did when they were on websites: which links they clicked on, the things they typed, and even the amount of time they spent on each page (WebWise, 2012). The innovation helped save people time. A person would not have to re-enter passwords when visiting websites, and if a shopper puts an item in an electronic shopping basket, it would be there when they returned (Coale, 1997). When you returned to the website, the cookie—stored in your browser—would send the information it recorded back to the website. DoubleClick used this technology to build detailed consumer profiles about what individual users were doing across the internet. It was essentially the start of tracking online user behaviour, not just readership. As an early *Wired* article explains:

> Let's say the last time you went online you clicked on pages about travel, surfboards, and Hawaii. The sites alert DoubleClick's software, which notes that those packets of data went to your Internet address. The software begins to build a profile of your characteristics, including email address, location, and consumer interests.
>
> (Voight, 1996)

DoubleClick's genius move was to connect ad delivery with customer profiling. This decision resulted in precision customer targeting now called "behavioural advertising." Once DoubleClick "gathered enough clues" about your potential interest in a "Pacific cruise," it would "instantly upload … a customized ad—all within milliseconds of your signing on" (Voight, 1996). Other companies were also pursuing this approach, but DoubleClick became the industry favourite. It quickly became a dominant player in the advertising world, buying up rivals like NetGravity (Napoli, 1999) and listing on the New York Stock Exchange (*CNET*, 1998).

By the early 2000s, Google was becoming the world's preferred search engine because it provided more accurate results than its competitors. Despite its rapid growth, Google was losing money because it had not found a way to monetize its search engine. They soon turned to advertising to generate revenue (Oremus, 2013). Decision makers within Google started giving other companies the option to purchase ad space next to specific keywords that would appear in searches. When a person entered a search term into Google search, they would also get a text advertisement related to the words they had typed into the search box (Google, 2000a). Google then developed a self-service process called AdWords, which allowed any business to manage its own campaign and monitor its progress "directly from the Google website" (Google, 2000b; Spurgeon, 2008). However, it was Bill Gross who devised the unique method that would revolutionize the embryonic market of online advertising.

In the late 1990s, Gross launched GoTo.com, which was a free-market enthusiast's platonic ideal of what a search engine should look like: an open auction. The system gave advertisers the opportunity to bid for search queries placement "with the highest placement going to the highest bidder" (Hillner, 1998). Information from not-for-profit companies and academic research would be placed at the bottom (Hillner, 1998). Prioritizing commercial interests shocked the search engine market because these companies had prided themselves on returning the most accurate results to users. GoTo.com had instead introduced a new way of paying for advertisements. Up until this point, companies had used a system referred to as Cost Per Mille (CPM) clients would pay a certain amount of money for every thousand people who *viewed* the advertisement (these were called "impressions").[1] Bill Gross's new method was called Pay Per Click (PPC) and charged companies based on the number of people who *clicked* on their ads (Hillner, 1998).

GoTo.com eventually gave up on the search engine and changed its name to Overture to focus on its growing advertising network. After this pivot, Gross quickly turned to Google founders Larry Page and Sergey Brin and suggested a merger. He reasoned that Overture's ads could appear alongside Google's search results, essentially helping to monetize the service (Oremus, 2013). In a move that would become increasingly common across the tech sector, the founders of Google declined the offer and went off to build a very similar system. Google's AdWords Select service launched in 2002, and Overture was eventually bought by Yahoo in 2003 (Oremus, 2013). This is how by the early 2000s, Google and Yahoo could each hold online auctions for ads and match companies selling and buying space on web pages with search results. The system was a precursor to programmatic advertising. However, whereas Google's automated service was a roaring success and served text ads against search results and web pages, Yahoo struggled to incorporate Overture. Executives from both companies fought over turf as the companies tried to merge their operations. As a result of organizational dysfunction, Yahoo's search engine eventually started to lose market share in online advertising (Vogelstein, 2007) and Google became the dominant provider of text advertising.

While Google had experimented with video and display, they were competing against DoubleClick, which also housed troves of valuable consumer data. Google's solution was simply to purchase DoubleClick for USD 3.1 billion in 2007 (Google, 2007). The Federal Trade Commission (Kawamoto, 2008) and the European Commission were concerned that the merger would give Google too much power across the advertising supply chain, but both parties ended up approving the deal anyway (Castle and Jolly, 2008). The purchase was the first and arguably the most important in a series of acquisitions by Google. The company went on to purchase several independent advertising companies to establish themselves across the supply chain, although the DoubleClick deal remains the most consequential in terms of understanding why news organizations became dependent on Google for advertising (Morton and Dinielli, 2020).

The first benefit of Google purchasing DoubleClick was that their customer targeting abilities were boosted. The second benefit was that Google now had access to DoubleClick's auction system. The *New York Times* referred to DoubleClick's auction technology as a "Nasdaq-like exchange for online ads" that brought "[w]eb publishers and advertising buyers together on a Web site where they can participate in auctions for ad space" (Story and Helft, 2007). In contrast to Google's auction site, which was offered to select partners, DoubleClick was open to anyone. Once the exchange was incorporated into Google's system, it helped transform the online advertising experience from a relatively sedate process into something reminiscent of a frantic NASDAQ trading floor.

From Mad Men to NASDAQ: Introducing programmatic advertising

The previous short history shows how customer targeting, the networked distribution of advertisements, detailed customer profiling, and auctioning of advertising space laid the foundation for online advertising. The interaction between these elements led to today's frenetic programmatic environment for advertising. Online advertising auctions are still conducted, only at a much faster pace (O'Kane, 2009) and often in real time. Advertisers can bid for ads to be served to individuals or chosen audiences who are actively browsing, and then publishers are matched with the best bid. This process is automated and happens within milliseconds. As Dan Andrew (2019, p. 82) explains:

> Every time a media user visits a website that is part of a programmatic trading network with available ad impressions, the user is identified and the opportunity to expose them to an advertising message is auctioned off to the highest bidder, all in the time it takes for the web page to load.

As companies collect a growing amount of consumer data, they can segment audiences by demographic data, location, or even previous browsing habits (Andrew, 2019; Braun and Eklund, 2019; Thomas, 2018). Matching advertisers, publishers, and audiences can only occur so quickly because automation and complex algorithmic systems are at the core of the bidding process. As a result, advertising was no longer associated with *Mad Men*-style long lunches and cocktails, or even the cocaine-fuelled parties of the 1980s and 1990s. Instead, at least in the online world, the sector became more like a loosely regulated stock market. Buyers and sellers operated like an exchange, watching prices rise and fall, and closing deals, all from behind a terminal.

The following description explains how these different parties interact. There are six key actors in the process (ACCC, 2020; Andrew, 2019; Braun and Eklund 2019; Thomas, 2018):

- The *advertiser* that wants to place an ad.
- The *ad agency* facilitates the purchase.
- The *demand-side platform* (DSP) provides an automated way to purchase inventory (ad space).

- The *supply-side platform* (SSP) is where publishers see who wants to place inventory on their sites.
- The *advertising exchange* is where the SSP and DSP trades are facilitated.
- The *ad servers* are used by publishers and advertisers. They help publishers manage inventory and advertisers manage and track campaign and advertising information.

Advertisers and ad agencies still speak to each other about strategies and branding; however, the interactions between agencies and publishers have largely become automated. The end-product of the bidding process should be familiar to anyone who has used a web browser recently. The most innocuous outcome of an online advertising auction is a vaguely relevant interactive advertisement. For example, as you browse the website of your favourite newspaper you might see an ad for a new car or clothes from a website you visited a few weeks ago. These systems operate across display (dominated by Google) and social (where Facebook rules). News generates most of its online advertising revenue from display advertising, and consequentially they are dependent on Google.

Advertising and anti-trust

Google and online advertising are inextricably linked. They are not simply a dominant player in the online advertising market. Google has a significant market share across the entire advertising supply chain. The United Kingdom's Competition and Markets Authority conducted a study into online platforms and online advertising and found that Google dominates the publisher and advertiser side of the supply chain, capturing around 90 per cent of the ad server market share. However, they also hold between 50 and 60 per cent of the SSP and DSP market (see Figures 3.1 and 3.2). Market dominance drives Google's revenue. While the company offers e-mail services (Gmail), an online video platform (YouTube), and a range of other products, they make most of their money from advertising, which represented 83 per cent of their revenue in 2019. While most of this revenue came from advertising hosted on their own sites, approximately 13 per cent came from hosting an advertising network for other companies (USSEC, 2019; Statista, 2021).

Politicians, regulators, and civilians are increasingly worried about the central role that Google plays in online advertising, the growing power of online platforms, and the tendency towards monopolization in the sector. Politicians have called on legislators to break up "Big Tech" (Warren, 2019). They want governments to use anti-trust laws, which were introduced to stop monopoly power and

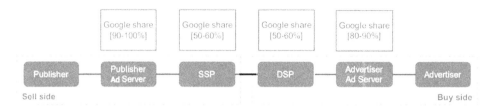

Source: CMA: We include Google AdX, Google Ad Sense and Google AdMob in our definition of SSPs and Google DV360 and Google Ads in our definition of DSPs.

FIGURE 3.1: Google's market share across the online advertising supply chain (CMA, 2020, p. 20).

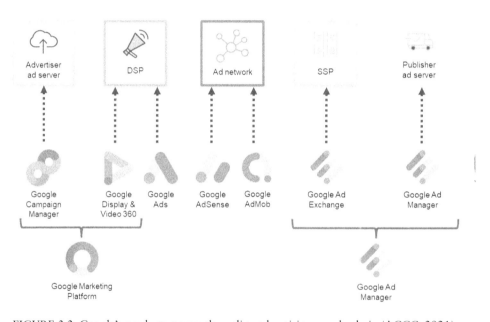

FIGURE 3.2: Google's products across the online advertising supply chain (ACCC, 2021).

intervene in online markets. These positions have been inspired by arguments from academics who argue that there is an inherent lack of competition in many online markets (Popiel, 2020). Authorities have acknowledged these arguments and are beginning to pay attention to the problem. Regulators are worried about several different online monopolies, but several inquiries and legal cases that were launched in 2020 focused specifically on the relationship between Google's properties and its online advertising business (McCabe and Wakabayashi, 2020).

The United States Department of Justice (DoJ) made the most consequential intervention when it launched *United States v. Google* in 2020. It is the biggest case since *United States v. Microsoft Corporation* in the late 1990s. In this case, Microsoft was found to be engaging in anti-competitive conduct to protect its operating system monopoly and secure a monopoly position in the internet browser market (Economides, 2001; Paul, 2020). If it is decided similarly, this latest anti-trust case could define the digital economy for the foreseeable future. The complaint argues that Google holds a monopoly position across the markets for "general search services, search advertising, and general search text advertising" and uses anti-competitive conduct to maintain this position (US DoJ, 2020).

I focus on the latter two markets, but a central criticism of Google is that their products work together to create a high barrier to prospective competitors. The dominance of search and active presence in areas like online video and e-mail allows the platform to collect lots of data. As the complaint states, because of its large user base, Google can deploy algorithmic systems to analyze its data and find out "which organic results and ads best respond to user queries" (US DoJ 2020, 5). Their varied interests across the advertising supply chain raise additional worries. The complaint notes that Google has the "power to manipulate the quantity of ad inventory and auction dynamics," can "charge advertisers more," and can restrict "the information it offers to advertisers about their marketing campaigns" (US DoJ, 53). These examples emerge from the complaint and are not yet findings of anti-competitive conduct. However, as we will see next, France has gone so far as to fine Google for anti-competitive behaviour and competition authorities in other countries are raising similar concerns (ACCC, 2020; CMA, 2020).

Facilitating dependence

In the online advertising sector, Google uses its market dominance to encourage the news media industry to stay dependent on its products. Recent inquiries in the United Kingdom and Australia have focused on digital advertising markets and in doing so have been able to reveal some of these emergent dependencies. As the image in Figure 3.1 makes clear, Google holds a dominant market share in publisher ad servers, through its product Google Ad Manager. These servers manage the advertising inventory of publishers and ultimately make decisions about which ad will appear next to content, based on the outcome of auctions. This means that the vast majority of news media companies must work with Google products to secure advertising income. The Australian arm of the *Daily Mail* calls Google Ad Manager "the default publisher ad server for the industry" (*Daily Mail*

Australia, 2021) and while it is possible to work with multiple publisher ad servers, most stick with Google (CMA, 2020).

There are more options when it comes to SSP, DSP, and advertising exchanges. As noted earlier, SSPs allow advertisers to place advertisements (SSP) and DSPs allow publishers to offer their advertising space for purchase. Increasingly, SSPs and exchanges are becoming hard to differentiate, with companies connecting advertisers with publisher ad space and conducting auctions in the same product. Google has a strong position in these markets, but they compete with other companies such as Xander (DSP/SSP), Adform (DSP/SSP), and Open X (SSP), amongst others. It is here where the issue of dependence becomes more interesting. While publishers are already dependent on Google's advertising server, they have more options at this part of the supply chain. Therefore, Google has the motivation to ensure that these news organizations (and other publishers) continue to use their products all the way through the transaction. Certain news companies have argued that Google has engaged in anti-competitive conduct in pursuit of this goal.

In submissions to Australian inquiries, News Corporation has provided the most detailed and exacting account of this charge, offering a deep dive into their interactions with Google's infrastructure. The core of their argument is that "Google is a participant in auctions that it holds on its own servers" (News Corp Australia, 2020, p. 32). Offering an exhaustive list of examples, News Corporation suggests it is theoretically possible for Google to self-preference AdX (its SSP and exchange) over other competitors. The possibility has also been raised by anti-trust expert Dina Srinivasan (2020). She reminds us that online advertising essentially operates like a giant financial market. However, unlike global financial markets, which have independent exchanges, Google is both an auctioneer and market participant, and could easily privilege its buy-side companies by slowing down the ability of competitors to bid in a fast-paced online market.

News Corporation lists several recent examples of self-preferencing, arguing that Google has set up bidding systems that prefer their networks. These include "last look" bids, which allowed Google's advertising exchange to witness all other competing bids and then place the lowest possible winning bid at the end. So, if a competition advertiser bid USD 5 for an advertising space, Google would step in and bid USD 5.01. Google also launched Enhanced Dynamic Allocation in 2015, which allowed Google to compete against advertising space that was directly pre-sold to (often high-value) advertisers. Google would set up an auction based on this price (somewhat adjusted) and auction off the space. Obviously, the result would be an increased yield for the publisher. However, the process arguably encouraged advertisers to battle to win this important real estate through Google's own ad exchange, at expense of direct engagements with publishers.

There were efforts to weaken Google's hold on the industry through the introduction of header bidding. This allowed exchanges to bid against each other for the right to auction the advertising space. It has often been described as an "auction of auctions." Google refused to participate and instead offered an alternative process called Open Bidding that operated in its own advertising server. This competing system favours Google. If publishers selected another exchange Google takes a 5 per cent fee, placing an additional premium on competing exchanges. However, publishers cannot ignore Google because of the significant amount of advertiser demand that comes through their products. What was interesting about this development is that regulators eventually found some evidence of self-preferencing here. France's Competition Authority (the Autorité de la concurrence) found that Google's "last look" mechanism was also in operation until September 2019. This meant that Google was able to witness the auction amongst the SSPs (or exchanges) and then let AdX bid one cent more to win the right to auction off the space (Kayali, 2021).

Publishers also remain stuck in the Google ecosystem because they need to access Google Ads, which sits on the advertiser side of the supply chain as a DSP. Google Ads plays a central role in programmatic display advertising. It focuses on smaller advertisers and allows publishers to see which ones are keen to purchase space. While publishers could theoretically use any exchange to purchase from Google Ads, there is some evidence that self-preferencing exists here too. In their Digital Advertising Services Inquiry, the Australian Competition and Consumer Commission (ACCC) found that "the vast majority of Google Ads demand is sent through Google's SSP" (ACCC, 2021, p. 101). Another way of phrasing this is that if a publisher wanted to see all of the Google Ads inventory, they should really use Google Ad Manager instead of a competing third party. Google launched Google Display and Video 360 in 2018, which promised to offer a wider spectrum of inventory when compared to Google Ads and provide a better service for enterprise advertising clients. France's ADLC argued that this new product also engaged in similar self-preferencing behaviours, favouring Google Ad Manager (ADLC, 2021, p. 53). The ACCC did not make as strong a finding but noted that "it is easier to access demand from Google's Display & Video 360 demand through Google's SSP" (ACCC, 2021, p. 104).

The above examples show how Google works to keep news publishers (along with other publishers) in their online advertising ecosystem. With subscription revenue not yet able to provide a strong foundation for the entire news media sector, news organizations are essentially dependent on Google for their revenue.

While there has been a significant focus on the risks associated with news organizations and platform news feeds, the opaque system of online advertising is much more consequential. Indeed, Google's self-preferencing and its hold over the entire advertising supply chain gestures to the lack of power that news publishers have in this relationship. News organizations have been in an asymmetrical relationship with Google, unable to meaningfully seek out alternative advertising options or break away from Google Ad Manager. To do so incurs significant switching costs with the numerous advertisers, who prefer Google because of its ability to build consumer profiles on the back of a massive number of data points, unlikely to follow.

Such dependence threatens the long-term health of the news media environment in several ways. Reliance on advertising can hasten the widening divide between large and small media players, in turn raising structural concerns around media pluralism and independence. As we saw with subscriptions, some news media companies are more powerful than others. They have the resources to wear the significant switching costs involved in moving away from Google, and the brand recognition to encourage advertisers to follow them. These publishers also have the capacity able to engage in a significant transition towards subscriptions or, as we will see later, build out their own advertising platforms. For now, it is enough to note this divide and reflect on what it means for most news organizations. Barring reform, smaller organizations will remain dependent on Google's advertising system. The ongoing reliance on Google's systems and supply chain for core revenue points to a growing lack of independence across the sector and an inability to independently control their own future. It also provides further evidence for the argument raised in the previous chapter, that while some major publications may be able to look towards the future positively, the future of a genuinely pluralistic media is at risk.

These findings naturally lead to a more existential risk for journalism. It is becoming increasingly evident that the contemporary online advertising ecosystem does not have the democratic goals associated with journalism at its heart and cannot guarantee its long-term future. These arguments have been present so long as there has been a commercially supported media (Baker, 2002; McChesney, 2008), and Victor Pickard (2019) has argued convincingly that today we need to look beyond commercial support to ensure a sustainable and democratic news media. However, such goals are difficult to achieve so long as news organizations remain reliant on advertising revenue and platforms like Google. Having proven a level of dependence, we now move beyond Google, to explore how this more general reliance on advertising has resulted in one of the more egregious democratic harms associated with the news media sector.

Whitelisting, blacklisting, and algorithmic defunding

Programmatic advertising might sound efficient to the average reader, but the system is flawed. It is incredibly easy for a publisher to paste code on their website and start monetizing their content. In many cases, major brands like L'Oreal and Canon are unaware of where their brands end up until activist groups contact them. Worryingly, some brands do not see this as a concern. As Joshua Braun and Jessica Eklund (2019) explain, companies are generally focused on targeting demographics rather than the context their ads are seen in. Smaller, less brand-conscious companies like local cafés may let their ads run anywhere because they assume generating some revenue is better than none. Ease of monetization is also how conspiracy theorists and people disseminating hate speech can start turning a profit (Edelman, 2020a). They simply set up a website, connect it with existing advertising networks, and start to earn income from display advertising. It functions because some advertising exchanges often do not care *where* ads go, as long as they reach a certain audience (Edelman, 2020a).

Larger brands have become increasingly concerned about what they call "brand safety." The issue picked up steam in 2017 when advertisers discovered that their brands' advertisements were appearing next to extremist content on YouTube. As a result, 250 brands refused to place ads on YouTube or any other Google product for a short period (O'Reilly, 2017; Solon, 2017). Ad tech businesses responded by developing digital tools that protected brands, which appeased the worried executives at these companies, even as it intensified the commercial crisis occurring across the news sector.

Brand executives who are faced with the uncertain world of online advertising often turn to intermediaries to solve their safety issues. These companies claim to use "advanced machine learning, artificial intelligence and semantic engines" to ensure that advertisements are not placed next to offensive content (Fou, 2020). However, the sector is not as technologically advanced as it claims. The most widely used tools are keyword and website flagging, blocking, and category exclusion. Flagging happens when intermediaries develop a *blacklist* of keywords, websites, or entire content categories (like adult content). Advertisers can also import their own blacklists. These lists ensure that even if advertisers win an auction, their ad will not be placed next to content that the brand deems problematic or offensive. These words usually cover terms associated with adult content, terrorism, and other "bad news" topics, which can be entirely subjective. The same actors can also *whitelist* words and websites that they approve of. Often, these words reference the brand itself or other words relevant to the product being advertised. However, it is the blacklisting that is of most concern to the news media industry.

Blacklists are incredibly simple to automate. Even when an advertiser wins an auction, brand safety intermediaries will simply stop advertisements from being uploaded to a website if they find a blacklisted keyword on a webpage. As Marla Kaplowitz, the President and Chief Executive Officer of the American Association of Advertising Agencies, notes, "imagine being next to a story about the death of an infant if you're a baby brand" (Moses, 2020). The problem for the news media industry is that important news is often bad news, which means that news websites often feature blacklisted terms. While these intermediaries claim to use technologies like artificial intelligence, the processes are anything but sophisticated. For example, they have blocked articles about Meghan Markle because the word "sex" appears in "Duchess of Sussex" (Southern, 2019).

Consider how this blocking process plays out on an online newspaper's website. The banner ad at the top of the website for the *New York Times* is prime online real estate. It is one of the most popular news websites in the world, with a growing, international, and well-educated audience (Djordjevic, 2021). For a brand, the top of the *New York Times* website is the place to be. However, in early March, the banner ad at the top of the home page was a series of static clouds placed randomly across a blue background (see Figure 3.3). At first glance, a visitor to the website might think it was an ad for an avant-garde streetwear brand, or perhaps a mental health initiative. But it turned out not to be an ad at all. Instead, it was the work of DoubleVerify, an ad tech intermediary focused on brand safety. They

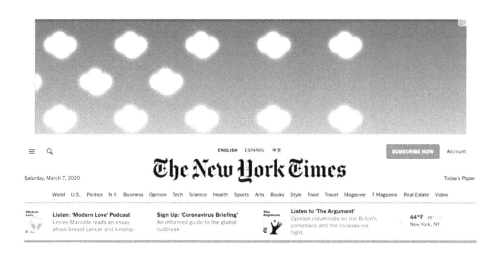

FIGURE 3.3: A blocked advertisement on the *New York Times* home page (source: https://twitter.com/aripap/status/1236455200845684736).

had somehow wrongly identified the *New York Times* as offensive content and stopped ads from being placed there. The advertiser could have chosen to whitelist the *New York Times* but had not done so, meaning the automated blacklisting process kicked into gear (@MattMcLaughlin, 2020). Publishers do not get paid when this occurs, and often cannot contact the shadowy intermediaries who work in the middle of this complex programmatic landscape (Slefo, 2020). As a result of arbitrary decisions made by other parties across the advertising supply chain, news outlets lose revenue.

The clouds appeared in March 2020 when COVID-19 started to dominate the headlines. Publishers assiduously covered the first truly global pandemic in over 100 years, but this vital public service caused something of a revenue crisis across the news media industry. Negative terms like "pandemic" are often on blacklists, which meant that more advertisements were withdrawn from news websites. Normally, this issue wouldn't be a major problem because news websites cover a range of content. However, the first global pandemic in over 100 years dominated the news cycle. The topic's ubiquity led to an automated advertising collapse across the news sector. Programmatic advertisements no longer appeared on news websites because they were filled with negative news, a process that was driven by automated blacklisting (Willens, 2020b; Summerfield, 2020; Slefo, 2020). Blocked advertisements were just one contributor to the broader post-COVID financial crisis in the sector, but it remains particularly important due to its broader democratic implications.

Further examples underscore the impact that blacklisting has on democratic debate. Following the Black Lives Matter protests, *Vice* revealed that some "ad blocklists [include] such terms as 'Black Lives Matter,' 'George Floyd,' 'protest' and—in one case—'Black people'" (Spangler, 2020). Indeed, *Vice* found "that content related to the death of George Floyd and resulting protests was monetized at a rate 57% lower than other news content" (Spangler, 2020; Wu and Winicov, 2020). Inequitable bias is also present within other niche media. Leading LGBTQIA+ media news outlets have found innocuous terms like "lesbian" or "same sex" blacklisted, resulting in "a 'death sentence' for their advertising revenue" (CHEQ, 2020). Industry analyses have also revealed tentative findings, which suggest that some journalists are more likely to be penalized for covering serious topics such as extremism or crime (Adalytics, 2021).

I term this process *algorithmic defunding* and argue that it is causing significant structural damage to the news media sector and leading to wider democratic harms. The advertising system punishes the news sector for pursuing serious journalism or journalism that is outside a highly inaccurate normative framing of society. Algorithmic defunding particularly harms specific content areas, like LGBTQIA+ media, thanks to rarely checked and automatically enforced keyword lists. Unscrupulous blacklisting appears to arbitrarily reduce revenues to the news media industry and (in the worst cases) completely defunds entire news genres. In response, many of these outlets are forced to exist on the fringes of the news and advertising ecosystem, surviving purely through revenue from memberships or subscriptions.

There was a clear economic downturn from COVID-19, and publishers in the United Kingdom stood to "lose as much as £50m in online ad revenue" (Stewart, 2020). There is evidence of long-term damage as well. A University of Baltimore study found that US news publishers were losing USD 2.8 billion a year from keyword flagging, which "amounts to [...] nearly one in every four dollars of potential programmatic ad revenue" (CHEQ, 2019). Intermediaries such as DoubleVerify claim that "under two percent" of advertisements are blocked on news websites, but it's clear that this still represents much-needed potential revenue (McLaughlin, 2020).

These tools clearly present an ongoing risk to news media businesses that still rely on an opaque and unreliable online advertising sector. In its current state, the online advertising sector cannot consistently and transparently fund journalism. Instead, the confluence of ad tech and detailed consumer profiles has also given advertisers power over the news ecosystem. They can target more risk-free topic areas (or "verticals") like sports and lifestyle. Worse, advertisers might "take the perceived 'safest' path and avoid" news entirely, "causing significant harm to news publishers" (McLaughlin, 2020; Marvin, 2020). Some individual marketers believe that agencies should whitelist news (Branded, 2020) but these requests are unlikely to be taken up by a sector that has concerns about readers drawing potential connections between reportage and brand content—consider the baby brand example above.

The current state of online advertising also causes real democratic harms. High-value advertisers can financially reward publishers for publishing content that they deem uncontroversial. Sadly, this means that advertisers tend to reward content that brands perceive as "neutral" rather than the negative news stories and political topics that comprise the news cycle. This process of preferring unobjectionable content to important content suggests that the fundamental democratic goals of news publishers are not embraced by the market. In addition, the process suggests that specific media operations struggle to generate meaningful revenue, as is the case with LGTBQIA+ media (Watson, 2020).

These developments are part of a significant change in the relationship between advertisers and the news media. Traditionally, there was a split between the commercial and editorial sides of a newspaper. Editors and reporters would cover the news and the commercial side of the paper would deal with the money—never the twain would meet. Of course, news outlets have always been driven by commercial imperatives and there never was perfect separation between the two sides of the house. However, there was a sense that boundaries should stand between the democratic role performed by news workers and the commercial necessities of the business. In recent years the boundaries between these two areas have converged as news organizations combine "established editorial values with the values of collaboration, adaptation and business thinking" (Cornia et al., 2020, p. 173). News outlets are choosing to engage with the commercial side of the business, and editorial departments have some agency with respect to business decisions. Now, algorithmic defunding actively takes revenue away from these outlets with little oversight or justification. No longer do we have to worry about the subtle influence of commercial decisions. Instead, its influence is blatant and out in the open.

Advertiser-supported news after cookies

Despite the democratic harms and state of dependence outlined earlier, recent developments in the online advertising sector may present something of an escape for larger and well-resourced media companies. These changes all centre around the third-party cookie, which opened this chapter. While privacy advocates had always been concerned about how commercial goals intersect with online privacy, their worries were sidelined until Edward Snowden revealed in 2013 that the US National Security Agency was conducting widespread online surveillance (Greenwald et al., 2013). Cambridge Analytica's use of personal Facebook data for political targeting also ensured that data privacy became a headline issue in 2018 (Cadwalladr and Graham-Harrison, 2018). These revelations have forced digital platforms to reassess their privacy protections. Google, Apple, and Mozilla (a non-profit organization) have decided to stop supporting third-party cookies in their browsers (Chrome, Safari, and Firefox, respectively) (Bohn, 2020). Google will continue to collect data but will place people in generalizable "cohorts" and stop individual targeting (Shields, 2020). The transition is clearly harder than expected as Google keeps pushing back their deadline to phase out the technology. Currently, Google is planning to deprecate cookies in 2024.

When the change does happen an online advertising industry that has relied on collecting personal data and individualized targeting will be radically changed. A significant portion of the online population (users of Safari and Firefox specifically) are already anonymized. Advertisers are unable to see them, forcing brands, publishers, and the industry at large to return to an older method: contextual advertising (Broughton, 2019). Instead of focusing on the individual customer, this method aligns advertisements with the content of web pages. As an article in *Wired* notes, the goal of contextual advertising is to:

> [G]et information about what the user is looking at. Pages and videos are tagged based on their content. Instead of targeting a certain type of customer, advertisers target customers reading a certain type of article or watching a certain type of show.
>
> (Edelman, 2020b)

The programmatic system for advertising would still function. But now, instead of personal data being added to the equation, website publishers would provide information about their sites to advertising servers (Automatad Team, 2020). What is significant in a shift towards contextual advertising is that some news publishers are moving away from complicated programmatic markets and developing in-house advertising platforms.

Prominent international news organizations are leading the charge. The *New York Times*, *The Guardian*, *Forbes*, *The Washington Post*, and new entrant *Vox* are all investing in bespoke advertising platforms (Fischer, 2019a, 2019b; Seale, 2020b). Apart from *Vox*, the other companies are well-established online publishers with a high-income customer base that is still attractive to advertisers. *The Washington Post* also has the backing of the owner and billionaire Jeff Bezos, who also owns Amazon, a competitor to Facebook and Google. With an infusion of Silicon Valley money, they are making the most aggressive moves in online advertising (Giuliani-Hoffman, 2019). *The Washington Post* launched the Zeus technology suite, which will not only collect first-party data and serve ads but can also be licensed by "local and national media companies." The newspaper also has ambitions to challenge Facebook by building a comprehensive advertiser network of local and regional news websites that local brands can turn to when they want to advertise (Sluis, 2019). Its goal is to get smaller companies to advertise through the Zeus platform—therefore supporting publishers—rather than immediately turning to Google or Facebook. In contrast, the *New York Times* and *The Guardian* have more modest goals to build platforms that can serve their substantial international readership.

These developments signal the emergence of a two-lane online advertising economy in the news media sector. Premium news brands can continue to rely on customer data—now collected in-house—and can also expect to collect revenue from online advertising. The Dutch public broadcasting organization Nederlandse Publieke Omroep also successfully built an advertising server and moved away from cookies. However, they had the benefit of being a leading news brand. They only had to invest in technology to build "descriptive metadata to enable more granular contextual targeting on video content" (Lomas, 2020). *BuzzFeed* recently purchased the *Huffington Post* from Verizon and established a partnership with the communications conglomerate (Bloomberg, 2020). The merger helps these two digital media businesses consolidate their operations, but the ongoing partnership also may give *BuzzFeed* access to Verizon's extensive collection of first-party data about its customers. In contrast, smaller news companies are not likely to have the money to develop bespoke advertising platforms or engage in strategic mergers. In addition, they will not have a sufficient audience to interest advertisers with first-party data (Edelman, 2020b). Instead, they will have to choose between licensing technology from a leading publisher like *The Washington Post* or continuing to work with Google's technology.

There are obvious reasons to applaud the efforts of *The Washington Post*. They are performing industry advocacy by calling for companies to advertise with publishers instead of Facebook and Google (TechXplore, 2019). But their advocacy comes at a price for other publishers; they can either pay a licence fee to manage their own advertising through Zeus or be subsumed into *The Post*'s own advertising network. This approach also presumes that Facebook and Google's overwhelming dominance in online advertising can be challenged. It is also important to note that the prospective challenger is owned by *another* platform company, Amazon (although the businesses are structurally separated). Alternatively, smaller news companies might find themselves at a disadvantage in this new data economy. They will no longer be able to collect behavioural data from users through Google and will have limited available funds to implement their own data strategy. This could further accelerate the decline of local news, and harm local and regional news ecosystems, challenging efforts to ensure a diverse media landscape.

We should be cautious about the potential of online advertising for premium news brands, and at the same time recognize how they benefit these companies. The news media may no longer be so dependent on Google and could establish closer relationships with advertisers. However, there is early evidence that problematic practices from the era of programmatic advertising will remain. For example, *The Guardian*'s in-house platform may keep using keyword blocking to ensure brand safety (Seale, 2020b). As a result, algorithmic defunding could endure unless these companies manage their in-house platforms carefully. News companies may well manage these issues in a more sensible fashion, but they will have to balance editorial imperatives with commercial demands. It is an open question whether news businesses can handle personal data with any more care than digital platforms, which have significant capital available to pay legal and technical experts.

There is a lot to dislike about the current state of the online advertising industry. It is opaque, unreliable, and presents genuine risks to media freedom and democracy. However, most news organizations still rely on advertising revenue and Google's supply chain to keep operating. The beginning of the pandemic revealed that news publishers were still dependent on Google's advertising supply chains than the algorithmic systems that operate platform feeds. Major news media organizations are just starting to transition away from online advertising and towards subscriptions (Meese and Hurcombe, 2020; Pathak, 2019; Willens, 2020a). However, what is even more concerning is that only premium news organizations have the capital and the audience to develop their own bespoke solutions. Smaller outlets will continue to rely on a questionable partner in Google and an opaque and unregulated programmatic advertising ecosystem.

NOTE

1. Mille is Latin for thousand.

4

The True Cost of News

The aggregators and plagiarists will soon have to pay a price for the co-opting of our content.

(Rupert Murdoch, World Media Summit, Beijing [Dawber, 2009])

The agreement with Facebook is a landmark in transforming the terms of trade for journalism, and will have a material and meaningful impact on our Australian news businesses.

(News Corp Chief Executive Robert Thomson, News Corp, 2021)

Rupert Murdoch used his speech at the inaugural World Media Summit in 2009 to denounce news aggregators and search engines. He termed these new intermediaries "kleptomanics" and said it was time to "decisively act to take back control of our content" (Dawber, 2009). Murdoch followed up this speech with a suggestion that his company, News Corporation, might remove their news content from Google's search results (Johnson, 2009). While the news baron never followed through with the threat, his speech represented a critical juncture when it came to the future economics of online news. A clear public statement from the chairman (and then chief executive) of a globally dominant media company set the stage for a battle between legacy media and these emerging digital actors. Murdoch's speech also exposed the growing resentment of news aggregators and search engines. Not only were these intermediaries capturing an ever-increasing slice of the online advertising market, but they were doing so while using free content provided by news outlets. Murdoch maintained this line of argument throughout 2009 and signalled that the era of free news was coming to an end.

As we have already seen, proprietors introduced paywalls in the early 2010s as an initial response to this problem. However, Murdoch and the legacy news media had a larger goal in mind. Their end game was to get aggregators, search engines, and anyone else who used their news content online to pay. Criticism was initially directed towards aggregation efforts from search engines like Google and emerging digital news competitors like *The Huffington Post* (Coddington, 2019). Both companies collected articles from across the web and presented audiences with headlines and either summaries or the first few lines of an article. Each aggregator mimicked a newspaper. Google News had sections for different news categories and early designs of *The Huffington Post* were reminiscent of a newspaper's front page. Once Facebook started to get involved in news in the mid 2010s, they were also incorporated into these critiques, with legacy media outlets arguing that their quality content was being used to draw people to the website.

The battle between online aggregators and media companies continued during the 2010s. Early efforts saw a few abortive attempts at legal reform in Germany and Spain to get Google to pay for news content (Furgal, 2021). As we will see, these reforms had a limited impact, and the search giant easily navigated them. To everyone's surprise, news payments came back on the international agenda when The European Union ratified the Directive on Copyright in the Digital Single Market (DSM) in June 2019. The reform attempted to deploy regional heft to force platforms to pay for online content from news media companies. France was the first Member State to transpose the directive to their national law and ended up in court with Google. On the other side of the world, the Australian Competition and Consumer Commission completed a multi-year review of digital platforms and recommended a voluntary code of conduct between platforms and publishers. A mechanism in the proposed code would require platforms to pay media companies for their news content. The Australian Government took up the suggestion and introduced a now-mandatory code in early 2021. In doing so, they engaged in high-stakes negotiations with Meta. The company did everything possible to stop the associated legislation from being passed, including deliberately blocking news and other sources of information from Australian citizens.

This chapter examines the development and subsequent outcomes of the above reforms, which saw France and Australia publicly clash with Meta and Google. I discuss the operation of each law and show how it was put into practice in each country. I go on to examine why Australian law became the preferred reform option for other countries, including for some European Member States who were already operating under (or planning to implement) the EU Copyright Directive. While this reform aimed to reset the relationship between the news media sector and platforms, the approach raises long-term risks for the news media sector. While there is justified celebration around the amount of money that the Australian reforms have secured for journalism, I suggest that reliance on financial contributions from platforms increases the risk of platform dependence and only further intensifies the relationship between news and platforms.

Europe, Google, and the Copyright Wars

European governments and publishers have always led the charge when it comes to securing news payments. So European publishers were keen to ensure that their copyrights were respected as Google News was rolled out across the region in the mid 2000s. European governments provided additional support through copyright law reform efforts throughout the 2010s. Facebook was only starting to encourage news content on its platform at this point, so legislators mainly targeted Google. These reforms directly influenced the creation of a new press publisher's right, which forms a critical part of the European Copyright Directive described above. Considering this legacy, it is worth exploring these early contestations in more detail before discussing the specifics of the directive and assessing its subsequent implementation in France.

The first shot in the battle around paying for the use of news content was fired in 2005 by Agence France-Presse (AFP). The agency sued Google for using their "photographs, news headlines [and] story leads" and sought damages and an injunction against further use (Cozens, 2005). Google eventually settled with AFP in 2007 and was able to keep using the content (Auchard, 2007). However, other countries quickly followed France's lead. Another copyright case quickly came in response to Google News' 2006 launch in Belgium. While Google had agreed to deal with "organizations representing journalists and photographers," Copiepresse—a company that managed the copyrights for a group of Belgian news-papers—did not agree to a proposed "revenue-sharing arrangement" (Crampton, 2007). Instead, they brought an action against Google. This case was more compli-cated and went on for some time. The court found against Google and the plat-form continued to lose as they moved up the Belgian court hierarchy, continually appealing the case. Google was ultimately forced to remove Copiepresse content from Google News. However, Google argued that the judgement also required them to remove their stories from search results. This was a step too far for Copiepresse, who clearly enjoyed the traffic that they were receiving from Google (Reisinger, 2011). Eventually, the two parties settled, with Google working with publishers "on a range of initiatives to increase their revenue, including paywalls and subscriptions, tapping Google's AdSense platform for site advertising, and collaborating on distribution of content to mobile devices" (Musil, 2012).

These early settlements revealed a growing tension between platforms and news publishers. While news outlets wanted licensing revenue from Google that they felt was rightfully theirs, they were also keen to keep receiving traffic from the search engine. AFP and Copiepresse took aggressive stances, but both parties eventually settled with Google and allowed their content to continue to be used. Realizing that individual lawsuits were not going to solve the problem; leading news publishers intensified their lobbying efforts (Tworek and Buschow, 2016). Some national governments responded and introduced laws forcing Google to pay when they linked to news content. Germany was the first to do so, introducing a "link tax" (*Leistungsschutzrecht*) in 2013. Google could reuse small snippets—a term that was not defined—but would be charged if they used a substantial amount of content (Best, 2014). However, publishers were not able to make use of the reform. As soon as the law passed, the major publishing consortium VG Media forced Google to stop using its content. Google acquiesced and only published headlines from news articles. In a matter of weeks, VG Media relented, explaining that "the experiment had caused traffic to its sites to plunge" (Wolde and Auchard, 2014). This opened the door for all German publishers to establish zero-cost licensing agreements with Google, effectively maintaining the status quo (Masnick, 2014).

Spain took a more aggressive stance and in 2015 introduced legislation that forced aggregation services to pay for even the most minor use of news content (Koch, 2014). In response, Google shut down Google News in Spain in late 2014, explaining that Spain's approach was "not sustainable" (Google Support, n.d.). Other smaller aggregators also shut down, concerned about being exposed to additional unforeseen costs (Masnick, 2015). The law was only "overturned" once Spain adopted the EU Copyright Directive in 2021, which cleared the way for Google News to return (Owen, 2022). France was considering adopting a similar approach but was essentially bought off by Google. High-level negotiations between then-President Francois Holland and then-Executive Chairman Eric Schmidt secured USD 82 million for the French news industry in 2013 (Reuters Staff, 2013).

Google was able to avoid a significant regulatory burden during this period. Publishers were still experimenting with paywalls and their business was still largely focused on online advertising (Carson, 2015). This meant that audience traffic was still a central metric for news media companies (Vu, 2014) and as a result, outlets were unable to resist giving their content to Google. However, the European Parliament was watching these battles closely and set about trying to find a solution. Their answer was to incorporate the "link tax" into a broader reform proposal around copyright and the DSM. The DSM aimed to translate the existing internal free market principles and efforts at harmonization that sustained the wider European political project to the digital environment. Copyright was a major tranche of the DSM process, which explains why a proposal for a new

Copyright Directive was tabled in 2016 (On Copyright in the Digital Single Market). Sitting alongside a range of reform options was "a new right for press publishers aiming at facilitating online licensing of their publications, the recoupment of their investment and the enforcement of their rights" (On Copyright in the Digital Single Market, 2016). Crucially, this reform did not address the foundational question about the copyright interests at stake when platforms used news content—they simply introduced an ancillary right that could be used as a mechanism to begin negotiations.

There were immediate concerns amongst the technology industry and sympathetic commentators that the European Parliament was seeking to introduce a strict "link tax." The core concern was that the reform would force businesses to pay whenever they linked to content. Freely directing people to other web pages sat at the heart of the philosophy that supported the world wide web, and they feared commercializing the process would disrupt a previously "neutral" internet. We explore this debate later in the chapter. For now, it's enough to know that while some Member States listened to this criticism and initially opposed the bill, the European Parliament eventually came to a working consensus (European Parliament, 2018). The Copyright Directive became European law in June 2019 and Article 15 was a core feature of the reform. The Article stated that when "information society service providers" used news content, "publishers of press publications" had to be compensated (Article 15, Directive (EU) 2019/790). It was also made clear that these revenues needed to be shared with the legal authors of the content. France was the first country to transpose these broad statements into national legislation and successfully enforce them. They were only able to do so after a long-drawn-out battle with Google, but their qualified success was telling. After years of resisting paying for news, why did Google eventually back down?

The directive in action

France moved quickly and by October 2019, Article 15 was transposed into national law. Google responded and immediately stopped showing content extracts or photos from French publishers on Google News (Gingras, 2019). However, they implied that publishers would be able to ask for these elements to be reinstated without cost, essentially establishing free licenses in France (as they did in Germany). The decision was a clear sign that Google was again going to do everything it could to avoid being forced to pay publishers for content. While the strategy had worked well in previous standoffs, this time the French were up for a fight. Organizations from the French publishing industry started to file complaints against Google with the French Competition Authority (Autorite de la Concurrence, or ADLC), arguing that Google had unlawfully refused to negotiate with them. These parties were bolstered by contemporaneous comments from President Emmanuel Macron, who declared that France was "going to start implementing the law" (Agence France-Presse, 2019).

Some months later, Google received bad news. In April 2020, the ADLC released a judgement that forced Google to open negotiations with the publishers who had brought the suit. The judgement was a significant development in the long-running debate around news payments. While the reform drew from copyright principles, the ADLC had taken a competition lens to the problem and found that Google's stonewalling would "constitute an abuse of a dominant position, as well as an abuse of economic dependence" (Autorité de la Concurrence, 2020).[1] Notably, the decision clearly stated that there *was* a level of dependence amongst news organizations with reference to Google.

The ADLC stated that Google's ability to give or withhold traffic to news organizations meant that both parties did not have equal bargaining power. The authority demanded web traffic data from 32 news titles and found that search engines provided between 26 and 90 per cent of the redirected traffic and since Google was the dominant provider in this market, dependence was established (Autorité de la Concurrence, 2020).[2] Such a finding is open to challenge. As we have already seen in earlier chapters, news outlets had varying levels of reliance on search engine traffic and certain outlets were doing their best to reduce their reliance on platforms when it came to distribution through building subscriber revenue. However, it was difficult to argue with the ADLC's more substantive finding that Google's immediate actions and subsequent attempts to ask news organizations for "free licenses" did not "reconcile with the object and the scope of the law" (Autorité de la Concurrence, 2020).[3] The practical outcome of the decision was that negotiations with publishers were to be opened immediately.

Google was also forced to reinstate "snippets" and associated media from news organizations on Google News (Autorité de la Concurrence, 2020). The platform appealed, but in October the Court of Appeal of Paris upheld the decision (Kayali and Larger, 2020). Google must have seen the writing on the wall because just before the Court of Appeal released its judgement it launched Google News Showcase. The USD 1 billion initiative would pay publishers for news content. The major difference would be that stories would be organized by publishers that would be paid for content, rather than by topic. The fact that Google was also trying to manage a battle over news payments in Australia influenced this decision to splash cash across the news industry. It, therefore, came as no surprise that around the same time, reports of more positive negotiations came from APIG, the group that published *Le Monde* (Rosemain, 2021). Google seemed to realize that they would have to pay for news. However, it was evident that they wanted to hand out money on their own terms rather than deal with restrictive legal frameworks.

Google eventually managed to agree to a deal with APIG in January 2021, with the platform handing over a reported USD 76 million for three years (Rosemain, 2021). While this was a victory for APIG, a group that represented over 120 publishers, other French publishers were left out in the cold. A few months later in July 2021, the ADLC fined Google EUR 500 million (Autorité de la Concurrence, 2021). The ADLC argued that Google's ongoing focus on the News Showcase foreclosed any discussions around remuneration for the "current use of content," essentially sidestepping the entire question of neighbouring rights (Autorité de la Concurrence, 2021).[4] They also accused Google of failing to negotiate with a range of outlets (including press agencies like AFP) and not providing a transparent account of how they came to a final valuation of news content. Google is planning to appeal the fine (France 24, 2021).

The French experience delivered mixed results. It became clear that Google had finally been worn down after a decade of ongoing lawsuits across Europe. The platform committed to paying news organizations for news content and set aside USD 1 billion to do so. APIG was also able to secure millions of dollars for its members. However, they had to share this windfall across their large member base. Google is also reticent about making agreements with other publishing groups and has been fined as a result. The company has also been cautious about handing over any additional information that could be used to establish the true value of news content such as user data.

Europe has also mainly focused on Google, with Meta not yet being forced to enter payment negotiations. However, the latter platform has already started to prepare for negotiations by launching its News Tab. Like Showcase, the News Tab is a more curated experience that sits apart from other content. It was launched in the United States in mid 2020 and the United Kingdom soon followed, with Meta giving millions of dollars to newspaper groups in the process (Waterson, 2020). Meta will have to pay European news organizations once other Member States transpose the directive into law. Indeed, Europeans were acutely conscious that while France was arguing with Google, a law introduced in Australia was starting to get results. The reform did not just bring Google *and* Meta to the negotiating table but also got them to hand USD 100 million to media companies.

Australia and the competition solution

Compared to Europe's drawn-out legal battles with Google, Australia was a late convert to news payments. Like many other countries, they first adopted a light-touch approach to platform regulation, allowing digital platforms to gradu-ally accumulate more users, data, and power (Flew, 2021). However, in contrast to the European story above, media companies in Australia did not immediately turn to the courtroom and seek to secure payments from platforms. This was no doubt related to Australia's common-law background and a century of relevant copyright jurisprudence that provided greater latitude to reuse small amounts of newspaper content and which confirmed that headlines and phrases were not protected by copyright.[5] This meant that while Rupert Murdoch remained a prominent global advocate around the issue, there were no drawn-out court battles between his Australian stable of News Corporation papers and Google across the early 2010s.

Australia started to get more interested in digital platform regulation and news payments in the decade that followed, thanks to a growing interest in two intersect-ing policy issues. The first was the collapse of the traditional business model that supported journalism. While this problem started to resonate with policy-makers from the late 2000s onwards, in the Australian case it took until 2017 for mean-ingful engagement to emerge at a national level. The Australian Senate led the conversation and formed a Select Committee on the Future of Public Interest Jour-nalism in May 2017. The committee had a broad remit, tackling media freedom, the commercial sustainability of journalism, and social and commercial issues associated with the emergence of digital platforms. The second policy issue was the growing power of digital platforms, which was signalled through concerns about market power, 'clickbait' and disinformation in the committee's terms of reference. This represented the early signs of an Australian "techlash," with legis-lators, policy-makers and regulators following their international counterparts and paying more attention to digital platforms (Flew, 2021).

The committee could have potentially made a substantive impact on plat-form regulation in Australia. However, the Senate was quickly overshadowed by the Australian Government. Only six months later, the government directed the Australian Competition and Consumer Authority (ACCC) to conduct an inquiry into digital platforms, focusing on how these institutions intersected with news media and advertising markets. The inquiry was launched because the government had made a deal with a minor party to establish this policy process in exchange for their support for media deregulation reform (Meese and Hurcombe, 2022a). However, the government's engagement with the ACCC suggested that they were also genuinely interested in solving some of these problems. The ACCC is responsible for competition law in Australia (also known as anti-trust) as well as consumer protection. However, it is also known informally within government circles as the "regulator of last resort" and is often asked to address difficult or complex issues (Danckert, 2019). That they—rather than Australia's media regulator, the

Australian Media and Communications Authority—received the inquiry suggested that the government wanted major reform. The ACCC's involvement also meant that the Senate inquiry vacated the field, largely leaving discussions around platforms to the newly launched Digital Platforms Inquiry.

The inquiry lasted over two years and the ACCC covered a lot of ground. The commission had a strong understanding of digital platform business models and was conscious that privacy and competition concerns not only intersected with one another but also had a potential downstream impact on media and advertising markets. They also took up concerns about misinformation and disinformation that were originally raised in the Senate Committee. The commission held wide-ranging discussions with stakeholders in the opening months, seeking to better understand how a reasonably complex market worked in practice. However, there was a sense that the ACCC was keen to establish a significant reform agenda, as confirmed in the release of a preliminary report in late 2018 (ACCC 2018). The commission proposed developing an independent regulatory authority for digital platforms and reforms associated with privacy. At this point, it also became evident that despite the reasonably neutral name of "digital platforms," there was a significant focus on Google and Facebook (soon to be Meta).

Interestingly, the issue of platform payments was not originally on the policy agenda and only started to emerge during stakeholder meetings in the months that followed. Everyone was conscious that the Cairncross Review in the United Kingdom had proposed a code of conduct to support bargaining between platforms and publishers and the idea started to circulate nationally (Flew and Wilding, 2021; Meese, 2021). People held different views about the proposal, with some supporting the idea and others lukewarm, but the ACCC took up the idea enthusiastically. By the time the final report and recommendations were released in late 2019, a voluntary bargaining code ensuring a revenue transfer from platforms to publishers was the centrepiece of reform. The government enthusiastically adopted the proposal and directed the ACCC to develop a voluntary code in consultation with stakeholders.

Negotiations were slow and stakeholders struggled to come to an agreement about what a code should entail. As the pandemic took hold and advertising revenue collapsed, the Federal Government stepped in and directed the ACCC to establish a mandatory code in April 2020 (Taylor, 2020). The draft code was released in July 2020 and core principles of the code that made it to the final legislated version were established. The ACCC would allow organizations to bargain with platforms that were designated under the code, either individually or separately. Parties would come to an agreement independently, but if that was not likely to occur a news organization could initiate a bargaining process.

The bargaining process would originally involve mediation but if no resolution was forthcoming, baseball arbitration would occur. Baseball arbitration is when the platform and publisher submit offers and an independent arbitration panel constituted by the Australian Communications and Media Authority makes a final binding determination. Alongside this central mechanism, the code also featured additional minimum standards that the platforms would have to abide by. In the initial release of the draft code, these standards included provisions that would allow news organizations to understand and access data about platform users that engaged with their content; warnings about forthcoming changes to algorithmic systems; the provision of additional tools to manage user comments; and appropriate recognition of original news content. Notably, there was no provision in the code ensuring that news outlets would spend any revenue sourced from platforms on public interest journalism.

The code was a direct threat to platforms because its core mechanism placed them in a corner. The presence of "baseball arbitration" not only ensured that some money would exchange hands but that if platforms continued to stonewall over payments, the financial determination about how much they would be charged would be entirely out of their hands. In worse news for Meta and Google, comments from the government and the ACCC not only suggested that Facebook and Google would be designated under the code but they would also target Google Search and Facebook News Feed as regulatable entities (Bossio et al., 2021). Moreover, the platforms also had to deal with several minimum standards that placed a set of novel obligations on them (such as a certain level of algorithmic transparency). In sum, Google and Meta were concerned that this draft code, which was much more detailed than the idea that emerged out of the Cairncross review, would offer inspiration to regulators across the world (Meese, 2021).

Google launched a lukewarm public relations campaign in August 2020 arguing that the code was going to "break" Google Search and did not account for the traffic and distribution value that platforms brought to news outlets (Bossio et al., 2022; Leaver et al., 2020). Meta also offered a robust critique of the code at points and threatened to stop featuring Australian news content on its platforms but did not engage in a similar public relations effort. These early complaints from platforms had some impact. A revised draft in December 2020 watered down the minimum standards, significantly reducing data transparency requirements. This was a win for platforms and small publishers. As we saw in the previous chapter, leading news companies were starting to transition into advertising platforms, and NewsCorp and Nine were no different. Securing data from platforms would boost their own advertising capacity. It would potentially weaken Facebook and Google's hold on online advertising but also deepen the gap between large and small publishers.

This development was the only victory for the platforms. Algorithmic transparency requirements were retained (albeit in a modified format) and the core problems of formal designation and the bargaining mechanism remained. Google's response intensified as the code made its way through parliament. In January 2021, the company threatened to pull Google Search from Australia, deployed a search pop-up, and experimented with removing local content from search results (Brook and Bonyhady, 2021). Meta also threatened to remove news from Australian products, explaining that they were already assessing how local news could be removed from the News Feed (Samios, 2021a). This was a notable development and signalled the extent to which these apparently complex and uncontrollable algorithmic systems (according to the platforms) could be finely tuned. It also revealed the independence of these new distributors, who were able to make politically charged decisions about how their algorithmic systems distributed content, with no existing legislation restricting their decision-making at all. Indeed, the Australian media could only watch as their content was "experimentally" removed, and the government had no power to intervene. So, legislators did the only thing they could do, which is push on with the reform. The bill started to proceed through parliament apace in February 2021. Australian politicians and regulators proclaimed that they had brought the digital giants to their knees while securing a future for journalism. It was at this point that Google, the most vocal opponent of the reform, acquiesced and started to sign deals with news organizations.

In contrast, Meta played hardball and followed through with their longstanding threat to remove news for the entire country. On 17 February 2021, Australians woke up and found that they were not able to access news on Facebook. Meta had not only removed news from people's feeds but the company had also blocked a range of additional pages including "the Australian Bureau of Meteorology, emergency services pages, health care pages, hospital pages [and] services providing vital information about the COVID-19 pandemic" (Leaver, 2021). They argued that the code had defined news too broadly. It eventually became evident that this was a deliberate ploy on behalf of Meta, who made a decision at the highest levels to adopt such a definition as a negotiation strategy (Hagey et al., 2022). Leaving aside the genuine public interest concerns, the move was a strategic masterstroke as it forced the government back to the negotiation table.

Over the next week, the Australian Treasurer Josh Frydenberg had ongoing meetings with Meta chief executive Mark Zuckerberg, eventually reaching a compromise. The platforms would avoid designation if the platforms were able to establish enough commercial deals with publishers. What was "enough" was not stated, so the threat of designation would always hang over Google and Facebook like a sword of Damocles. The outcome was something of a détente between platforms and the news media. Platforms avoided the strict bargaining mechanism and associated minimum standards so long as they handed over money to news organizations. The agreement was enough for the government, and the Australian News Media and Digital Platforms Mandatory Bargaining Code became law.

With designation no longer on the table, Meta joined Google to quickly establish commercial agreements with Australian news publishers. Within a matter of months, several deals had been done, and the total sums were an order of magnitude larger than those secured in France. While details of the deals were commercial in confidence, approximately AUD 200 million a year was given to the Australian news media sector (Hannam, 2022). Some of the larger players even secured deals on their own that match Google's deal with multiple French outlets. For example, Google agreed to give Nine Entertainment over AUD 30 million per year over five years (Samios, 2021b). Of course, the size of deals differed between outlets and between platforms. Reports suggest that Google is paying more than Facebook and offering more beneficial deals, including fee discounts on technology and additional revenue-sharing opportunities (Whitehead, 2021). What is clear is that Google has established more deals with more publishers. While not every media company has managed to secure a deal, the vast majority of the Australian news sector has a deal with at least one platform. The Australian code focuses on the production of "core news content," a definition that captures "issues or events" that are of public significance or relevant in "engaging Australians in public debate and in informing democratic decision-making" (Treasury Laws Amendment [News Media and Digital Platforms Mandatory Bargaining Code] Act 2021, s52A). A concern with core news content meant that outlets solely producing lifestyle journalism like restaurant reviews, entertainment, or travel originally struggled to secure compensation from platforms. However, a year after the code was introduced, Google secured deals with a broader range of outlets, which included lifestyle publisher *Time Out* and property publisher *Australian Property Journal*. A lack of designation also gives platforms the choice to ignore certain publishers and risk designation. This has seen Meta refuse to deal with certain outlets that were expecting payment.

The lack of designation means that the code is technically not active, with deals being done in the free market. Despite this, the code has been viewed as a success and countries across the world are now considering adopting Australia's competition approach (Meese, 2021; Furgal, 2021). In contrast to the European approach, Australia's model avoids modifying an already complicated national copyright law. The threat of forced bargaining and designation also pressures platforms to deal with news outlets and hand over money. Canada and New Zealand have both signalled that they will be pursuing news payments and will be informed by the Australian approach (Shakil, 2022), and there is currently a bill before the United States Congress that provides an exception to existing anti-trust law, allowing publishers to negotiate with platforms collectively and share information about the progress of negotiations (Cox, 2021). Most notably, Denmark seeks to go beyond European law and also incorporate collective bargaining mechanisms (Barsoe, 2021). While these proposals are not exactly like Australia's law, their focus on competition and market power aligns with Australia's approach. Canada's legislation is the most advanced and is on track to be enacted by the time this book is published.

Taken together, Australia and France have weakened Meta and Google's resolve. As we saw earlier in this chapter, platforms had resisted paying for news content and removed services from jurisdictions where new laws applied. After a series of bruising policy battles, we are now seeing platforms hand over millions of dollars to news organizations in multi-year deals. Considering this outcome, many politicians, regulators, and journalists have declared victory, arguing that securing payments has saved journalism and alleviated other problems associated with platforms. To provide one commonly cited downstream effect, advocates argue that entrenching the presence of news on platforms helps to drown out misinformation by providing quality information sources (Lu, 2021).

However, we should not welcome platform payments uncritically. In the next section, I explore the ACCC's analysis, which argued that a growing dependence on platforms for audience traffic was a justification for the above reform. I go on to argue that not only is this account only partially correct, but the proposed solution simply accepts the platformization of news and could potentially entrench platform dependence. The subsequent implementation allows digital platforms to shape the news market and further intensifies the role they play across the news sector.

Referrals and dependence

The beginnings of the ACCC's argument were outlined in their preliminary report. As a government authority, the commission was able to request access to sensitive industry data, which meant that their analysis was one of the more comprehensive studies of a complex media market. The core plank of their argument rested on data about referrals that they had received. The commission noted that in 2017, "Google and Facebook account[ed] for over half of referrals to Australian news websites, often providing more traffic than direct visits to the website" (ACCC, 2018, p. 31). They went on to outline the impact of referrals on specific media sectors, explaining that referrals from these two platforms accounted for "more than 80 per cent of traffic to news websites operated by radio broadcasters," more than 50 per cent for "the news websites operated by print and digital native publishers," and "more than of 40 per cent of traffic" to the news websites of television broadcasters (ACCC, 2018, p. 31).

At this early stage, there were already some issues around the framing of the problem. While the ACCC had a legitimate interest in ensuring a healthy news ecosystem overall, radio and television broadcasters were incorporated in the analysis even though their respective websites were not core business in many cases. The businesses of print and digital native publishers were more reliant on the ongoing success of their online websites. In any case, these overall numbers were used to make the preliminary finding that Google and Facebook were likely to hold substantial market power in the "supply of news referral services" (ACCC, 2018, p. 9) and were crucial partners in delivering audiences to media outlets. Supporting information was also provided in submissions from media outlets, with television broadcaster Seven West Media stating that around two-thirds of its traffic came from Google and Facebook and multi-platform media company Nine who said that their website received 30 per cent of referral traffic from Google and 10 per cent from Facebook (ACCC, 2018).

The ACCC did recognize that not all traffic from social and search was a direct substitute for someone accessing the website directly. Some people may have come across news on platforms that they would not have otherwise sought out. The commission also noted that the news media also clearly received a minor benefit from promoting their news content through these intermediaries. However, these were minor concessions and the commissions' preferred interpretation was made clear in the release of the final report. Interestingly, the ACCC did not find that the two platforms had substantial market power in the news referral market. They also restricted their focus to news publishers in the concluding analysis, excluding radio and television. However, even with these qualifications, the commission found that "Google and Facebook have become unavoidable trading partners for many media businesses" (ACCC, 2019, p. 253). In response, they recommended a code of conduct that would incorporate the sharing of revenue between platforms and news businesses or compensation. This would eventually become the bargaining code.

The above argument was framed around traffic and the audience. Adopting this perspective is entirely understandable in one respect, as audiences have long been accepted as the central product of media businesses (Napoli, 2003; O'Regan et al., 2002). However, the entire argument was soon challenged by the rapid pace of the media industry itself. As we already know, not every news media organization was wholly reliant on platforms for traffic and the relationship between platforms and publishers with respect to distribution is changeable. We know that at present,

Google is a more reliable ongoing source of referrals. The business models of many major news organizations are also in a critical transitory phase. While they are still reliant on advertising (and therefore referral traffic), many large news media companies are attempting to move to subscription models, which reduces the importance of referral traffic. We are also seeing messaging services and new social media platforms also emerge as places where people access news. Therefore, while there is some level of dependence with respect to referrals in certain contexts, the argument may become less robust as the sector continues to develop.

A hollow victory?

The focus on referrals also risks missing the forest for the trees. We have already identified a wide spectrum of dependencies across the news media sector. Considering this wider context, mandatory platform payments are likely to *increase* the level of platform dependence across the news media sector. In this section, we see how this policy intervention formalizes platforms as a central news distributor and further integrates platforms in the overall news media ecosystem. In short, it is a policy framework that embraces platformization.

The obvious initial evidence of integration is that platforms are now enrolled—however unwillingly—in the ongoing sustainability of news media companies. News outlets are struggling to generate revenue, major outlets are still in the middle of a transition towards subscription revenue and independent advertising platforms, and smaller outlets don't even have the luxury of these possible futures. This could appear to be a dramatic claim. For larger media companies these platform deals represent welcome but not transformative sums of money. Amounts are confidential but if we take reports and rumours at face value, platforms are not propping up the Australian news industry by themselves. Table 4.1 situates these payments in relation to the broader financial situation of selected major Australian media companies.

It is necessary to contextualize these numbers. Nine, Seven West, and News Corp are multi-platform companies and have interests in broadcasting and publishing. Nine and Seven West own Free-to-Air television stations that feature news and a limited amount of current affairs, whereas News Corp has a network of cable channels called the Australian News Channel (best known for Sky News). In terms of publishing, Nine has its own long-running news website as well as major newspaper mastheads in populous cities (Melbourne and Sydney). News Corp is the other major competitor, dominating the printed news media landscape in Australia, to the extent that their publications are often the only printed masthead in certain capital cities. Seven West has more limited publishing holdings, owning

TABLE 4.1: Rumoured amounts of deals made with Google against annual revenue for FY 21–22.

Media organization	Revenue FY 21–22 (m)	Revenue FY 21–22 (inc. broadcast)	Payment p.a. (m)[6]	Payment as per cent of revenue	Platform
Nine	593.5*	1964	30	5.95*	Google
ABC	1183[7]		12	1.01	Google
Seven West	169*	1537	30	17.7*	Google
News Corp	1,088*,†	4449*,†	70[8]	6.43*,†	Google

*Publishing revenue only.
†Australian revenue only.

a major newspaper in West Australia. Strictly, platform payments are agnostic and and are meant to simply recompense media companies for news content in general. However, as is common in many nations, the bulk of these companies' broadcast content is not news oriented and rely heavily on entertainment. As a result, while accounting for revenue from broadcast and publishing is strictly accurate in one sense, it may not actually provide a clear picture of how much is actually being earned from news content alone. As such I have decided to give primacy to the publishing revenue. While this excludes broadcast entirely, it gives a slightly better sense of the payments to news content ratio.

To provide a brief example, the multi-platform news and entertainment company Nine Entertainment is one of Australia's two major media companies with a broadcasting and publishing revenue of AUD 1,964 million for the 2021–22 financial year. The company's deal with Google is reported to be anywhere from AUD 30 million to AUD 45 million. This represents between 1.5 and 2.2 per cent of category revenue (Samios, 2021b). Taking the publishing revenue alone (AUD 593.5 million) offers a slightly higher percentage of 5.95 per cent. The table adopts the latter method to analyze reported (but unconfirmed) payments to the television station Seven West and News Corporation. Of course, the truth sits somewhere between these two sets of publicly available numbers (Table 4.1; Turvill, 2021). Seven West's numbers should be treated particularly lightly as they have a much smaller publishing business, in comparison to Nine and News Corp.

A final few clarifications relate to the ABC and News Corp. The ABC's numbers incorporate broadcast and online as the public service media organization has never had a printed offering. I have also only accounted for News Corp's Australian publishing and broadcast revenue. While News Corp's deal with Google was global and included payments to *The Wall Street Journal* and *The Times* as part of Google News Showcase, it was clear that the main focus of this deal was the Australian legislation. While these additional international properties no doubt bumped up the numbers somewhat, it is impossible to disentangle these different properties when it comes to accounting for Google's payment. These challenges are due to the limitations associated with corporate financial reports and the general lack of transparency around these deals. However, as noted earlier, they do not stop us from seeing that these payments make up a small to moderate amount of annual revenue at first glance. Indeed, they become seriously overshadowed by broadcast revenues, once they are taken into account.

Whole of industry analyses provide some additional context. The newspaper publishing and television sectors (incorporating Free-to-Air, cable, and streaming) in Australia bring in an annual revenue of AUD 13.8 billion which means that AUD 200 million from platforms are only a drop in the ocean for the sector (Calabria, 2022; Kyriakopoulos, 2022; Reeves, 2022). It is clear from the above data that these agreements do not secure the future of major media companies on their own. However, many of these sectors are running on relatively thin profit margins. Australian newspaper publishing industries are turning an annual profit of USD 108 million and the sector has declined by 10.8 per cent over five years (Reeves, 2022). Profit margins are higher for Free-to-Air television at USD 266 million and growth is somewhat stagnant (Kyriakopoulos, 2022). While pay television and streaming is looking more robust with a similar level profit (USD 258 million) and a stronger growth rate (6.8 per cent), much of this activity is supported by transnational streaming companies like Disney and Netflix, and does not directly relate to the production of news.

Subsequently, these payments represent a stable source of revenue that news media companies will rely on in a changeable market and may well boost profit margins (presuming that platforms are forced to keep paying). From here, it is clear to see how dependencies emerge. Platforms will also only make these payments so long as news organizations continue to let them use the content for their products and services. This creates tension, as companies must choose between stepping away from platforms or accepting a lucrative (and easy) revenue source. Unsurprisingly, most media companies have chosen to take the money. The decision means that despite diversification around distribution strategies and revenue, news organizations will be financially motivated to keep engaging in wider platform ecosystems. Greater integration should worry media companies considering they have traditionally struggled to remain sustainable in such a context.

When thinking about dependencies, it is also worth noting what was left out of the legislation. While politicians and policy-makers in Australia celebrated the deals, the reform did not address existing dependencies, many of which we have considered throughout this book. The proposals Google and Meta were likely to have been most worried about were requests for data sharing and algorithmic transparency, and they managed to block or significantly water down these reform efforts. Forcing platforms to share data about how their users interact with news content would give major media companies access to valuable data points that they could then incorporate into new advertising platforms. Algorithmic transparency would similarly force these platforms to reveal closely guarded corporate information to another sector. In contrast to these more aggressive interventions, payments allow Google and Meta to hand over money with little additional scrutiny while embedding news organizations more deeply within platform ecosystems.

As in other chapters, we can also connect these dependencies to wider examples of democratic harm. Critically, mandatory payments contribute to the widening gap between a select few news media organizations and the rest, threatening the long-term sustainability of a diverse media environment. The Australian legislation remains dormant, which means that platforms are not required to deal with any outlet that wants payment. As a result, the current situation gives Google and Meta the ability to influence the shape and structure of the news market. They can give money to some outlets and ignore others. Google has been relatively open to dealing with a range of publishers and has established deals with the vast majority of the Australian news media sector. However, Meta has refused to establish deals with the Special Broadcasting Service, a multi-cultural public service media organization, and The Conversation, an outlet that works with academics to publish relevant news content. In France, the agreement with Google has only enriched publishers associated with APIG. Such bias is likely to be of little concern to major news organizations. Whether a publisher secures a deal and more critically, the subsequent size of these payments could, if not deepen the gap between larger and smaller players, at least reinforce the status quo.

In the Australian context, simply enforcing the legislation may not provide a solution. Karen Lee and Sacha Molitorisz (2021) note that even if platforms *were* designated under Australian legislation, smaller companies may have little expertise to engage in negotiations with corporate giants. In Australia, there are exceptions to competition law that will allow smaller players to band together, but even if this does occur, it may not save some companies. If a small media company was struggling financially, and even if they were part of a larger consortium, they may not be able to survive through the long, drawn-out bargaining process.

There are also suggestions that Google's overarching approach to news does not integrate well with smaller outlets. Matt Nicholls is an editor of *Cape York Weekly*, a publication based in the far north-east corner of Australia, and he raised these issues in a 2022 Federal Government Inquiry into Australia's regional newspapers. He explained that Google requires publishers to "upload a minimum of six stories per day" (*Cape York Weekly*, 2022, p. 2), which in total represents twenty additional stories that a regional newspaper needs to produce. Many of these papers are already struggling and are unlikely to be able to double their production. Google has made deals with some regional outlets, but in his submission, Matt suggests that some of these outlets are "uploading a lot of press release material and generic content" to meet these targets (*Cape York Weekly*, 2022, p. 2).

The current state of affairs is clearly oriented towards establishing a détente between major media organizations and these two platforms, leaving small media organizations with little choice in the matter. Small outlets are likely to just accept what Meta and Google offer. They are also likely to have few resources available to seriously assess or even contest the offer without outside support. We also see clear evidence of the asymmetry present in the relationship between media organizations and platforms, which is at the heart of any form of dependence. Not only can Meta and Google pick and choose how much money they give to each party, but there are rumours that Google sets standards around the rate of publication that news media organizations must meet. There is also nothing stopping platforms from asking news organisations to ensure that the payments to support specific activities. This is evidence of a power imbalance and encourages news organizations to produce "filler content" or set up specific projects to keep receiving payments. While most large and small media outlets have secured a deal with at least one platform (in most cases, Google) there are still ongoing inequities that need to be accounted for.

Questions about media independence also come to the fore. Even though the Australian Government played a central role in establishing the payment scheme, these mandatory deals are done in secret. This means that despite the best efforts of books like these, we do not know the extent of Google and Meta's influence on the news media sector. The obvious focus is on the amount of money being transferred from platforms to news media organizations. However, more subtle details are potentially more revealing. Google's standard rates of publication suggest platform intervention in news production and distribution. These innocuous base standards, no doubt sitting somewhere in these confidential agreements, reveal a lot. They tell us about the inequities between platforms and certain publishers and the new arrangements that are shaping the long-term future of our news ecosystem.

Conclusion

The chapter has explored the debate around news payments and tracked the decade-long effort to get digital platforms to pay for news. Focusing on Europe and Australia, I outlined the two regulatory models that these jurisdictions used—competition and copyright—and identified the success of the Australian model and its potential adoption in other countries. I went on to examine and critique how platform dependence was constructed in the Australian policy process, which largely focused on traffic and referrals. In addition to noting the more complex nature of platform dependence, I suggested that news payments simply contributed to the problem. In the chapter that follows we turn from mandatory payments to voluntary contributions and explore the growing role of Meta and Google as a patron of news media. We will see how these companies use these gifts to avoid the sort of regulatory interventions described above, and to maintain dependencies on certain products and services.

NOTES

1. From the translation: "constitueraient un abus de position dominante, ainsi qu'un abus de dépendance économique."
2. From the translation: "les moteurs de recherche—et donc Google pour une large part—représentent, selon les sites, entre 26% et 90 % du trafic redirigé sur leurs pages."
3. From the translation: "ce choix paraît difficilement conciliable avec l'objet et la portée de la loi."
4. From the translation: "pour les utilisations actuelles de leurs contenus."
5. The relevant case here is *Fairfax Media Publications Pty Ltd v. Reed International Books Australia Pty Ltd*.
6. Reported by not confirmed annual payments. The length of these deals also differ for each company.
7. ABC is a public service broadcaster and so most of its revenue comes from government.
8. These deals have been reported as the result of a global partnership, with Google paying for News Corp's content across the world. Select UK and US publishers will be given money but the available detail specifically refers to the Australian content. With much of this money presumptively being booked as revenue for Australian publications, revenue in Table 4.1 only refers to News Corp's Australian publishing arm.

5

Platforms as Patrons

We're announcing a new program to establish stronger ties between Facebook and the news industry.
(Public statement accompanying the launch of the Facebook Journalism Project, January 2017)

The GNI will build on these efforts and deepen our commitment to a news industry facing dramatic shifts in how journalism is created, consumed, and paid for.
(Public statement accompanying the launch of the Google News Initiative, March 2018)

Every January, the small tourist town of Davos, Switzerland welcomes billionaires, chief executive officers, policy-makers, politicians, and the occasional activist to the World Economic Forum. The event creates space for the global elite to discuss pressing challenges around an overarching theme, supported by a public agenda filled with speeches and panels. The event also features a backchannel, where constellations of participants catch up in conference rooms to advance their agendas. In 2015, the gradual collapse of the news media sector was the topic of one Davos conference room (Bell, 2018).

Google was worried that its business model would be criticized, as it was capturing online advertising revenue that the news media relied on to stay afloat. In response, European policy-makers called on Google to pay media companies for news content, raising concerns about Google's anti-competitive practices and asking awkward questions about how Google's respect for fundamental privacy rights. Keen to avoid being cast as the "bad guy," Google met with 26 publishers at Davos and asked what they could do to help. As Emily Bell (2018, p. 251) narrates, while "[t]he answer was couched in many different ways, [it was] essentially the same from everyone sitting in the awkward circle of chairs: money."

Google took the hint and responded with the Digital News Initiative (DNI), a 150-million-euro fund to support innovative digital journalism and developing new business models. The contribution represented a major change in how the search giant would continue to engage with news. Google made a one-off contribution to French publishers in 2013 to stave off demands that they pay for news content but declined to make a sustained financial commitment to journalism (Marchive, 2013). The DNI saw Google offer millions of dollars to European news outlets and represented the first of many news-oriented "initiatives" from Google. Even at this early stage, some early trends were notable.

The money for the DNI came out of Google's marketing budget (Bell, 2018), and the initiative was launched in response to concerns across the news media sector and rumours of increased regulatory activity (Gonzalez-Tosat and Sadaba-Chalezquer, 2021). The DNI eventually went global and in 2018, it was renamed the Google News Initiative (GNI). Google continues to focus on innovation, but the company has also established new projects for subscription growth, media literacy, and the introduction of machine learning into newsrooms (Schindler, 2018). As we've already heard, they also launched the Google News Showcase in late 2020 and started paying certain news publishers for their news content.

Meta was less enthusiastic about financially supporting the news media industry and had a reputation of being more distant than Google. Money only changed hands when the news sector was producing content that aligned with Facebook's wider strategic goals. They were willing to pay news organizations to produce video content, but they had little interest in financially supporting the wider news ecosystem. Their reticence became untenable after the 2016 US election, once it was revealed that Russian-backed disinformation efforts were circulating across Facebook's network prior to election day. As we already know, the fallout motivated Meta (then Facebook) to move away from journalism and deprioritize news content in their news feed. However, it also produced an additional, somewhat paradoxical, response.

With regulators watching Facebook closely, the platform needed to respond to the disinformation problem. It also needed to manage growing discontent amongst news publishers, who were concerned about the role that Facebook was playing in the wider news ecosystem. In a matter of months, the Facebook Journalism Project (now the Meta Journalism Project, or MJP) was launched. The project offered news organizations financial support to keep up with changes in digital technology and journalism training while establishing specific projects to improve fact-checking and address misinformation and disinformation. In addition to these specific initiatives, Meta also started to pay news publishers for the content featured on Facebook News in mid 2020 (Statt, 2020).

The GNI and the MJP represented another significant change in the relationship between platforms and the news media sector. In the late 2000s and early 2010s,

Google and Facebook did not respond to the economic challenges and structural transformations facing journalism. Now both platforms were voluntarily transferring millions of dollars to the news media sector for training initiatives, content, and projects.

In this chapter, I approach Meta and Google's contributions as a form of patronage. Google and Meta were handing out millions of dollars to support the news sector and (at least initially) little was required in response. The following chapter examines the growing role that platforms play as patrons of news and outlines the risks of patronage for an independent media. I map the programmes that have been launched before and after the GNI and the MJP. Further details of these interventions are provided through studies that clearly show how such patronage encourages news media organizations to rely on platform infrastructure. In turn, these platforms use patronage to stave off regulatory attention and generate positive public relations. In other words, the risk of a news outlet becoming financially dependent on platforms or being encouraged to adopt news production and distribution processes in exchange for revenue is of concern. Meta and Google do not engage in editorial interference, but their interventions present new challenges for media independence.

Mapping platform patronage

It is worthwhile to start an analysis of platform patronage by thinking about why Google and Meta have contributed so much money to the news media sector. For Google, headline figures are relatively easy to come by. At the end of 2020, the GNI provided USD 189 million to news partners across the world (Google News Initiative, 2020). This money only accounted for money expended through the GNI from 2018 onwards and did not include the USD 1 billion given to selected news outlets through Google News Showcase, USD 100 million of additional marketing spend in response to the pandemic, or the EUR 305 million (approximately USD 345 million) distributed through the earlier DNI. Taken as a whole, Google has given around USD 1.63 billion to the news media sector.

Numbers for Meta are harder to come by. The company does not produce reports about its overarching programmes but instead releases funding information haphazardly. As such, it is difficult to tally how much money Meta has given to the sector. However, their contributions have been substantial. At the start of 2019, Facebook committed USD 300 million to news programmes (Brown, 2019) and promised an additional USD 100 million in response to the pandemic (Brown, 2020). While Meta often launches new projects supported by a few million dollars, it is unclear whether these funds are separate from these top-line figures. In addition, the company has also voluntarily paid certain news companies anywhere from USD 500,000 to several million dollars each year to feature their content in Facebook News (originally known as the Facebook News Tab). Interestingly, these contracts are unlikely to be renewed (Fischer, 2022). The rumoured top-line payment was USD 10 million per year and Meta's contributions were estimated to run into the mid-hundreds of millions of dollars at a minimum. These were multi-year deals, which meant that news companies could rely on these payments for some time (Mullin and Patel, 2019; Tobitt, 2021). However, Meta's recent change of direction highlights the risks associated with accepting platform largess.

Having gotten a sense of how much money is involved in patronage, we can now discuss where these platforms are directing their money. Looking at the 38 programmes launched by Google and Meta gives us a good idea of what is being funded. A vast majority of programmes are framed around innovation and sectoral transformation, a trend that started with the launch of the DNI, which focused on encouraging innovation throughout European journalism. Google and Meta both have added programmes that focus on improving the subscription revenue of selected news partners, encouraging these outlets to seek income beyond advertising. They also offer a variety of training courses, from basic introductions to digital journalism (see Meta's Reuters Digital Journalism Course), to approaches inspired by the technology sector (such as Google's Introduction to Machine Learning). In addition to the above, Google offers various labs that improve the capacity of news publishers to work with data (GNI Data Labs) and support building the audience of news websites (GNI Audience Labs). The platform has also created tools that they claim produce positive outcomes for online news organizations (GNI Data Tools).

A commitment to innovation and sectoral transformation is also seen in their more experimental funding initiatives, which are heavily influenced by the culture of Silicon Valley. Google is the central player in this area, supporting the GNI Startups Lab, which aims to help digital news entrepreneurs set up news organizations, and the Local News Experiments Project, which aims to "create sustainable, all-digital news organizations in communities currently underserved by local news" (Google News Initiative n.d.). Google has also launched the GNI Innovation Challenges (n.d.), which they believe supports "new thinking in online journalism." In all the above projects, the value to the technology company is clear; platforms are positioning news organizations as stagnant institutions, which struggle to adopt new data-oriented business practices and adapt to a changing online environment. Meta and Google look like pro-social actors that offer programmes to revitalize the moribund institution of journalism. The news media sector is always seen as lacking essential skills or knowledge that would allow businesses to succeed. The GNI Startups Lab and Local News Experiments Project go one step further and support the creation of new media companies, implying that these new entrants are better aligned with digital technology.

In addition to the above programmes, Meta and Google also support projects that directly manage external criticism. As we have seen, local and regional news has struggled to adapt to a platformized news environment, and so these two platforms have launched programmes in response, focused on local news. Meta has established the MJP Community Network, which provides grants of up to USD 25,000 to local news outlets, and Google supported the creation of Newspack, an open-source, pre-loaded WordPress platform that can be deployed by small and medium news businesses. Google then hosted GNI Community News Summit in 2021, which united community news producers from the United States and Canada. As noted earlier, a significant amount of funding has also been directed to media literacy and fact-checking initiatives. Google and Meta have provided training around these issues for journalists, courses for the public, and grants to address disinformation and misinformation, which many people view as a growing problem.

Infrastructure and strategy

Despite Meta and Google's best efforts to frame their patronage as pure generosity, it is clear that their patronage forms part of a broader public relations effort. The fact that initial forays in this area were funded by Google's marketing budget is telling. As we have already seen, platforms launch these initiatives to manage regulatory debates and their relationships with the news sector. However, these contributions are also informed by an agenda driven by platform dependence. Many of these programmes encourage news organizations to deepen their relationship with the platform infrastructures that Meta and Google own. News organizations are offered financial support to align their businesses' production with the financial goals and priorities of Google and Meta. The platformization process ensures that news organizations embrace relevant platform products, thereby establishing dependencies favourable to Google and Facebook.

Google encourages news organizations to embed themselves in Google's ecosystem through these targeted initiatives. Consider GNI Data Tools; their overarching goal sounds promising, as Google promised to develop tools for news organizations to use. These tools included: a News Tagging Guide, which allows news organizations to identify which data they should be collecting to understand their readers; News Consumer Insights, which provides data analysis to identify opportunities to engage with readers or convert them to subscribers; and Realtime Content Insights, which allows news organizations to identify real-time trends and deploy data visualizations. These are all useful tools, but they all require news organizations to use Google Analytics. News organizations are likely to already be using the service since it is one of the most popular web analytics products globally (Statista, 2021) and is used across the news sector (Fanta and Dachwitz, 2020). Offers like GNI data tools are deeply embedded in existing Google infrastructures.

The role of infrastructure is also evident in the GNI Cloud Program, which has given 200,000 small and medium news organizations free access to Google's cloud-based workspace, reminiscent of Microsoft Office. These organizations also received credits for Google's cloud computing infrastructure. In contrast to the example above, while most news organizations already used Google Analytics, in this case Google was encouraging the sector to incorporate other products into the foundational infrastructure that supports journalism. There are clear benefits for Google, as it allows them to capture market share around office suites (Statista, 2021b) and cloud computing in a key industry (Richter, 2022). Google has also been keen to highlight the benefits for news partners, which can stop paying for servers and more easily track edits to stories (Google News Initiative, 2020). However, even though the goals of the news and tech sectors may align, Google's generosity also exacerbates platform dependence. Once we add GSuite, Google Cloud, and Google Analytics to Google's extensive control over the advertising supply chain, for many newsrooms, journalism can't be produced without Google products and services.

Other areas of the GNI highlight how Google uses algorithmic systems to ensure a continued role in news distribution. As we saw earlier, Google has now overtaken Facebook in audience referrals to online news websites. In fact, GNI training reinforces the view of Google as a central intermediary for the news media. For example, the GNI Audience Lab has a strong focus on search discoverability and search engine optimization (SEO), a process that ensures Google search will present your website to relevant searchers. These seminars can lead to significant internal change. The US-based Center for Investigative Reporting noted that they had "implemented a stronger SEO workflow into our editorial processes" (News Revenue Hub, 2020), and Bridge Michigan reported "improved search engine optimization" because of their participation (Emkow, 2020). The fact that participants have organized their websites to favour Google search algorithms shows how these training sessions are more than just about upgrading journalistic skills. They allow Google to reinforce its position as a crucial intermediary for news distribution.

In contrast, Meta's programmes do not focus on Facebook and Instagram's roles as intermediaries. Keen to distance itself from news distribution, the company's programmes do not teach news organizations how to publish on their platforms. Instead, they encourage other forms of dependence by carefully aligning news media business models with platform products. Meta has concentrated on providing supporting emerging subscription business models through the MJP Accelerator Program, which is focused on building reader revenue streams for news organizations.

At first glance, Meta's approach does not appear to invoke the spectre of platform dependence. News organizations are actively encouraged by Meta to move away from the viral strategies adopted in the mid 2010s and work towards more sustainable solutions. However, there are subtler examples of dependence at play throughout these programmes. Promoting subscription products on Facebook means that news media organizations will continue to engage with the platform. While most companies would prefer to have subscribers sign up through their own independent websites, Meta still retains a significant audience and many people continue to source information about the world through their products. As such, news media organizations may have to keep focusing on Facebook as a central location for securing reader revenue, an outcome that the Accelerator Program reinforces.

In addition, while Meta does not publicly welcome news distribution on their products, its programmes do not completely disavow Meta products. One success story from the Accelerator tells of a French publisher using a Facebook Messenger bot to discover what readers were interested in. The publisher then wrote stories in response targeting their interests (Grant and Fritsch, 2020). A lifestyle publisher in Hong Kong reported success using Facebook's much-criticized Instant Articles format (Ng and Yeo, 2021). They reported that using Instant Articles improved their ability to secure strong SEO results, which required the alignment of Facebook products with Google's algorithms. The above cases show that the Accelerator Program can also encourage dependencies at the product level. It is unlikely that the French publisher will stop using the Messenger bot so long as it helps build their readership.

Supporting local news

These platforms have also contributed to local news organizations and small publishers. Google is working with partners to locate a viable business model for local news, and Meta has distributed funds to local and community publishers. In addition, both companies also provided relief funding for small- and medium-sized newsrooms during the global pandemic. There are good reasons for their generosity. Google and Meta's capture of the online advertising market damaged the business models of many mid-tier or smaller publishers. Larger national outlets could still survive due to economies of scale. In many cases, they had enough resources to start establishing alternative revenue streams (as discussed earlier).

In contrast, other publishers have struggled throughout the digital transition, and many were simply forced to shut down. In many countries, this has resulted in the appearance of "news deserts," where communities have little to no access to local media (Abernathy, 2020).

Therefore, Meta and Google's generosity must be understood as an effort to repair damaged business relationships. Local news and small publishers have been an obvious (albeit unintended) casualty of platforms moving into a dominant position in online advertising markets. There is also an imbalance at the heart of their patronage relationship with news media organizations. As noted earlier in this chapter, platforms are not interested in directly interfering with editorial decisions. However, the impact of their funding on the operation and function of local news economies is still of genuine concern. Indeed, with many of these news organizations in perilous financial situations, interventions from platforms raise genuine questions about whether new dependencies are being established.

To take one example, Google's Local News Experiments work to "create sustainable, all-digital news organizations in communities currently underserved by local news." Google meets community needs by partnering with local media organizations (Google News Initiative n.d.). The initiative is largely focused on cities with "a half million people because that's where local news decay is worst" (Fischer, 2019c). At the time of writing, seven new online news sites have been launched across the United Kingdom (Peterborough), the United States (Longmont, CO; Oakland, CA; Mahoning, OH; San Diego, CA; Coulder, CO), and Canada (Village Media). From the public records of funded news organizations, it becomes clear that Google has played the role of a start-up funder. *The Oaklandside* revealed that the business "received $1.56 million in seed funding from the Google News Initiative" (*The Oaklandside*, 2022), which illustrates the level of financial support other news organizations likely received from Google. *The Boulder Reporting Lab* also notes that Google will also offer an unspecified amount of "technical and product expertise" for two years (*The Boulder Reporting Lab*, 2022).

Google is not encouraging these organizations to rely on them for the rest of their operating lives. The platform is quite happy to provide initial funding as start-up news media businesses gradually build revenue sources. However, the presence of Google during these critical first two years of these businesses reveals systemic dependencies that emerge out of this patronage relationship is evident that in an impoverished media market, Google is one of only a few actors with the resources and capacity to fund local news organizations and remediate gaps in news coverage. As a result, Google has become a crucial part of the local news infrastructure. Of course, there are several organizations that invest in local news production through grants and training from the Institute of Non-Profit News or ProPublica (both US-based). However, Google stands alone as one of the few companies with the capacity, and critically, the interest to start up local newsrooms with millions of dollars. In such a situation, patrons like Google encourage local communities and democracies to rely on them. Dependencies become systemic because in certain cases local reportage simply *doesn't occur* without Google's contributions.

On Facebook, dependence has emerged in a different fashion. Meta has been less generous to local news organizations. Their patronage largely consists of gifts of around USD 25,000 for recipients to support community engagement or newsroom projects. To choose some quick examples, grants have been used to support community meetings that help local papers identify salient issues, develop voter guides, and establish community connections. These interventions suggest that Facebook is aware of its democratic role since grants often go to community-level democratic projects. However, the nature of these grants means there is little risk of dependence associated with Meta's patronage.

The threat from Meta is more existential. In some cases, local organizations are using Facebook as an information infrastructure to share news instead of their local newspaper. A group of Michigan researchers found that many local organizations preferred to post on Facebook, and local news media were "considered less and less important as intermediaries for local information" (Thorson et al., 2020, p. 1248). In addition, community residents can independently set up hyperlocal Facebook Pages or Groups, where news and information can be shared (Freeman, 2020; Turner, 2021). Facebook Pages serve to supplement an already existing local paper but can also replace it. The obvious risk here is that the very infrastructure of Facebook becomes a critical source of community information and knowledge. In such a situation, a more serious form of dependence may well occur; a Facebook Page or Group will replace the local newspaper (Meade and Hanna, 2022; Hess and Waller, 2020).

Platforms are not interested in running local news companies. Grants and initiatives are carefully structured so that news media companies do not continue to rely on them. As a result, there is a low risk of a small news organization becoming financially dependent on these platforms. There is also a little risk to editorial independence, as the operation of news organizations is clearly separated from platform funding. However, what this discussion around local news and patronage has shown is that platforms are becoming vital information infrastructures for democracies. Google is actively offering funding to fill gaps in reporting coverage and Meta is giving money to local projects focused on democratic engagement. Therefore, the risk of dependence is more of a systemic issue. Platforms play a market-shaping role through their patronage, as they choose which areas are deserving of local news. They also offer more foundational support for democratic activity through discrete projects associated with local news. Alongside these forms of patronage, they can also replace local newspapers and essentially function as a site of community engagement.

Considering that Google and Meta remain for-profit companies, allowing platforms to address news coverage gaps and support reporting is interesting, to say the least. It may well be that like the commercial newspapers of old, the companies will do their best to manage corporate commitments with a vague and imperfect commitment to positive democratic outcomes. The more worrying possibility is that platforms have little interest in supporting local communities, and these initiatives simply form part of a wider public relations effort. At a minimum, the emergence of platform patronage and the growing use of Facebook as a platform to maintain community connections suggests that we increasingly depend on platforms as core democratic infrastructure.

Google News Showcase and Facebook News

The earlier sections have detailed several journalism projects that Google and Meta have provided money under the auspices of the GNI and the MJP. However, there is one form of patronage that stands alone when it comes to expenditure: voluntary payments to news organizations for their content. As already noted, Google and Meta have set aside hundreds of millions of dollars for this effort and have launched Google News Showcase and Facebook News to facilitate these payments. These products launched in 2020 and only news organizations who have been paid for their content are able to host content on them. As always, there are strategic reasons behind the boundless generosity of platforms. In this case, payments formed part of a wider response to the debate around whether news organizations should be recompensed for the aggregation or hosting of their content.

In the previous chapter, we saw how platforms fought against paying for news content and managed to ignore numerous European initiatives before succumbing to the momentum of an Australian reform agenda. Meta and Google were effectively forced to establish agreements under the threat of further regulatory action (Bossio et al., 2021). This example showed how legal challenges and legislative reforms had been used to secure platform payments. We now turn to the extensive additional patronage that Meta and Google undertook to avoid this sort of regulation. These contributions reveal that Google and Meta are not as worried about giving money to news organizations as they are about being regulated by governments (Flew, 2021).

Google and Meta's fear of regulation explains an additional motivation behind voluntary payments. Meta and Google are acutely conscious about the spread of misinformation and disinformation on their platforms, which is drawing the attention of governments worldwide. In response, they are launching initiatives to address the problem and avoid direct regulation of their content. These efforts have not stopped some jurisdictions from imposing strict legislative requirements on platforms (most notably in Germany). However, many other countries are hedging their bets and seeing whether the media literacy programmes, stronger private enforcement, and supporting products provided by platforms reduce misinformation and disinformation (Meese and Hurcombe, 2022b). Showcase and Facebook News are supporting products and should be understood as forming part of the platform's overall response to misinformation and disinformation. Google and Meta have created exclusive environments for news and information, where only certain brands are allowed to contribute. Such restrictions stand in stark contrast to earlier examples of how these companies used to treat news. Google News functions as a more general aggregator of news, and Facebook's News Feed allows a wide array of content to be posted, which can potentially feature on someone else's News Feed (now simply called "Feed").

Platforms started seriously considering giving money to the news sector as the Australian reform process was concluding in mid 2019. With the prospect of news payments becoming a firm policy proposition, both Google and Meta launched new products in response. Governments working to introduce legislation addressing misinformation and disinformation probably also influenced their decision-making. Suddenly news organizations in other countries were being offered money for their content, in some cases after years of railing against platforms to no avail. The rollout of these new products proceeded apace. Now Facebook News is available in the United States, the United Kingdom, Germany, and Australia, and Google News Showcase is available in India, Japan, Germany, Brazil, Austria, the United Kingdom, Australia, Czechia, Italy, Colombia, Argentina, Canada, and Ireland.

Considering the regulatory context, these payments may not look like patronage at first glance. Instead, it could be argued that Google and Meta were simply trying to outmanoeuvre their competitors by securing deals with news media organizations before they were forced to do so. However, a closer look at the deals challenges this view. Reports show that they were basically money transfers with few strings attached. One anonymous participant revealed that when dealing with Meta, "no audience hurdles and no minimum thresholds" needed to be met (Turvill, 2020a). Instead, their business automatically made around 10 per cent of their content available on the platform on an ongoing basis. Similarly, there have been mixed reports on the effectiveness of Google News Showcase. Some partners claim that they received "minimal traffic from the aggregation site" (Turvill, 2021).

While Google has strongly defended the value of their new product, it could simply use News Showcase as a way of justifying paying certain media companies over others. Google and Meta's approaches do not provide any insight into the value of news to their business models. These platforms simply hand over money and expect news organizations to take it without further questions. Considering the above examples, patronage seems like the appropriate term (Turvill, 2021; 2022).

Research from journalism studies points to worrying trends in media pluralism. These voluntary payments appear to be predominantly directed towards "dominant international and national news brands" that already have large audiences (Myllylahti, 2021). While some small or medium-sized publishers have also been given money, deals appear to be done on a random basis. There is little justification given for why some outlets are funded over others. As Merja Myllylahti (2021, p. 14) suggests, the behaviour of platforms has real potential "to strengthen the 'winners'—dominant international and national news brands—and weaken the 'losers'—including regional and local news publishers and independent news outlets." The extent of these contributions points to the potential market-shaping role that voluntary platform payments play in the news media economy.

Platforms argue that they are entitled to choose the news that they feature on their platforms. As private companies, they should not be compelled to fund every news organization in the world. Google has said as much, explaining that "not all publishers produce the volume and type of content necessary for the product, and our level of funding can't account for all news organisations" (Mayhew, 2021). Meta has made a similar statement, explaining that they prefer to pay for "quality, premium news content" (Submission to Senate Economics Legislation Commission, 2020). These arguments are understandable. While platforms have a role to play in supporting the overall health of media systems, they are not responsible for them in the same way that democratic governments are. We should not rely on Meta or Google to fund journalism.

However, it is impossible for these companies to maintain the fiction that they are entirely removed from the news media sector, operating only as disinterested and generous benefactors. Google and Meta, like all patrons throughout history, hold significant institutional power and influence. These companies are naturally going to ensure that any funded news organizations align with their wider strategic goals. As such, any contributions are going to influence the future of the news media sector. While this chapter has focused on various forms of patronage, voluntary payments are the largest contribution and so carry the greatest impact on the wider media economy. The problem for liberal democracies is that Google and Meta are loathe to recognize or account for this impact.

While giving private money to certain newspapers or broadcasters has always been a feature of the news media markets (Baker, 2002; Tambini, 2021), funders have been committed to the media itself, politics, economic outcomes or a combination of all three. It is a strange situation to see two companies voluntarily fund news purely to avoid regulation and to address their own public relations failings. These motivations are political but of a different calibre to the party-political interests that are found throughout the history of the press. Meta and Google's self-interest means that they are not focused on the downstream problems that come from their interventions across the sector. Rather, they leave dealing with the impact of their arbitrary funding of selected news organizations to others. Meta's sudden decision to no longer pay US news media for content is a salutary example of how erratic and disruptive these payments can end up being without supporting legislation (Fischer, 2022).

In terms of these downstream impacts, there is a significant crossover with the discussion around mandatory payments in the previous chapter. Whether voluntary or mandatory, some news organizations may become reliant on these regular sources of revenue and in turn, align themselves with platform requirements. There are also concerns that payments may influence the long-term structure of the news media sector and in so doing, affect media diversity. With these issues discussed in Chapter 5, I now turn to the most obvious issue associated with platform patronage, that of media independence. Patronage clearly implies some level of obligation and influence, which presents a challenge for a sector that is supposed to be independent. Of course, the news media has never been free from political and commercial interference, but the growing influence of platforms presents novel challenges. The issue is not whether the news media is "free" in some ideal sense, but rather how to realize practical media independence in the context of growing platform dependence.

(In)dependence and transparency

In liberal democracies, the news media are presumed to be independent (Tambini, 2021).[1] However, it is not enough to simply proclaim this independence. Instead, an environment that fosters autonomy must be established around a set of normative standards. Rather than detailing all these standards, here I note two basic principles relevant to our discussion around platform patronage. Firstly, news organizations must be able to "operate autonomously" (Tambini, 2021, p. 138), free of editorial direction or subtle influence wielded by potential funders. Secondly, any funding requirements must be subject to "procedural standards and independence" (Tambini, 2021, p. 164), ensuring that platform revenue is transparently and logically distributed while considering the impact of these contributions on the wider media environment. Of course, as we have already seen, both normative conditions are not reflected in the growing patronage activity in platform dependence.

Editorial independence is not threatened by platform payments. Google and Meta have consistently claimed that they are not interfering in the production of stories. Indeed, interfering with news production would be a strange move for platforms based in the United States, home of the First Amendment. German researchers have interviewed German journalists and managers who were recipients of Google's Digital News Initiative (Fanta and Dachwitz, 2020). Participants in the project rejected any suggestion of direct interference or influence from Google. However, these findings do not let Google or Meta off the hook, as the interviewees discussed alternative ways Google's patronage was more subtly deployed.

Google's investment in journalism training and the industry means that they naturally seek to influence the future of the profession (Fanta and Dachwitz, 2020). From what we have seen through their patronage, one such goal is encouraging news organizations to increasingly rely on Google infrastructure. Many news organizations now rely on the platform for news distribution through search or for revenue. Google's advertising and patronage efforts around cloud infrastructure and office tools have only expanded their territory. Meta has not contributed as much money, but their programmes similarly have encouraged the news media sector to view their platforms as a source of audience traffic and an opportunity to experiment with new products. Taken together, these efforts allow each company to reframe their attempts at "infrastructural capture" (Nechushtai, 2018) and platform dependence as well-meaning patronage.

Headline contributions from both platforms form part of the same strategy. These contributions have come in the form of voluntary platform payments, where millions of dollars have been transferred from Meta and Google to news organizations. Both platform companies remain focused on influencing prospective reform agendas rather than engaging in direct editorial influence. Much like other forms of patronage, dependence is assumed by these deals. As with the more stringent Australian reforms, news organizations are required to post content on Facebook News or Google News Showcase to receive revenue. As such, these payments function as simply another type of "capture" (Nechushtai, 2018). They also point to the conflicting motivations of platform companies. Google and Meta are keen to disavow their interest in and reliance on news content. However, their patronage efforts encourage platform dependence amongst news organizations. These conflicting outcomes suggest that these two companies are clearly not that worried about platform dependence and are primarily focused on managing threatening regulatory proposals from various jurisdictions. Indeed, the ongoing focus on regulatory movements can be seen in Meta's decision to more or less abandon news entirely, to avoid the regulatory hassle of paying for content. Along with refusing to renewing content payments, the company also recently laid off staff who were apparently central to these patronage efforts (Fischer, 2022; Scire, 2022).

Such financial contributions present challenges around media independence. The arbitrary funding of news organizations as determined by platforms is not a fair or reasonable way to secure the future of the news industry. Confidential voluntary payments also mean that news organizations are negotiating in an information vacuum, making exact amounts paid and the services rendered the subject of hushed rumours. It is impossible for anyone to know just how much money Google and Meta are providing to news organizations. They are simply encouraged to take any money they are offered. The lack of funding transparency is a net loss for the general public, as there is limited information about the extent of the financial relationship between platforms and news organizations. In addition, with platforms as decision-makers, additional revenue is distributed with their long-term goals in mind, rather than thinking about wider democratic outcomes.

The media cannot continue to function with platforms providing variable and largely unchecked funding to selected partners. The problems are clearly seen in these voluntary payments, but it is notable that even with more stringent requirements, the Australian reform experiment ended up in a similar situation (Bossio et al., 2021). While Google has been quite generous with who it deals with, Meta has been unwilling to negotiate with small and medium players. Platforms can pick favourites and can even simply cancel contracts if they no longer want to serve news content. It is up to the Australian Government to designate Meta and start another regulatory battle to ensure compliance. Of course, if Meta is legitimately no longer interested in supporting or hosting news content, whether they should be forced to pay money to support an unrelated sector is a genuine question. At a minimum, greater transparency around these payments and more sustained intervention from policy-makers and industry are required to ensure that platforms do not distort the news media market. Governments, policy-makers, and regulators should also consider incorporating patronage efforts in their overall assessment of news media environments.

NOTE

1.   There has been a longstanding international bifurcation of media freedom doctrines. The United States has adopted a strong negative rights tradition focused on avoiding government control, whereas the European Union have been more comfortable with placing duties on media. Nevertheless, there is broad agreement around these top-level beliefs, albeit with no formal consensus.

6

Solutions for a Dependent Press

I suspect that soon we will have five, 10, 15 countries
adopting similar rules.
(Canadian Heritage Minister Steven Guilbeault on mandatory
platform payments in Ljunggren, 2021)

It's no use. I'm stuck.
(Winnie the Pooh from *The Many Adventures*
of Winnie the Pooh, 1977)

We begin our final substantive chapter in Salzburg, Austria, via the soundstages of Los Angeles. I am talking of course about *The Sound of Music*, a movie and eternal family favourite that depicts the love between a trainee nun and a strict naval officer, amidst the background of the lead up to the Second World War. One of the stand-out songs in the Oscar-winning musical is "How Do You Solve a Problem Like Maria?" Composed by musical theatre royalty Richard Rodgers and Oscar Hammerstein, the scene features a group of nuns ruminating on the problem of Maria Rainer, an enthusiastic but somewhat forgetful nun who isn't committed to convent life. In the chorus, Reverend Mother sings about the impossibility of controlling such a character, asking "How do you hold a moonbeam in your hand?" In the context of a mid 1960s musical, her reflections were a useful way of placating a group of frustrated nuns. Unbeknownst to Rodgers and Hammerstein, the lyrics also gesture to the seemingly intractable problem of platform dependence.

It can appear impossible to ensure the long-term sustainability of sectors that are increasingly reliant on platforms like Google and Meta. As technology companies start functioning as infrastructure, other sectors depend upon them to run their businesses. To complicate further matters, platforms offer infrastructural capacity at various points of the news media supply chain, which means that we cannot just focus on one problem area. When looking at the news media sector, it is not enough to consider how Facebook's algorithmic systems influence the production, consumption, and distribution of news. We must also account for Google's control over the advertising supply chain, the impact of platform patronage efforts, and the adoption and use of platform tools. One may well find solace in the words of the Reverend Mother when reflecting on platform regulation. Trying to intervene in this dense web of infrastructural dependencies is like trying to "catch a cloud and pin it down."

At least, the Reverend Mother had the option of sending Maria off to be a governess. She became the Von Trapp family's problem—and eventual matriarch. Policy-makers and regulators have no such luck. With citizens and politicians increasingly concerned about platforms, public officials have been tasked with the difficult job of working out how to regulate platforms (Flew, 2021). Laudably, government agencies across the world have taken on the challenge and have introduced a series of regulatory interventions to minimize the growth of "platform power" (Moore and Tambini, 2018). We already know that there is a growing consensus around the use of platform payments as a critical intervention—yet these reforms do little to solve platform dependence. In this chapter, I consider how regulators and governments could best address the problems associated with platform dependence in the news sector.

Many existing reforms are ineffectual because they treat the symptoms of platform dependence rather than the cause—an approach supported by a constrained framing of the relationship between platforms and publishers. I outline alternative solutions here and see how direct interventions focused on platform's market dominance over the advertising supply chain, as well as reforms that allow third parties to observe platform behaviours carry more impact. Following a section on why current interventions haven't been effective, I discuss more targeted reforms that aim to address more immediate concerns about how platform dependence impacts journalism.

The wrong target

The fact that mandatory platform payments do not address platform dependence should come as no surprise. The proposed solution is situated within a highly specific market context—the relationship between platforms and publishers. We see this type of intervention in the Australian example, where Meta and Google are framed as unavoidable trading partners for news media organizations who depend on these companies for audiences. Reforms aim to address this power imbalance by establishing better bargaining conditions, which force platforms to pay for news content. The stated policy goal is to create a balanced and regulated arena for negotiation to take place, but one could also view this intervention as an attempt to transfer advertising revenue from one to the other. With the market now operating efficiently and news media organizations boosted by additional revenue, society will start to see positive downstream impacts.

The reasoning about Australian-style mandatory platform payments has a comforting logic. News media get some additional revenue and platforms are duly punished. However, as noted earlier, focusing purely on referral traffic and the exchange of advertising revenue fails to correctly diagnose the scope of the problem. News organizations can secure some audiences without the assistance of platforms, and many are adopting different business models that avoid relying on referrals. There is also extensive and growing evidence that the collapse of journalism's business model had little to do with platforms (Lotz, 2021; Giblin and Doctorow, 2022). We can turn to the evidence of a decline in news circulation and city-based competition between dailies from the 1940s onwards (Lotz, 2021), or business histories of the news media sector, which tell stories of publications floundering in a changing communication environment (Abramson, 2019; Dunlop, 2013; Ryan, 2013). The answer is not to ignore or explain away the reality of platform dependence but address it at its source. We know that the news sector is still reliant on a platform-dominated advertising market for revenue. Therefore, it makes more sense for the news sector to place its hopes in recent policy efforts that work to address dependence at its source—the advertising supply chain.

Some of the most interesting work around the supply chain is occurring in the United Kingdom and Australia. Regulators in these jurisdictions have proposed reforms to limit Google's dominance, which I consider below. If successful, these regulatory efforts will produce an improved online advertising market while freeing up revenue from Google to see it sent on to publishers or returned to advertisers.

Fixing the supply chain

Regulators in Australia and the United Kingdom have correctly identified the biggest problem in the online advertising market: each platform can share data across its various products, which they are biased to treat favourably (ACCC, 2019; Competition and Markets Authority, 2020). In response to these concerns, the UK Competition and Markets Authority (CMA) and the Australian Competition and Consumer Commission (ACCC) have suggested similar reforms. Their proposals include introducing a new set of rules for the sector that would force Google to share data with competitors where feasible, ensuring greater transparency of Google's operations, and establishing "data silos" that limit Google's capacity to capture and combine information from across their supply chain. These are merely recommendations at this stage, but the obvious aim is to weaken Google's capacity to deploy its market power for its own benefit.

What is interesting for our purposes is that these reforms borrow from regulatory approaches that are already in operation in adjacent markets. In doing so, they take us closer to solving Mother Superior's problem at the start of this chapter. It turns out that other sectors have already had to work out "how to catch a cloud." As Terry Flew (2021, preface) notes, "although digital platform regulation presents many complexities and challenges, these are not inherently greater than those associated with other industries that deal with intangible global commodities for instance banking and finance." Early recommendations for online advertising suggest that regulators are starting to recognize that regulation is not only achievable but there may well be similarities between sectors. Indeed, as noted earlier in this book, Dina Srinivasan has been one of this idea's key advocates, arguing that there are clear similarities between financial markets and online advertising markets.

Srinivasan explains that these markets function in similar ways, and "access to information, speed, and the routing of buy and sell orders are the linchpin of a healthy, competitive market" (2020, p. 77). US financial markets are strictly regulated to protect against the problems that have been witnessed across the online advertising sector. If you run a stock exchange, you usually cannot also be involved in trading. However, even if a firm is given permission to perform both activities as a multi-service firm, they "must manage their conflicts of interest and cannot simply route their customers' buy and sell orders (order flow) to the firm's own electronic trading venue" (Srinivasan, 2020, p. 82). Alongside these protections, brokers who buy and sell stocks for customers cannot use information about widespread trading activity—gathered through the operation of their business—to trade for their own financial gain. In addition, rules on insider trading ensure a generally transparent market with information made as public as possible.

These rules are not applicable in the current online advertising market. As we have already seen, Google has been reportedly self-preferencing throughout the advertising supply chain. They have allowed its exchange to engage in "last-look" bids and ensure that the full ad inventory from Google Ads can only be seen on Google Ad Manager. Srinivasan's proposed solution to these problems is to weaken Google's dominance by requiring "exchanges to provide all traders with non-discriminatory access" (Srinivasan, 2020, p. 173) to both consumer data and speed. This looks like separating "conflicting operations" (Srinivasan, 2020, p. 162) and regulating conflicts of interest by establishing ethical walls. Communication scholar Dwayne Winseck notes that the regulatory toolbox of telecommunications offers similar solutions with "bright line" rules drawn around market structures and firewalls within the business itself (Winseck, 2020; also see Rahman, 2018a, 2018b). With respect to online advertising, a similar approach would see these "firewalls" introduced "between different layers, actors and activities" across Google's "advertising stack" (Winseck, 2020, p. 268–69).

At first glance, these reforms do not appear to immediately benefit the news media. It is easier to see value in Meta and Google handing over millions of dollars to selected publishers, instead of a code of conduct for advertisers or structural separation. However, these latter reforms are likely to have a more meaningful impact, by allowing outlets across the board to secure advertising revenue. A fairer online advertising market means that less revenue would go to Google, and more revenue to publishers and advertisers. The Competitions and Market Authority notes that "intermediaries capture, on average, at least 35% of the value of advertising bought through the open display channel" and that "greater competition and transparency would put downward pressure on these fees and help ensure that publishers can get a better deal" (2020, p. 211). Similarly, the ACCC found that "fees for the four key ad tech services made up 27% of advertiser expenditure on programmatic advertising in Australia in 2020" (2019, p. 48). They go on to argue that a more competitive market would reduce these fees and free up more revenue.

Considering the lack of maturity in the news subscriptions market, most news publishers continue to have a vested interest in the successful operation of the online advertising market. As noted earlier, many News Corp submissions to Australian government inquiries have focused extensively on ad-tech systems. As such, it makes sense to focus regulatory attention on this area, to ease dependence and support the potential success of the news media. The trajectories identified in this analysis also provide some insight into emerging two-stage solutions to platform dependence. The CMA and ACCC want to introduce more competition into this market and weaken Google's dominant position. Doing so would ensure that no outlet would wholly rely on Google for advertising revenue. However, even if Google continues to control the market, they are also proposing targeted regulations that ensure that a fair and equitable relationship can be established between dominant platforms, advertisers, and publishers.

Watching the platforms

Problems with the ad-tech supply chain mean that there is a macro trend towards platform dependence across the news media sector. News companies can also become dependent on platforms for distribution but, as we already know, these dependencies are more dynamic. We have seen this play out when Facebook served as a distribution source. Several companies oriented their distribution strategy around Facebook's algorithmic systems in the mid 2010s, only to turn to Google, Instagram (also owned by Meta), TikTok, or in-house distribution methods (like newsletters), when Meta altered how Facebook distributed news across its platform in January 2018. Of course, around that same time, several populist websites discovered that they found favour with the new parameters that informed Facebook's algorithmic systems and invested significant resources into the platform. The always-changing context around distribution means that we need to consider an alternative approach.

Thankfully, Bernhard Reider and Jeanette Hoffman present a way forward with their concept of *platform observability*. These authors note that scholars, policy-makers, and governments have been largely concerned about the transparency of platforms' algorithmic systems. To this end, they have advocated for more algorithmic transparency and called for platforms to open their "black box" systems to scrutiny. Common regulatory tools they have proposed include asking for source code disclosures or running algorithm audits that examine algorithmic decision-making and processes at a particular point in time (Seaver, 2019). However, Reider and Hoffman explain that it is incredibly difficult to locate, dissect, and analyze algorithmic systems. The systems owned by platforms are highly distributed deep learning systems, making decisions through the opaque analysis of billions of data points. The provision of source code or assessment of an algorithm at a point in time doesn't account for the "dynamic, and distributed materiality of contemporary computing technologies and data sets" or "the evolving interactions between changing social practices and technical adjustments, which may, in turn, be countered by user appropriations" (Reider and Hoffman, 2020).

Reider and Hoffman argue that a more effective solution is to continue to observe platforms. Doing so allows researchers and regulators to understand and assess their impact on different sectors. There are already examples of data sharing between platforms and the wider community, which allow for some of this observation. Until recently, Twitter had a relatively open application programming interface (API) that allowed researchers, hobbyists, and regulators to collect and analyze activity on the platform (Burgess and Baym, 2020). Meta has been more reticent following the Cambridge Analytica scandal and dramatically restricted outsider access to its API (Bruns, 2019a). In its place, the company has enacted formal research partnerships with selected researchers, which in some cases includes the provision of platform data through Social Science One. Meta also provides access to CrowdTangle, which gives industry and academic users basic information about the content on their platform. In addition to these platform-led initiatives, regulators can also compel the provision of information when conducting inquiries, forcing platforms to provide details about how their systems work.

The European Union (EU) and the United States have gone so far as to develop legislation that forces platforms to provide research data. The EU is planning to introduce the Digital Services Act, a significant proposal that aims to establish regulatory parameters for significant (or as they call them, "Very Large") online platforms. The current text addresses several important issues, but Article 31 is of most immediate relevance to this discussion. Article 31 would require platforms to make data available to academic researchers who would use the data to identify and understand "systemic risks." The Platform Transparency and Accountability Act, proposed in the United States Senate, has similar aims. It proposes that platform work with the National Science Foundation to enable approved research projects to access platform data (Coons, 2021).

These efforts represent largely intermittent efforts at collecting and analyzing data. Regulators can only ask for data when specific inquiries are happening, and researchers can only request data for discrete projects. An important aspect of Reider and Hoffman's (2020) argument is that observation must be *continuous* and *ongoing* because the interactions between platforms and the wider environment are so unpredictable. One step forward in this regard is the development of platform observatories, in which citizens donate selected data to researchers. These donations allow researchers to develop a more granular account of how these technical systems function and can operate with the tacit approval of platforms. Early efforts have seen people work with researchers to study search personalization (Bruns, 2022). With a growing number of democracies establishing specific agencies tasked with regulating the digital environment, developing legislatively backed digital observatories would allow policy-makers to better understand the ongoing interactions between platforms and critical sectors like the news media industry.

Many individual news organizations have already set up their own digital observatories. Newsrooms are now awash in metrics, and editors know exactly where their traffic is coming from and how well a story is doing (Christin, 2020; Petre, 2021). Individual organizations can, if not wholly understand, at least make an informed guess about how their distribution strategy intersects with algorithmic systems. However, an industry-led platform observability effort is unlikely. Internal information is incredibly sensitive and individual companies will not share it with competitors. Therefore, at this stage it looks like this effort will need to come from the government and academia rather than the industry itself.

Targeted observability

Platformization is a society-wide development that has revealed new opportunities and created new problems, of which platform dependence is just one. It stands to reason that the most effective way to address these problems is at its source through structural reforms. A focus on observability also accounts for the dynamic nature of dependence, particularly when it comes to distribution. As we have seen, while news organizations are often broadly dependent on platform infrastructure, specific dependencies are often dynamic and therefore difficult to track. Of course, it is also important to address the specific challenges that platform dependence presents to the normative goals of journalism: informing the citizenry, maintaining a diverse media environment, and ensuring media independence. We begin by considering what reforms have been proposed in the first two areas and see how platform observability offers opportunities for positive interventions. We are now less worried about directly alleviating dependence and are instead focused on the downstream risks that emerge from news content circulating on platforms, and the platformization of the news media industry.

Ensuring quality information

One great challenge of the networked information environment is that any speaker can reach and potentially command a large audience. Content from media companies must compete to be heard in an increasingly noisy online communication environment. Influencers, nation states, individual politicians, meme accounts, and ordinary people are all potential competitors for vital real estate. Platforms use algorithmic systems to curate this content and play an important role in deciding what content ends up on an individual user's feed. Such critical decision-making power means that these technology companies will be partially responsible for supporting the circulation and consumption of quality information for the wider public.

After years of waffling (Napoli and Caplan, 2017), platforms have started to take some positive steps with content moderation. Meta has established an Oversight Board for Facebook, which allows an independent body to adjudicate on the most challenging moderation decisions. The growth in disinformation activity and the spread of misinformation during COVID-19 pandemic has also forced platforms to recognize that the general health of the information ecosystem is a critical concern. Several jurisdictions are actively introducing reforms that force platforms to actively commit to reduce disinformation and/or misinformation. At the most interventionist end, Germany's Network Enforcement Act (or NetzDG) forces social media platforms with two million users to:

- Allow users to report content easily;
- Remove "manifestly unlawful content" within 24 hours;
- Remove "unlawful content" within seven days;
- Produce transparency reports.

While the law focuses predominantly on hate speech and content moderation, the prevalence of misinformation was an additional motivation for passing this Act. The EU (of which Germany is a part) and Australia have decided to embrace a more consultative approach, starting with voluntary co-regulatory initiatives and later scaling up to more enforceable regulatory instruments (Hurcombe and Meese, 2022).

These developments show that platforms are increasingly answerable for the wider information environment on their products. As a result, they are being incentivized to support the wider circulation of quality news. Initial efforts from governments mostly focus on transparency, but adjacent proposals from civil society give us a sense of what may be possible with platform observability. At the start of the COVID-19 pandemic, the activist group Reset Australia called on Big Tech to provide a live list of COVID-19-related URLs to "public health officials, government, academics, and journalists." The list would help decision-makers and analysts see which sources were "gaining traction on social media"[1] and help them better understand how misinformation was circulating online. While the proposal was largely ignored by platforms, it is an example of a targeted observability measure that could provide ongoing insights into information quality across the online ecosystem.

Exposure diversity

Observability also has a crucial role in assessing media diversity. As noted throughout this book, democracies rely on a plural and diverse media and many actively work to bolster it. Therefore, understanding what content circulates through our media systems becomes an important task that increasingly implicates platforms. So long as the news media sector continues to distribute content on products like Google Search and Facebook, platforms will make decisions about the types of content that people see based on their expressed interests and associated data points. With algorithmic systems largely focused on establishing a curated list of content, understanding exposure diversity—what sort of content is being presented to whom—becomes an important issue (Helberger, 2012).

We know that initial concerns about people being stuck in "filter bubbles" and not having access to alternate viewpoints have been productively challenged (Bruns, 2019b). While there is still only limited empirical work available, we can start to get a sense of how platforms shape people's news diets (Bandy and Diakopolous, 2020; Diakopolous, 2019; Trelli and Diakopolous, 2019). Google's Top Stories box regularly selects stories from major national news organizations (Trelli and Diakopolous, 2019), which points to the more general bifurcation in the sector discussed throughout the book. However, personalization may be much less of a problem than we think, as studies show that different user personas or participant cohorts often receive the same (or similar) information (Haim et al., 2018; Möller et al., 2018; Nechushtai and Lewis, 2019). These findings suggest that we need to adopt a more nuanced approach to the way that platforms sort news content.

A lack of intense personalization does not mean that we can ignore platforms and algorithmic systems. Instead, it suggests that, when thinking about media diversity, we should treat platforms as part of the wider media environment. There have been long-running efforts to measure media plurality through the European Media Pluralism Monitor and United Kingdom's Ofcom measurement framework. Existing systems tend to focus on traditional metrics associated with media diversity, such as media concentration, independence and freedom, and the extent to which the media environment suitably addresses social issues. The Ofcom measurement framework is slightly more advanced and attempts to account for the presence of online intermediaries like Google, but still struggles. A recent Ofcom consultation notes that,

> The introduction of online intermediaries, and the lack of transparency as to the algorithms they use to serve news, has made this role much harder by challenging our ability to measure accurately what news people are consuming, and to understand the significance and influence of different news sources.
>
> (2021, p. 48)

As a result, we are still in the dark about how news and other media content circulates online. We struggle to identify the prominence of news on platform feeds, account for the curation performed by algorithmic systems, and understand how these processes intersect with people consuming content (Diakopolous, 2019). Here, observability comes to the fore.

Working towards observability as a policy goal allows us to keep an eye on how news circulates, which benefits industry, government, academia, and the wider public. The long-term task is to examine the impact that algorithmic selection and curation have on the news media sector and on news consumption more generally. There is a knowledge gap when it comes to understanding platformized news media. We are never going to get an overarching view of the system, but by establishing policies that allow government departments to establish observatories and supporting data access more generally, we can get a better understanding of these dynamic news flows and examine how these different platforms mediate and distribute news content.

Size matters

We now move away from platform observability while continuing to consider the relationship between platform dependence and media diversity. One of the key takeaways from this book is that we are witnessing a growing divide across the news media sector, with larger media companies better able to function in a dependent environment. Indeed, in some cases we have seen these larger news outlets able to build new forms of infrastructure that could potentially reduce their dependence while securing new revenue streams from platforms. Conversely, smaller outlets have less capacity to extract themselves from dependencies. At the most extreme end, we have even seen local news companies be replaced by the infrastructure itself, with communities choosing to rely on Facebook for information sharing over a local newspaper. The growing bifurcation of the sector requires us to think about media diversity through a more traditional lens and consider source diversity and media concentration.

Many governments are actively considering how to limit further concentration caused by platform dependence by directing public funds to the news media. Notably, these interventions go beyond the standard grants regularly provided to public service media organizations to maintain their operations and involve the direct funding of private media. Public support for the private media sector is not a completely new phenomenon. In Scandinavia, private media news outlets have received indirect government subsidies such as VAT exemptions to support their journalism (Allern and Pollack, 2019) and there is growing interest in this area (Ots and Picard, 2018). Governments are funding news media, particularly at-risk outlets like smaller local, rural, regional, and start-up news organizations. Examples include Australia's Public Interest News Gathering Fund, New Zealand's NZD Public Interest Journalism Fund, the BBC Local Journalism Partnership, and France's Strategic Press Development Fund. These funds all operate in slightly different ways, but money is commonly given to support innovation initiatives or to address reporting gaps.

As the advertising market transforms and readership dwindles, in many cases, smaller outlets have nowhere else to turn than to the provision of public funds. However, it is unlikely that the influx of capital is enough to allow these smaller businesses to avoid existing dependencies. These funds are generally provided through government processes, which come with bureaucratic application processes, expenditure rules, and (particularly in the case of innovation) a clearly specified project or initiative. Government procedure also means that funds are usually highly restricted. For example, while New Zealand's Public Interest Journalism Fund supports projects that could improve a news company's strategic direction in response to platformization, it also has money earmarked for training and the funding of specific roles. Even if additional capital could be used to address platform dependence, an outlet couldn't use these funds like a private war chest and respond quickly to subsequent platform developments. Of course, the obvious tensions around the use of public funds to support private, for-profit companies need to be carefully managed.

Considering the limitations of public funding, the best that regulators and governments can do is establish a watching brief on the long-term sustainability of the news media sector. Several inquiries across the Anglosphere have already focused on the relationship between platforms and the news media (Meese, 2020). However, these were time limited and, as we have already seen, many outcomes were highly pragmatic, ultimately focusing on the transfer of revenue from platforms to the news sector. The ongoing challenge is to ensure that these payments and the wider context of platform dependence do not simply entrench existing major players who can at least operate in such an environment.

An independent media?

Discussions around the role of government in funding media and the role of platforms in the news media ecosystem naturally take us to the final normative goal addressed throughout the book: media independence. We have seen news outlets struggle as they have ceded control of online distribution channels to platforms that make decisions about curation and prominence. Addressing this loss of autonomy can be partially addressed through platform observability, which, as noted above, can illuminate platform operations. Arguably more challenging problems emerge around the provision of funds and opportunities to selected news organizations. There is no evidence of editorial interference, but the risk of subtle influence is more of a concern. Currently, platforms and news organizations can establish commercial agreements privately, with little oversight from governments (and indeed, encouragement in some cases). In many cases, these agreements simply involve Google and Meta handing over money to news organizations, but there is also evidence that certain platforms are making strategic contributions across the news ecosystem and working to establish closer relationships with the news media. These engagements see platforms encouraging news organizations to orient their production and distribution processes around platform infrastructure, which in some cases results in dependence.

There are obvious solutions that can be easily implemented. In short, some sort of transparency is key. This does not mean that agreements between companies need to be widely publicized, but at the very least, policy-makers and relevant departments need visibility around these deals. If platforms are forced to become involved in the long-term sustainability of the news media sector, their interventions must be trackable, reportable, and accounted for so parties can maintain a working oversight of the news media sector. There is already some evidence that countries are working towards this goal. Australia's News Media Bargaining Code has successfully introduced mandatory payments but allowed platforms and news organizations to claim that the amounts transferred were confidential. Jurisdictions adopting the legislation (like Canada) are unlikely to maintain this principle and are looking towards enforcing transparency requirements through annual reports.

Similar efforts should also be introduced for voluntary contributions to the sector made by platforms. Currently, platforms report gifts in a variety of ways, with some offering lots of detail and others offering a cursory survey of their activities and contributions. Considering the importance of the news media to democratic health, regulators may consider engaging with platforms to work towards common reporting schemes and even collaborative projects focused on targeted funding for areas of need. These efforts would at least help policy-makers understand the impact of platform contributions across the market and identify emerging revenue dependencies. With Meta already choosing to withdraw voluntary funding and scale down other patronage efforts, attention may increasingly turn to Google in this regard. Of course, such requirements would need to be extended to all private companies that make significant donations to the news media sector, beyond the purchase of advertising.

Media companies also have some agency about how they engage with platforms. As we have seen, major news organizations are better equipped to navigate risks associated with platform dependence. There is growing evidence that these companies are careful about the types of opportunities they accept, particularly after watching the rise and fall of the social news moment around the mid 2010s (Hurcombe, 2022). These decisions are potentially the most consequential when it comes to maintaining some sense of autonomy and independence in a platformized environment. Companies are already building out alternative infrastructures that replace what is on offer from platforms, from first-party data collection processes and advertising systems to internal automated systems that curate content. However, it can be hard to resist the offer of free support or revenue and it is the rare media company that has completely withdrawn from discussions with platforms.

Looking beyond Meta, Google, and Big Tech

As this discussion of how to potentially solve platform dependence ends, it is worthwhile to reflect on the wider narratives that have emerged from this original period of regulatory activity. When addressing the emergence of platformization across the news media sector, governments, and regulators have been relatively upfront about who they will target. Inquiries and reforms have spoken generally about platforms, but their central focus has mainly been Facebook and Google. There are, of course, good reasons for such a narrow approach. These two companies have actively intervened in the news media sector, and media companies have complained for years about how these two companies have impacted their businesses. Indeed, this book is no exception. With a decade or more of contestations between Google, Meta (and specifically their product Facebook), and the news media sector behind us, I have largely followed this approach and primarily focused on these two companies.

The issue is whether it is worth continuing to focus on Facebook and Google at the expense of the wider platform economy. There remain strong arguments for doing so. Google dominates the online advertising and search engine market and, along with Facebook, remains an important distribution channel for many news outlets. However, we have also seen variability across the platform economy when it comes to distribution. News organizations are turning to platforms like Instagram (owned by Facebook's parent company Meta) and TikTok to capture younger readers who are abandoning Facebook as a social platform (Heath, 2021). People are using messaging services like WhatsApp (again owned by Meta), Discord, iMessage (owned by Apple), and Snapchat to share content (Vázquez-Herrero et al., 2020; Lee, 2019). Apple News has also emerged as a new distributor and has established a position in the market. These developments present challenges to regulatory narratives circulating around the news media sector that identify Google and Facebook (or their parent company Meta) as the obvious enemies.

Of course, it is important to recognize that even when audiences and news media companies move away from Facebook, they may still end up on Meta products (such as Instagram and Whatsapp). However, it would serve all stakeholders well to consider that even when thinking about market dominance (as represented by the FAANG companies) there is still room for change. In such a context, ensuring a steady supply of empirical information becomes especially critical. We must understand how the news media sector *actually works* in the context of platformization, and in so doing, ensure that we do not continue to focus on old enemies at the expense of new ones. Such an approach requires ongoing investment in understanding how these novel news ecosystems function and consider regulation focused on broad criteria rather than targeting specific players.

Meta and Google were always in the regulatory firing line in Australia, with legislators keen to make an example of these two companies (Bossio et al., 2021). However, Europe is showing leadership around a more neutral approach that can help account for the variance that may occur across platform ecosystems. The incoming Digital Services Act introduces the definition of "Very Large Online Platforms" that are the primary reform targets. These platforms are those "which have a number of average monthly active recipients of the service in the Union equal to or higher than 45 million" (*Official Journal of the European Union* 2022). While such a definition still clearly targets major operators like Google and Facebook, at least transparent criteria avoid suggestions that forthcoming regulation is focused on two players at the expense of the rest of the market. Future reforms addressing platform dependence need to acknowledge the power that Google and Facebook have historically held while also establishing frameworks that can account for change, particularly around distribution.

Also, we should not lose sight of the news sector itself. It is evident that technology companies need to be regulated (Flew, 2021), but the momentum of the "techlash" has contributed to a relatively sterile and unsophisticated debate. Platforms have been placed on one side of the boxing ring and the news media on the other. With governments and regulators largely focusing on platforms, at points the complexity of the news media market has been ignored in favour of securing a regulatory compact. In writing this book, one goal has been to place a critical lens on the news media market and understand how various companies are responding to platforms. Indeed, while it is evident that the news media sector relies on platforms to some extent, it does not then follow that individual companies are simply resigned to their fate.

Indeed, we have seen a gradual change in news business models and the wider economics of journalism that, in turn, suggests that we also must be aware of changes across the sector. While regulators and scholars continue to point out the imbalances that can emerge through platformization and platform dependence, we must remember that not all news media companies are the same. To a certain extent, major media companies have relished the emergence of a policy discourse that has positioned themselves as the aggrieved party against an obvious enemy. These narratives ignore the fact that major news media companies have expended significant financial capital to survive (and possibly thrive) in a platform environment.

Governments and policy-makers would do well to recognize this significant variance across news media markets. Major media companies have struggled to navigate platformization, but they are making progress and at least have the capacity to establish strategies to combat platform dependence. Smaller companies that are at the most risk have limited capacity to innovate or develop. Broad narratives focused on securing "news" or "public interest journalism" do not necessarily account for these different capacities or indeed for subsequent changes in the news media market. In addition to hierarchical differences, there are also genuine contrasts in distribution strategies, business models, and audiences *within* these different sections of the market.

Considering the changing nature of the sector, an ongoing focus on the news media market itself is required. While there are clearly imbalances between media companies and platforms (Vos and Russell, 2019), interested parties must also attend to developments and inequities within news media markets. Adopting such an approach will involve establishing ongoing research on news media business models and the wider economics of journalism. We may even extend the chapter's ongoing interest in platform observability and call for greater observability of these sectoral trends. Not all news companies are the same, and their distinctions cannot be subsumed to promote the simplistic narrative of a wider battle with technology companies. Indeed, we may well find that some of these major media companies are able to build financial independence through subscriptions and independent advertising platforms to better manage their relationships with platforms. These possible futures underscore the fact that while platform dependence needs to be treated as a currently existing phenomenon for the sector it may not be in the future of every single news outlet.

Conclusion

The above proposals show that it is possible to address platform dependence through targeted interventions. Importantly, these approaches do not focus on the specific relationship between platforms and the news media sector. Instead, they are concerned with rectifying wider structural problems that do not just impact journalism but affect society more generally. Widening our perspective allows us to see how problems faced across the news media sector are also shared by other businesses dealing with platformization. It is yet possible to learn lessons from other sectors or the history of media and telecommunications regulation and translate these outcomes to the platform environment. Platform dependence is a complex phenomenon, but to return to the Austrian abbey for a moment, these reforms show that we can at least try to "catch a cloud."

Other solutions are also required to understand how platformization and platform dependence are impacting the normative goals that support journalism as an institution. Observability, ensuring that governments and policy-makers have visibility of platform contributions to the news media sector and the provision of public funds to media companies stand as promising avenues worthy of further consideration. Alongside these targeted reforms, this chapter has also noted the need for a more nuanced policy debate around platforms and Big Tech. It has called for more attention to be paid to the significant differences and divides that emerge across the news media sector. The conclusion advocates for new perspectives and future work that needs to be done, moving from policy-oriented solutions to scholarly considerations. Along with summarizing the central arguments and noting emerging trends identified throughout the book, I discuss how the field should think about researching the news media sector and platform dependence.

NOTE

1. See https://au.reset.tech/campaigns/a-live-list-of-viral-covid-information/.

Conclusion

Digital Platforms and the Press has examined the relationship between two key platforms, Facebook and Google, and the news media sector. The central argument is that there is a growing macro-trend of platform dependence occurring across the sector. The conceptual framework supporting this analysis was based on neo-institutionalism. Adopting this approach allowed the book to account for policy framework and legislation, historical path dependencies as well as the beliefs and expectations that circulate within these two institutions (Katzenbach, 2012; Mansell and Steinmueller, 2020). I went on to engage with recent scholarship on platformization, cultural production, and the news media sector (Nielsen and Ganter, 2022; Poell et al., 2022; van Dijck et al., 2019) and introduced a model that shows how platform dependence manifests across the news sector.

The model and the overarching argument do not present a simplistic or reductive account of dependence, suggesting that news organizations are only focused on Facebook's algorithm, for example. Along with identifying a general trend, the goal of the book is to offer a richer account of dependence as a phenomenon. Taking such an approach means broadening our perspective and looking beyond distribution and traffic. Scholars and policy-makers have mainly focused on the ability of platforms to attract large audiences and send referral traffic to the websites of news media organizations through algorithmic systems. The intermediary role that platforms play through the distribution channel is important but these institutional relationships are also changeable. Early chapters discussed the dynamic nature of online news distribution and identified emergent strategies that saw various news media organizations work to reduce their reliance on social media for traffic and the subsequent advertising revenue and build out subscription strategies (Bakke and Barland, 2022). Of course, certain news organizations became heavily dependent on these algorithmic systems at points, and it is hard for any news organization to wholly ignore these platforms. However, these relationships between platforms and news media organizations continue to be in flux (Chua and Westlund, 2019, 2022; Meese and Hurcombe, 2021; Wang, 2020), and some larger companies may escape, or at least moderate platform dependence through business model innovation.

More pervasive forms of dependence were identifiable further down the economic hierarchy. The transition to subscription revenue is underway but news media organizations continue to rely on advertising for revenue. Obviously, advertising requires an audience and social intermediaries provide significant amounts of traffic, but the news media sector has some flexibility in choosing its distribution channels. Conversely, when it comes to the advertising supply chain, these companies are deeply dependent on Google products. The Silicon Valley giant owns products across the online advertising supply chain and there are few options for those who need to engage with advertisers to secure revenue. These dependencies are pervasive and barring reform look likely to continue for some time. That being said, privacy reforms offer a possible way out for large news organizations that can afford the significant capital expenditure involved in building out their own advertising and analytics platforms.

Mandatory and voluntary platform payments emerged as another increasingly stable form of dependence worthy of consideration. We saw Australia slowly break down Google and Meta's resistance through strategic regulatory intervention and secure around USD 200 million per annum for Australian news outlets. Chapters 4 and 5 went on to identify a growing international consensus around platform payments that seems to be solidifying despite Google and Meta's desperate last-minute patronage efforts, which saw them granting millions to news media companies to stave off similar regulation. While new revenue streams for journalism are always welcome, the book noted that these mandatory payments entrench news organizations in a state of platform dependence. It forces them to continue producing content for platforms, often with platforms setting terms and conditions around production and in some cases, ultimately makes them reliant on these payments to fund important but otherwise unprofitable reporting ventures.

Beyond the direct and voluntary provision of revenue to news media companies, other forms of patronage represented a more subtle form of engagement with the news sector that can still generate dependencies. We saw Google and Meta offer training sessions to news organizations where they provided advice about business models and recommended specific platform tools for adoption. Through conferences and other interpersonal interactions, platforms worked to establish their presence across the sector. In addition, funding was given to specific "news deserts" and communities, in some cases to engage in discrete projects and in others to start up a new media business. Like distribution channels discussed at the beginning of the book, dependencies emerged and were reinforced through these engagements but were also dynamic. While Google funding a local start-up in news deserts gestured to potential long-term dependencies when it came to innovating around local news production, news organizations often had variable engagements with other forms of patronage (Fanta and Dachwitz, 2020).

Throughout the book, I also discussed how specific normative principles that supported journalism's important role within the wider system of liberal democracy were challenged by platform dependence. These were journalism's need to support an informed citizenry, the maintenance of a diverse media environment, and media independence and autonomy. Starting with the question of an informed citizenry and news quality, we saw that at points, Facebook's algorithmic systems aligned with populist news content (perhaps unwittingly). These moments point to the increasing editorial function of these platforms (Napoli and Caplan, 2017) and the need to better align these distribution systems with the public interest (Napoli, 2019). Despite productive early recommendations from inquiries (Meese, 2021) when it comes to the news media sector, international regulatory activity has avoided these more difficult reforms around oversight of private algorithmic systems and has largely focused on revenue transfers. Currently, reforms around news quality have largely focused on misinformation and disinformation (Meese and Hurcombe, 2022b; Wilding, 2021). However, this is just the start of the regulatory moment (Flew, 2021), and more specific reforms that focus on engagements between algorithmic systems and platforms as well as substantive structural interventions may be placed on the agenda soon (Meese and Bannerman, 2022).

The concept of platform dependence seems to directly challenge any notion of media independence or autonomy. This was recognized by the book, which picked up and developed a growing thread across the literature, which sees the news media sectors relinquish control over certain aspects of their business. Once they share content with platforms, news outlets no longer have sole control of their distribution channels. In a similar fashion, they can no longer manage online advertising deals independently, and most rely on Google products to some extent. These examples and many others point to what Mike Ananny calls a sociotechnical press, which in turn suggests that issues to do with media freedom and independence also become relevant to platforms and their various technical systems (Ananny, 2018; Tambini, 2021). There is no evidence from early studies that platforms are directly threatening editorial independence in any way (Fanta and Dachwitz, 2020; Gonzalez-Tosat and Sadaba-Chalezquer, 2021) but it is clear that many media companies are losing the ability to independently chart their own futures. Of course, as we consider our final normative principle of media pluralism, we come to realize that some media companies may be able to establish new strategies to lessen platform dependence. A central finding was that the platformization of news is encouraging a growing bifurcation across the sector. Many small companies had limited options when it came to replacing platform infrastructure or rejecting patronage. In contrast, major (and often, internationally oriented) media companies could spend money on new subscription strategies or, in a more extreme example, build new advertising platforms. This sort of limited autonomy does not mean that *every* major company can establish a future free from platforms, but it does suggest that certain companies may well be able to establish more equitable relationships with Facebook and Google. These interactions can be thought of much like planets drawn into orbit around a star with a large gravitational pull. While most will remain in orbit, larger planets will be able to escape.

The central focus on market structure necessarily meant that the book often focused on structural aspects of diversity (or source diversity). However, the book also addressed exposure diversity at points. Chapters 1 and 2 discussed how business models of platforms and the news media sector along with algorithmic systems interacted to surface certain types of news over others. Chapter 3 turned to online advertising and showed how obscure blacklists worked to selectively fund "non-controversial" news over more pressing (or diverse) topics. The debate between news companies and platforms even went so far as to raise the critical (and as yet unanswered) question of who should be in charge of news distribution channels, following Meta's blackout of news in Australia. These are still active policy concerns and Chapter 6 highlighted some possible solutions that may assist scholars and policy-makers still working to solve a complex balancing act. Decision-makers will have to carefully weigh up the rights of citizens to read what they want, the freedom of private companies to present information in a manner that suits them, and the wider public interest (Napoli, 2019; Helberger et al., 2016).

The overarching trend towards dependence and the arguments that support this finding are meant to be the start of a conversation. Facebook and Google have been dominant intermediaries for the news media over the last decade and many news companies now depend on them for a range of reasons. However, these platforms may not be key news distributors in the future. Indeed, we have seen some variance between genres and across the sector as algorithmic systems have changed and different business models have been implemented. There are also constant rumours about these platforms' long-term commitment to the news media sector, and at any point, they may simply decide to stop serving news content. Meta's recent decisions highlight the speed at which funding and support can be pulled from the news sector (Fischer, 2022). Therefore, future studies of platform dependence in the news sector need to acknowledge its dynamic nature and attend to changing market conditions on both sides. As the rest of the conclusion goes on to argue, scholarly work will need to get more specific about what we are studying, and exactly what outcomes we want as a society.

Beyond platforms

I have used the term platforms liberally throughout the book as a general term to represent Google and Facebook (or Meta). This is a common trend across the field, with much of the 2010s dedicated to understanding and critiquing these new sociotechnical formations that transformed the internet and society more generally (Gillespie, 2010; Mansell and Steinmueller, 2020; Poell et al., 2021). There is much to like about the term. It helps to capture these complex companies that seem to mediate much of our everyday existence and in the context of the news sector helps to frame the activities of a business that is engaged in multiple activities, from running a search engine to offering a dedicated section for news. However, the term can also obfuscate by providing a short-hand language to describe a range of social, economic, cultural, and technical elements that inform, to take one example, the design and implementation of a news feed.

These sorts of generic terms become less illuminating the more we look at specific technologies and their impacts. When thinking about the news media and platforms (there's that word again), future work may wish to go one level further and talk more directly about news media and "the recommender system that Google uses" or "Apple News's editorial decision-making." There is laudable work already occurring in this area (Bandy and Diakopolous, 2020; Diakopolous, 2019; Trelli and Diakopolous, 2019; Vrijenhoek, 2021) but from the perspective of media and communication studies, more could be done. Getting specific about technologies means developing a deeper technical understanding of how these systems work (as best as we can) and being attentive to the similarities *and* differences between Google's various technical systems (for example), or indeed between how Google and Facebook handle the news. Of course, many of these systems are opaque, but there is scope for scholars to place more focus on automated systems in recognition of the increasingly sociotechnical nature of the news sector.

In turn, such an approach forces us to avoid broad jeremiads about platforms and Big Tech and understand the specific problems that are emerging in this space. It is evident that platforms have presented challenges for the news media sector and democracy. The recent wave of critique productively pointed out these problems, and as part of this response, the recent (and currently ongoing) regulatory response was understandable. However, these broad critiques often fail to diagnose specific problems. As the regulatory moment progresses, it is not enough to simply rail against Big Tech and algorithms. Instead, it is beholden on scholars and policy-makers to show evidence of harm or deleterious effects. A greater focus on the function of technical systems in specific contexts can help to identify actual outcomes of the relationship between platforms and the news media sector, and not narrow in on certain actors at the expense of others. This book focused on existing debates across the news media industry and so focused on Facebook and Google. However, there may well be other actors or specific systems we should be particularly concerned about.

Democracy and the press

Moving beyond a reductive debate also means maintaining a critical eye on the press. The book has highlighted areas where the conflation of platforms and the news media sector may cause democratic harm and has focused on three normative principles which seem to be most at threat. While the study presumes that a functioning press can support democracy at a normative level, it does not assume that positive democratic outcomes will naturally flow from a prominently commercial press (Pickard, 2020). Policy analysis and public discussion around platform dependence presume the support of the press in a battle against dominant platforms (ACCC, 2021; CMA, 2020). However, most of the press function in a commercial system that only occasionally aligns with democratic outcomes. Indeed, many of the developments that have led to the current state of platform dependence can be linked to a competitive and highly commercialized culture.

Work is already emerging that critiques the commercial nature of the press (Pickard, 2019, 2020) and the limited imagination of these organizations, which focus on readers that often look like themselves (Usher, 2021). The trend may intensify as news media companies turn to audiences (presumably rich ones) for ongoing revenue. When thinking about some of these normative challenges, we must recognize that it is news media companies who are ruthlessly (and understandably) ensuring their own survival, often at the expense of smaller publications. The sector also has some agency and at times actively tries to align with platform imperatives for a presumed short-term gain. Alongside this sort of commercial decision-making, we have seen that the press can also deliberately or accidentally amplify misinformation and are not necessarily "better" than platforms on that front (Bruns et al, 2021). Of course, the perfect cannot be the enemy of the good and reporters at news media companies continue to write and publish important news. However, scholars and policy-makers must be careful about presuming that saving the status quo is a net win for democracy and instead be open to alternate sectoral futures.

As part of this process, future work would do well to consider what citizens and communities need, rather than what the commercial news media sector requires. Nikki Usher (2021, p. 247) calls these requirements "basic information needs" and lists a range of elements from information about the weather to updates on local events. Regulators have also done work in this area, with the US Federal

Communication Commission exploring the critical information needs of local communities a decade earlier (Waldman, 2011). Scholars who provided input into the process noted a series of essential information areas that citizens needed access to in a timely fashion. The overarching categories were emergencies and risks, health and welfare, education, transportation, economic opportunities, the environment, civic information, and political information. The team went on to note that a changing media landscape presented new challenges for Americans seeking to meet information needs, particularly in local and regional areas (Waldman, 2011).

As the authors of the above report anticipated, much of what journalism used to do has been taken up by other actors in the wider "informational ecology" (Broersma and Peters, 2017, p. 6). These developments have disaggregated the newspaper and threatened the primacy of the broadcast news, and audiences can now turn to apps, social media platforms, search engines, and even the websites of individual organizations to source information. In such a context, the role of journalism *must* be different, and so we must ensure that we do not perpetuate "discrepancy between journalism's rhetoric and the tasks it fulfils in the daily lives of individuals and society at large" (Broersma and Peters, 2017, p. 6).

These changes also suggest that new conceptual work may need to be undertaken. As the social role of the press changes, scholars and policy-makers cannot proceed on the presumption that the normative principles that have served us so well in the past will continue to do so in the future. Of course, the field does not need to throw all that hard work away and start again. For example, I cannot think of a reason why democracies would reject the possibility of a diverse media environment. However, it does provide an opportunity to carefully reconsider these core concepts and identify exactly what is linking the production and distribution of journalism through a specific institution to positive democratic outcomes. In an increasingly inclusive scholarly environment that is recognizing the need for greater diversity across race, gender, class, and geography, we may well see a more sophisticated theorization of this relationship.

To take one possible intellectual thread, we may consider the continual tension between news about politics, crime, and the economy, and softer news stories focused on television or bar openings. The former topics have often been seen as central to the journalistic mission as they focus on the workings of democracy, community safety, and the financial health of the nation. In contrast, the latter has been viewed as optional extras, not deeply aligned with journalism's normative principles, and potentially even able to be sloughed off from what we think of as contemporary journalism and handed over to niche websites. There is a heavily gendered element to this divide, with many news categories associated with women journalists historically derided as "soft" despite their social importance (and commercial viability) (Steiner, 2017). As we rethink these normative concepts, we may want to think about the democratic potential of culture and entertainment, and the extent to which understanding and engaging with these topics leads to positive democratic outcomes through understanding how society is represented through culture (television) or citizens building connections with one another (bar openings). Understanding what democracy means in terms of how people actually live their lives and perform citizenship, and how journalism fits into that, may well be the next challenge for the field.

Policy and economics

Digital Platforms and the Press also aims to contribute to emergent scholarly trends found across existing journalism scholarship. One central goal of the study was to focus on the economics and associated business models that sustain the contemporary news media and understand how these are changing in response to the emergence of platforms. Journalism research has often been focused on the newsroom, with numerous projects exploring what journalists think or focusing specifically on production processes and rituals (for similar critiques see Nielsen, 2018; Usher and Poepsel, 2021). These studies have provided wonderful insights at a critical moment of transformation, and there have been detailed accounts of how individual newsrooms have managed multiple waves of digital transformation. However, when thinking about the news media as a sector, these studies can only capture the production (or supply) of journalism as a good. As we have seen throughout, we can take a wider perspective on journalism as a business and account for engagements with various actors across the supply chain.

The book has charted broad trends across the sector, drawing on fieldwork and other data sources. In doing so, we have come to understand the continual reliance on advertising for revenue, the move from advertising to reader-revenue strategies and how much platform payments contribute to existing revenue streams. However, this project simply represents a small step in a direction and more could be done. These trends do not account for the specifics of individual news companies and there is scope for future research to deeply engage with media economics methods and analyses, or more critical approaches found in the political economy tradition. This would see greater attention paid to financial reports, a better understanding of what profitability looks like in the context of the news media sector and more work on critical issues, such as working out the actual social and economic value of news.

Another goal of the book was to engage deeply with policy and legislation and examine how governments and regulators were conceptualizing platform dependence as a policy problem. Scholarship on journalism and media policy rarely engages with each other, often due to an incorrect assumption that journalism is separate from government or heavy-handed regulation (Napoli, 2020; Pickard, 2019; Usher and Poepsel, 2021). Once we expand our perspective from the newsroom to account for platforms, automated decision-making systems, business models and so on, the absence of policy becomes much harder to justify. Policy-makers are concerned with the long-term future of journalism but they also focused on a range of policy issues that go well beyond the sector's sustainability. These topics include the relationship between platforms and the news media sector, the operation of recommender systems, and the spread of misinformation, to name a few. Such developments suggest that we can no longer cleanly separate journalism from media policy and, on the contrary, demand more work at the intersection of these two sub-fields.

The press as platform?

In closing this book, I wanted to reflect on what inspired me to start this project and in doing so, gesture to one final trend that only started to emerge at the end of this research journey. I was acutely conscious of the growing influence of platforms in the news sector throughout the 2010s but suspect that my interest in this specific area also emerged because I was living in Australia. The country has a small population and struggles to support a diverse media sector. As such, the internet provided a great opportunity for several local and global businesses to establish news start-ups here, some who embraced the "social news" formula (Hurcombe et al., 2019). These new entrants genuinely disrupted the small market that had previously existed, particularly for younger demographics, and were hard to ignore (Hurcombe, 2022). It soon became clear that alongside these developments, the country becaming a central node in the global battle between platforms and the news media sector. The Australian Government also welcomed the opportunity to create policy options that might address the relationship between platforms and the news media sector, and it was something of a global first mover in that regard (Flew, 2021; Meese, 2021; Meese and Hurcombe, 2022). These concurrent developments signalled a possible critical juncture emerging around these two institutions, a perfect time to start researching.

In beginning this work, I was familiar with early scholarship on the topic and on platforms more generally. To identify a broad trend, there was a persistent focus on algorithmic systems and a presumption that news media organizations would be helplessly drawn towards Facebook as a distribution source (Google was rarely mentioned) (see generally, Lewis and Molyneux, 2018). These analyses were not wrong, and indeed captured a moment in time for many news organizations. For example, Robyn Caplan and danah boyd (2018) productively noted that news media organizations were becoming increasingly dependent on Facebook and risked adopting isomorphic behaviours. They argued that these developments would see Facebook increasingly able to "exert change on other organizations that rely upon them" like the news media (Caplan and boyd, 2018, p. 5). In starting the project, I wondered if Facebook's decision to change its algorithmic systems in January 2018 would alter these relationships. I also wanted to look beyond the news feed and capture a wider set of dependencies to better map out the relationship between these two sectors.

I ended up offering a detailed account of the relationship, challenging the presumption that "complex and variable relationships between platforms and publishers are fixed in an ongoing state of platform dependency" (Meese and Hurcombe, 2021, p. 13). However, as I developed these early studies into a book, I eventually found myself ultimately acknowledging that currently the news media sector seems to be dependent on platforms, with only a few outlets feasibly able to chart an escape path. I now turn to this small collection of well-resourced, major news media companies, because their possible future presents a new trajectory that we may want to consider when discussing platforms and the news media sector.

Essentially, these larger news outlets are starting to take on the features of platform-based businesses, like Instagram or YouTube. Throughout the book we have seen major outlets increasingly using logins to collect first-party data, increase internal efforts to improve in-house recommender systems, and establish back-end solutions for advertisers (see Lindskow, 2020). These companies are likely to intensify these innovations in the future, particularly if these developments help them secure an independent future that is not as reliant on platforms. We might return to Caplan and boyd's (2018) discussion about isomorphism and keep thinking about how mimesis manifests through the adoption of platform features. This is less about metrics and journalistic production, or algorithmic systems and more about how platform features form part of news media business models. Of course, the *New York Times* (*NYT*) is not going to turn into Google and release an *NYT* e-mail client or a video-based social media platform. However, we may well see greater adoption of features and processes as these larger organizations turn to readers to ensure a major revenue stream. There is also a risk of a power imbalance within the sector, with larger news media companies possibly contracting out things like advertising platforms to smaller outlets as an additional revenue stream.

The press has been genuinely concerned about platform dependence and has managed to influence a global policy debate to such an extent that platforms are finally handing over money to news media organizations. At the same time, the most powerful news media organizations are actively learning from platforms and considering strategic trajectories that may well see a lucky few establish an independent future away from these technology companies. As part of this process, they may instigate patterns of dependence with smaller outlets, leave the rest of the sector to continue to struggle in a dependent relationship with platforms, or do both. This is an interesting development, which sees major news media outlets acknowledge the strategic innovations of platforms and adopt them for their own ends. While the press was once worried about platforms, now a select few are trying to become more like them.

This final trend offers a neat story of how my argument has ended up where I started. The book has offered a complex account of platform dependence across the news sector and has tried to avoid a continual fixation on one company or one type of dependence. The conclusion has also sought to sketch out possible scholarly trajectories for future work in this area that can help us better understand these relationships and avoid simple conclusions. However, in many ways we have not come much further than the early findings of Caplan and boyd (2018) who were investigating Facebook at the peak of the "social news" moment. The sector has changed dramatically in a few short years, a transformation this book has mapped, but the news media are still dependent on platforms. Along with algorithmic systems, this includes advertising supply chains, platform payments, and a range of patronage efforts that encourage ongoing engagement between these two sectors. And as this final example has pointed out, we have even got to the stage where certain news media organizations are even trying to mimic platforms and potentially replicate these dependencies themselves. I have tried to contextualize this dependence and signal that it may well change in the future. Whether or not it does, is up to decisions made by both platforms and the news media sector, how governments and regulators approach the ongoing task of digital platform regulation, and the consumption preferences and information needs of everyday citizens.

References

@MattMcLaughlin. (2020, March 8). "Hey @aripap..." Twitter. https://twitter.com/MattMcLaughlin/status/1236528424757403648.

Abernathy, Penelope. (2020). "News deserts and ghost newspapers: Will local news survive?" *Hussman School of Journalism and Media*. Chapel Hill: University of North Carolina.

Abramson, Jill. (2019). *Merchants of Truth: Inside the News Revolution*. London: Bodley Head.

AdAge. (2018, March 21). "Google to sweeten publisher deals as tech woos media." *AdAge*. https://adage.com/article/digital/google-sweeten-publisher-deals-tech-woos-media/312824.

Adalytics. (2021, February 2). "Tens of thousands of news articles are labeled as unsafe for advertisers." *Adalytics*. https://adalytics.io/blog/tens-of-thousands-of-news-articles-are-labeled-as-unsafe-for-advertisers.

ADLC. (2021, July 26). "Decision 21-D-11 of June 07, 2021: Regarding practices implemented in the online advertising sector." https://www.autoritedelaconcurrence.fr/en/decision/regarding-practices-implemented-online-advertising-sector.

Agence France-Presse. (2019, October 8). "Google can't escape copyright laws: France's Macron." *RTL*. https://today.rtl.lu/news/business-and-tech/a/1413436.html.

Albrecht, Jim. (2018, March 20). "Introducing subscribe with Google." Google News Initiative. https://blog.google/outreach-initiatives/google-news-initiative/introducing-subscribe-google/.

Allern, Sigurd and Pollack, Ester. (2019). "Journalism as a public good: A Scandinavian perspective." *Journalism*, 20:11, pp. 1423–39.

Alpert, Lukas I. (2020, October 26). "BuzzFeed expects to break even this year, thanks to heavy cost cuts." *The Wall Street Journal*. https://www.wsj.com/articles/buzzfeed-expects-to-break-even-this-year-thanks-to-heavy-cost-cuts-11603738660.

Ananny, Mike. (2018). *Networked Press Freedom: Creating Infrastructures for a Public Right to Hear*. Cambridge: MIT Press.

Anderson, C. W. (2011). "Between creative and quantified audiences: Web metrics and changing patterns of newswork in local US newsrooms." *Journalism*, 12:5, pp. 550–56.

Andrew, Dan. (2019). "Programmatic trading: The future of audience economics." *Communication Research and Practice*, 5:1, pp. 73–87. https://doi.org/ 10.1080/22041451.2019.1561398.

Apple. (2015, June 8). "Apple announces news app for iPhone & iPad." *Apple Newsroom*. https://www.apple.com/newsroom/2015/06/08Apple-Announces-News-App-for-iPhone-iPad/.

Associated Press. (2006, October 10). "Google buys YouTube for $1.65 billion." NBC News. http://nbcnews.com/id/wbna15196982.

Auchard, Eric. (2007, April 7). "AFP, Google News settle lawsuit over Google News." *Reuters*. https://www.reuters.com/article/us-google-afp-idUSN0728115420070407.

Australian Competition and Consumer Commission (ACCC). (2018, December 10). *Digital Platforms Inquiry – Preliminary Report*. Canberra: Commonwealth of Australia. https://www.accc.gov.au/focus-areas/inquiries-finalised/digital-platforms-inquiry-0/preliminary-report.

Australian Competition and Consumer Commission (ACCC). (2019, July 26). *Digital Platforms Inquiry – Final Report*. Canberra: Commonwealth of Australia. https://www.accc.gov.au/publications/digital-platforms-inquiry-final-report.

Australian Competition and Consumer Commission (ACCC). (2020, March 10). *Ad Tech Inquiry: Issues Paper*. Canberra: Commonwealth of Australia. https://www.accc.gov.au/system/files/Ad%20tech%20inquiry%20-%20issues%20paper.pdf.

Australian Competition and Consumer Commission (ACCC). (2021, 28 September). *Digital Advertising Services Inquiry: Final Report*. Canberra: Commonwealth of Australia. https://www.accc.gov.au/publications/digital-advertising-services-inquiry-final-report.

Automatad Team. (2020, July 9). "What is contextual advertising and how it works today?" Automatad. https://headerbidding.co/contextual-advertising-publishers/.

Autorité de la Concurrence. (2020, April 9). "Droits voisins: l'Autorité fait droit aux demandes de mesures conservatoires présentées par les éditeurs de presse et l'AFP." https://www.autoritedelaconcurrence.fr/fr/communiques-de-presse/droits-voisins-lautorite-fait-droit-aux-demandes-de-mesures-conservatoires.

Autorité de la Concurrence. (2021, July 13). "Rémunération des droits voisins: l'Autorité sanctionne Google à hauteur de 500 millions d'euros pour le non-respect de plusieurs injonctions." https://www.autoritedelaconcurrence.fr/fr/communiques-de-presse/remuneration-des-droits-voisins-lautorite-sanctionne-google-hauteur-de-500.

Bailo, Francesco, Meese, James, and Hurcombe, Edward. (2021). "The institutional impacts of algorithmic distribution: Facebook and the Australian news media." *Social Media + Society*, 7:2, pp. 1–13.

Baker, C. Edwin. (2002). *Media, Markets, and Democracy*. Cambridge: Cambridge University Press.

Bakke, Nils A. and Barland, Jens. (2022). "Disruptive innovations and paradigm shifts in journalism as a business: From advertisers first to readers first and traditional operational models to the AI factory." *SAGE Open*. https://doi.org/10.1177/21582440221094819.

Bandy, Jack and Diakopoulos, Nicholas. (2020). "Auditing news curation systems: A case study examining algorithmic and editorial logic in Apple News." In *Proceedings of the International AAAI Conference on Web and Social Media*, vol. 14, pp. 36–47. Geogria, Atlanta, 8–11 June.

Barsoe, Tim. (2021, June 29). "Danish media firms join forces to seek payment deal with Facebook, Google." *Reuters*. https://www.reuters.com/technology/danish-media-firms-join-forces-seek-payment-deal-with-facebook-google-2021-06-28/.

BBC. (2017, November 23). "Facebook to expose Russian fake news pages." *BBC News*. https://www.bbc.com/news/technology-42096045.

Bell, Emily. (2018). "The dependent press: How Silicon Valley threatens journalism." In M. Moore and D. Tambini (eds), *Digital Dominance, The Power of Google, Amazon, Facebook and Apple*. Oxford: Oxford University Press.

Bell, Emily and Owen, Taylor. (2017, March 29). "The platform press: How Silicon Valley reengineered journalism." *The Tow Centre for Digital Journalism*. https://www.cjr.org/tow_center_reports/platform-press-how-silicon-valley-reengineered-journalism.php.

Benton, Joshua. (2020, November 23). "Another bit of good news from Apple: Publishers can now offer targeted discounts in the App Store." *NiemanLab*. https://www.niemanlab.org/2020/11/another-bit-of-good-news-from-apple-publishers-can-now-offer-targeted-discounts-in-the-app-store/.

Best, Jo. (2014, December 11). "Google cans Spanish Google News after new law means it has to pay publishers." *ZDNet*. https://www.zdnet.com/article/google-cans-spanish-google-news-after-new-law-means-it-has-to-pay-publishers/.

Bilton, Ricardo. (2016, April 13). "A year into its new content strategy, *UpWorthy* is focusing on do-good videos instead of clickbait." *NiemanLab*. https://www.niemanlab.org/2016/04/a-year-into-its-new-original-content-strategy-upworthy-is-focusing-on-do-good-videos-instead-of-clickbait/.

Bishop, Katie. (2020, July 27). "Why are millennials and Gen Z turning to Instagram as a news source?" *The Guardian*. https://www.theguardian.com/lifeandstyle/2020/jul/27/instagram-news-source-social-media.

Blanchett, Nicole. (2018). "The evolution of analytics in journalism." *Digital Journalism*, 6:8, pp. 1041–51.

Bloomberg. (2020, November 22). "*BuzzFeed* buys *HuffPost* from Verizon in latest new media deal." *The Middle Market*. https://www.themiddlemarket.com/latest-news/buzzfeed-buys-huffpost-from-verizon-in-latest-new-media-deal.

Boczkowski, J. (2005). *Digitizing the News: Innovation in Online Newspapers*. Cambridge: MIT Press.

Bohn, Dieter. (2020, January 14). "Google to 'phase out' third-party cookies in Chrome, but not for two years." *The Verge*. https://www.theverge.com/2020/1/14/21064698/google-third-party-cookies-chrome-two-years-privacy-safari-firefox.

Bossio, Diana. (2017). *Journalism and Social Media: Practitioners, Organisations and Institutions*. London: Palgrave Macmillan.

Bossio, Diana and Bebawi, Saba. (2016). "Mapping the emergence of social media in everyday journalistic practices." *Media International Australia*, 161:1, pp. 147–58.

Bossio, Diana, Flew, Terry, Meese, James, Leaver, Tama, and Barnet, Belinda. (2022). "Australia's news media bargaining code and the global turn towards platform regulation." *Policy & Internet*, 14:1, pp. 136–50.

Boulder Reporting Lab. (2022, n.d.). "About *The Boulder Reporting Lab*." https://boulderreportinglab.org/about-us/.

Bødker, Henrik. (2017). "Vice Media Inc.: Youth, lifestyle – And news." *Journalism*, 18:1, pp. 27–43.

Branded. (2020, March 19). "Blacklisting 'coronavirus' is not helping anybody." *Substack*. https://branded.substack.com/p/blacklisting-coronavirus-is-not-helping.

Braun, Joshua A. and Eklund, Jessica L. (2019). "Fake news, real money: Ad tech platforms, profit-driven hoaxes, and the business of journalism." *Digital Journalism*, 7:1, pp. 1–21. https://doi.org/10.1080/21670811.2018.1556314.

Broersma, Marcel and Peters, Chris. (2017). "Introduction: Towards a functional perspective on journalism's role and relevance." In M. Broersma and C. Peters (eds), *Rethinking Journalism Again: Societal Role and Public Relevance in a Digital Age*. London: Routledge, pp. 1–17.

Brook, Stephen and Bonyhady, Nick. (2021, January 13). "Google admits to removing local news content in 'experiment.'" *The Sydney Morning Herald*. https://www.smh.com.au/politics/federal/google-admits-to-removing-local-news-content-in-experiment-20210113-p56tux.html.

Broughton, Matthew. (2019, December 18). "Predictions 2020: The rise of contextual advertising." *Exchange Wire*. https://www.exchangewire.com/blog/2019/12/18/predictions-2020-the-rise-of-contextual-advertising/.

Brown, Campbell. (2019, January 15). "Doing more to support local news." Meta Journalism Project. https://www.facebook.com/journalismproject/facebook-supports-local-news.

Brown, Campbell. (2020, March 30). "Facebook invests additional $100 million to support news industry during the coronavirus crisis." Meta Journalism Project. https://www.facebook.com/journalismproject/coronavirus-update-news-industry-support.

Bruns, Axel. (2012). "Journalists and Twitter: How Australian news organisations adapt to a new medium." *Media International Australia*, 144:1, pp. 97–107.

Bruns, Axel. (2019a). "After the 'APIcalypse': Social media platforms and their fight against critical scholarly research." *Information, Communication & Society*, 22:11, pp. 1544–66.

Bruns, Axel. (2019b). *Are Filter Bubbles Real?* Cambridge: Polity Press.

Bruns, Axel. (2022, March 17). "Australian search experience project: background paper." *ARC Centre of Excellence for Automated Decision-Making and Society*. https://apo.org.au/node/316976.

Bruns, Axel, Harrington, Stephen, and Hurcombe, Edward. (2021). "Coronavirus conspiracy theories: Tracing misinformation trajectories from the fringes to the mainstream," pp. 229–249. In M. Lewis, E. Govender, and K. Holland (eds), *Communicating COVID-19: Interdisciplinary Perspectives*. Cham: Palgrave Macmillan.

Bucher, Taina. (2012). "Want to be on the top? Algorithmic power and the threat of invisibility on Facebook." *New Media & Society*, 14:7, pp. 1164–80.

Bunce, Mel. (2015). "Africa in the click stream: Audience metrics and foreign correspondents in Africa." *African Journalism Studies*, 36:4, pp. 12–29.

Bunce, Mel. (2019). "Management and resistance in the digital newsroom." *Journalism*, 20:7, pp. 890–905.

Bunz, Mercedes. (2009, December 2). "Rupert Murdoch: There's no such thing as a free news story." *The Guardian*. https://www.theguardian.com/media/2009/dec/01/rupert-murdoch-no-free-news.

Burgess, Jean and Baym, Nancy. (2020). *Twitter*. Cambridge: Polity Press.

Cadwalladr, Carol and Graham-Harrison, Emma. (2018, March 18). "Revealed: 50 million Facebook profiles harvested for Cambridge Analytica in major data breach." *The Guardian*. https://www.theguardian.com/news/2018/mar/17/cambridge-analytica-facebook-influence-us-election.

Calabria, Tim. (2022). *Pay television and internet protocol television services in Australia*. IBISWorld. Report OD5546. https://www.ibisworld.com/au/industry/pay-television-internet-protocol-services/5546/.

Cape York Weekly. (2022, n.d.). "Submission 12 to Standing Committee on communications and the arts inquiry into Australia's regional newspapers." https://www.aph.gov.au/Parliamentary_Business/Committees/House/Communications/Regionalnewspapers/Submissions.

Caplan, Robyn and boyd, danah. (2018). "Isomorphism through algorithms: Institutional dependencies in the case of Facebook." *Big Data & Society*, 5:1. https://doi.org10.1177/2053951718757253.

Carlson, Nicholas. (2014, February 11). "Facebook changed how the news feed works – And huge wesite *UpWorthy* suddenly shrank in half." *Business Insider*. https://www.businessinsider.com.au/facebook-changed-how-the-news-feed-works-and-huge-website-upworthy-suddenly-shrank-in-half-2014-2.

Carlson, Matt. (2015). "When news sites go native." *Journalism*, 16:7, pp. 849–65.

Carlson, Matt. (2018). "Facebook in the news: Social media, journalism, and public responsibility following the 2016 trending topics controversy." *Digital Journalism*, 6:1, pp. 4–20.

Carlson, Matt and Lewis, Seth C. (2019). "Temporal reflexivity in journalism studies: making sense of change in a more timely fashion." *Journalism*, 20:5, pp. 642–50.

Carlson, Matt and Usher, Nikki. (2016). "News startups as agents of innovation: For-profit digital news startup manifestos as metajournalistic discourse." *Digital Journalism*, 4:5, pp. 563–81.

Carson, Andrea. (2015). "Behind the newspaper paywall – Lessons in charging for online content: A comparative analysis of why Australian newspapers are stuck in the purgatorial space between digital and print." *Media, Culture & Society*, 37:7, pp. 1022–41.

Carson, Aandrea and Fallon, Liam. (2021). "Fighting fake news: A study of online misinformation regulation in the Asia Pacific." *Facebook Research Report*. Melbourne: La Trobe University.

Castle, Stephen and Jolly, David. (2008, March 11). "Europe approves Google's merger with DoubleClick." *New York Times*. https://www.nytimes.com/2008/03/11/technology/11cnd-google.html.

CHEQ. (2020, n.d.). *The Economic Cost of Keyword Blacklists for Online Publishers*. Baltimore: University of Baltimore. https://info.cheq.ai/hubfs/Research/The%20Economic%20Costs%20of%20Keyword%20Blacklists%20covid%2019%20update.pdf.

Chokshi, Niraj. (2018, November 29). "Mic, a news site for millennials, lays off most of its staff." *New York Times*. https://www.nytimes.com/2018/11/29/business/media/mic-staff-layoff.html.

Christians, Clifford, Glasser, Theodore, McQuail, Denis, Nordenstreng, Kaarle, and White, Robert. (2010). *Normative Theories of the Media: Journalism in Democratic Societies*. Chicago: University of Illinois Press.

Christin, Angèle. (2020). *Metrics at Work: Journalism and the Contested Meaning of Algorithms*. New York: Princeton University Press.

Christin, Angèle and Petre, Caitlin. (2020). "Making peace with metrics: Relational work in online news production." *Sociologica*, 14:2, pp. 133–56.

Christensen, Nic. (2015, March 31). "Nine confirms it has bought stake in online youth site Pedestrian.tv." *Mumbrella*. https://mumbrella.com.au/nine-confirms-it-has-bought-stake-in-pedestrian-tv-284719.

Chua, Sherwin and Westlund, Oscar. (2019). "Audience-centric engagement, collaboration culture and platform counterbalancing." *Media and Communication*, 7:1, pp. 153–65.

Chua, Sherwin and Westlund, Oscar. (2022). "Platform configuration: A longitudinal study and conceptualization of a legacy news publisher's platform-related innovation practices." *Online Media and Global Communication*. 1:1, pp. 60–89.

CMA. (2020, July 1). *Online Platforms and Digital Advertising*. Competition & Markets Authority. London: Crown Copyright. https://assets.publishing.service.gov.uk/media/5efc57ed3a6f4023d242ed56/Final_report_1_July_2020_.pdf.

CNET. (1998, March 18). "DoubleClick hot, set to expand." https://www.cnet.com/news/doubleclick-hot-set-to-expand/.

Coale, Kristi. (1997, March 17). "DoubleClick tries to force hand into cookie jar." *Wired*. https://www.wired.com/1997/03/doubleclick-tries-to-force-hand-into-cookie-jar/.

Coddington, Mark. (2019). *Aggregating the News: Secondhand Knowledge and the Erosion of Journalistic Authority*. New York: Columbia University Press.

Cohan, William. (2020, October 24). "Vice gets squeezed." *Air Mail*. https://airmail.news/issues/2020-10-24/vice-gets-squeezed.

Constine, Josh. (2013, October 22). "Facebook's referrals to media sites up 170% YOY, new 'Stories to Share' tells pages what to post." *TechCrunch*. https://techcrunch.com/2013/10/21/facebooks-referrals-to-media-sites-up-170-yoy-new-stories-to-share-tells-pages-what-to-post/.

Consultancy.com.au. (2020, October 26). "News Corp Australia hires McKinsey for Growth Strategies." https://www.consultancy.com.au/news/2679/news-corp-australia-hires-mckinsey-for-growth-strategies.

Coons, Chris. (2021, December 9). "Coons, Portman, Klobuchar Announce Legislation to ensure transparency at social media platforms." https://www.coons.senate.gov/news/press-releases/coons-portman-klobuchar-announce-legislation-to-ensure-transparency-at-social-media-platforms.

Cooper, Mex. (2021, April 27). "Newsletter dashboards measure dozens of metrics at Sydney Morning Herald." *Age*. INMA. https://www.inma.org/blogs/value-content/post.cfm/newsletter-dashboards-measures-dozens-of-metrics-at-sydney-morning-herald-age.

Cornia, Alessio, Sehl, Annika, and Nielsen, Rasmus Kleis. (2020). "We no longer live in a time of separation: A comparative analysis of how editorial and commercial integration became a norm." *Journalism*, 21:2: pp. 172–90.

Cox, Kate. (2021, 13 March). "US lawmakers propose Australia-style bill for media, tech negotiations." *Ars Technica*. https://arstechnica.com/tech-policy/2021/03/us-lawmakers-propose-australia-style-bill-for-media-tech-negotiations/.

Cozens, Claire. (2005, 21 March). "AFP sues Google over copyrighted content." *The Guardian*. https://www.theguardian.com/technology/2005/mar/21/media.newmedia.

Crampton, Thomas. (2007, February 14). "Google said to violate copyright laws." *New York Times*. https://www.nytimes.com/2007/02/14/business/14google.html.

Crook, Jordan. (2015, January 28). "Snapchat launches Discover." *TechCrunch*. https://techcrunch.com/2015/01/27/snapchat-launches-discover/.

Crunchbase. (n.d.a). "*UpWorthy*." https://www.crunchbase.com/organization/upworthy.

Crunchbase. (n.d.b). "Mic Network." https://www.crunchbase.com/organization/mic-network.

Crunchbase. (n.d.c). "Buzzfeed." https://www.crunchbase.com/organization/buzzfeed.

Crunchbase. (n.d.d). "Vice." https://www.crunchbase.com/organization/vice.

Danckert, Sarah. (2019, June 29). "Watchdogs at ten paces: How the ACCC is raising ASIC's hackles." *The Sydney Morning Herald*. https://www.smh.com.au/business/consumer-affairs/watchdogs-at-ten-paces-how-the-accc-is-raising-asic-s-hackles-20190627-p521w3.html.

Dawber, Alistair. (2009, October 10). "Murdoch blasts search engine 'kleptomaniacs'." *The Independent*. https://www.independent.co.uk/news/media/online/murdoch-blasts-search-engine-kleptomaniacs-1800569.html.

Del Ray, Jason. (2017, April 24). "BuzzFeed is building a team of writers to sell you stuff you didn't know you wanted." *Vox*. https://www.vox.com/2017/4/24/15379964/buzzfeed-commerce-shopify-partnership-affiliate-network-links.

Diakopolous, Nicholas. (2019). *Automating the News: How Algorithms Are Rewriting the Media*. Cambridge: Harvard University Press.

Dick, Murray. (2011). "Search engine optimisation in UK news production." *Journalism Practice*, 5:4, pp. 462–77.

Directive (EU). (2019, April 17). *On Copyright and Related Rights in the Digital Single Market and Amending Directives 96/9/EC and 2001/29/EC*. https://eur-lex.europa.eu/legal-content/en/TXT/HTML/?uri=CELEX:32019L0790.

Dunlop, Tim. (2013). *The New Front Page: New Media and the Rise of the Audience*. Melbourne: Scribe Publications.

Dwyer, Tim and Wilding, Derek. (2022). *Media Pluralism and Online News: The Consequences of Automated Curation for Society*. Bristol: Intellect.

Economides, Nicholas. (2001). "The Microsoft antitrust case." *Journal of Industry, Competition and Trade*, 1, pp. 7–39.

Edelman, Gilad. (2020a, July 28). "Follow the money: How digital ads subsidize the worst of the web." *Wired*. https://www.wired.com/story/how-digital-ads-subsidize-worst-web/.

Edelman, Gilad. (2020b, August 5). "Can killing cookies save journalism?." *Wired*. https://www.wired.com/story/can-killing-cookies-save-journalism/.

Edelman, Gilad. (2020c, August 13). "She helped wreck the news business. Here's her plan to fix it." *Wired*. https://www.wired.com/story/she-helped-wreck-the-news-business-heres-her-plan-to-fix-it/.

Ember, Sydney. (2016, October 24). "New York Times Company buys *The Wirecutter*." *New York Times*. https://www.nytimes.com/2016/10/25/business/media/new-york-times-company-buys-the-wirecutter.html.

Emkow, Bill. (2020, August 6). "How Bridge Michigan turned new readers into paying members." Google News Initiative. https://blog.google/outreach-initiatives/google-news-initiative/how-bridge-michigan-turned-new-readers-paying-members/.

European Commission. (2016). *Proposal for a Directive of the European Parliament and of the Council on Copyright in the Digital Single Market*. https://digital-strategy.ec.europa.eu/en/library/proposal-directive-european-parliament-and-council-copyright-digital-single-market.

European Parliament. (2018, September 12). "Parliament adopts its position on digital copyright rules." https://www.europarl.europa.eu/news/en/press-room/20180906IPR12103/parliament-adopts-its-position-on-digital-copyright-rules.

Eyears, S. (2019, December 10). "How BBC News built a more engaged audience on Instagram." Meta Journalism Project. https://www.facebook.com/journalismproject/bbc-news-instagram.

Fanta, Alexander and Dachwitz, Ingo. (2020). "Google, the media patron: How the digital giant ensnares journalism." Otto Brenner Foundation. Frankfurt: Otto Brenner Foundation.

Ferrer-Conill, Raul and Tandoc Jr., Edson C. (2018). "The audience-oriented editor: Making sense of the audience in the newsroom." *Digital Journalism*, 6:4, pp. 436–53.

Ferrucci Patrick and Tandoc Jr., Edson. C. (2015). "A tale of two newsrooms: How market orientation influences web analytics use." In *Contemporary Research Methods and Data Analytics in the News Industry*. Hershey: IGI Global.

Fischer, David. (2016, September 23). "An update on Facebook video metrics." Facebook for Business. https://www.facebook.com/business/news/facebook-video-metrics-update?mod=article_inline.

Fischer, Sara. (2019a, September 17). "Washington Post builds ad network for publishers to take on Big Tech." *Axios*. https://www.axios.com/washington-post-zeus-prime-advertising-8f356787-5f66-4fc2-9d34-a62516d4762d.html.

Fischer, Sara. (2019b, December 30). "Vox Media launches new privacy-focused ad-targeting platform." *Axios*. https://www.axios.com/vox-media-ad-targeting-platform-forte-b44146cd-de35-4b97-94f7-e341768c792a.html.

Fischer, Sara. (2019c). "Exclusive: Google partners to fund new local media sites." *Axios*. https://www.axios.com/2019/03/26/google-local-news-sites-funding-mcclatchy.

Fischer, Sara. (2022). "Scoop: Meta officially cuts funding for U.S. news publishers." *Axios*. https://www.axios.com/2022/07/28/meta-publishers-news-funding-cut.

Flew, Terry. (2021). *Regulating Platforms*. Cambridge: Polity Press.

Flew, Terry and Wilding, Derek. (2021, January 1). "The turn to regulation in digital communication: The ACCC's digital platforms inquiry and Australian media policy." *Media, Culture & Society*, 43:1, pp. 48–65.

Fou, Augustine. (2020, June 19). "The importance of brand safety in digital advertising – It's not what you think." *Forbes*. https://www.forbes.com/sites/augustinefou/2020/06/19/the-importance-of-brand-safety-in-digital-advertisingits-not-what-you-think/?sh=505f5b3b62dd.

France 24. (2021, September 1). "Google to appeal 'disproportionate' €500 million French fine in copyright row." https://www.france24.com/en/technology/20210901-google-to-appeal-disproportionate-%E2%82%AC500-million-french-fine-in-copyright-row.

Freeman, Julie. (2020). "Differentiating distance in local and hyperlocal news." *Journalism*, 21:4, pp. 524–40.

Friedland, Lewis, Napoli, Philip, Ognyanova, Katherine, Weil, Carola and Wilson III, Ernest. J. (2012, July 16). "Review of the literature regarding critical information needs of the American public." Communication Policy Research Network. https://transition.fcc.gov/bureaus/ocbo/Final_Literature_Review.pdf.

Furgał, Ula. (2021). "The EU press publishers' right: Where do member states stand?." *Journal of Intellectual Property Law & Practice*, 16:8, pp. 887–93.

Fürst, Silke. (2020). "In the service of good journalism and audience interests? How audience metrics affect news quality." *Media and Communication*, 8:3, pp. 270–80.

Giblin, Rebecca and Doctorow, Cory. (2022). *Chokepoint Capitalism: How Big Tech and Big Content Captured Creative Labor Markets and How We'll Win Them Back*. Boston: Beacon Press.

Gillespie, Tarleton. (2010). "The politics of 'platforms.'" *New Media & Society*, 12:3, pp. 347–64.

Gingras, Richard. (2019, September 25). "Nouvelles règles de droit d'auteur en France: notre mise en conformité avec la loi." https://france.googleblog.com/2019/09/comment-nous-respectons-le-droit-dauteur.html.

Giomelakis, Dimitrios and Veglis, Andreas. (2016). "Investigating search engine optimization factors in media websites." *Digital Journalism*, 4:3, pp. 379–400.

GNI Innovation Challenges. (n.d.). "Google News Initiative." https://newsinitiative.withgoogle.com/innovation-challenges/.

Gobry, Pascal-Emmanuel. (2014, March 31). "What Vice's stunning financials tell us about the future of media." *Forbes*. https://www.forbes.com/sites/pascalemmanuelgobry/2014/03/31/vice-media-ipo/?sh=6326c4f41a9e.

Gold, Ashley. (2018, April 10). "Zuckerberg: Facebook contacted by Mueller probe." *Politico*. https://www.politico.com/story/2018/04/10/zuckerberg-facebook-mueller-russia-probe-512493.

Google. (2000a, August 16). "Google's targeted keyword ad program shows strong momentum with advertisers." *Google News*. http://googlepress.blogspot.com/2000/08/googles-targeted-keyword-ad-program.html.

Google. (2000b, October 23). "Google launches self-service advertising program." *Google News*. http://googlepress.blogspot.com/2000/10/google-launches-self-service.html.

Google. (2007, April 13). "Google to acquire DoubleClick." US Security and Exchanges Commission. https://www.sec.gov/Archives/edgar/data/1288776/000119312507084483/dex991.htm.

Google News Initiative (2020, n.d.), "About as: Local news experiments project." https://news-initiative.withgoogle.com/local-news-experiments-project/about-us/.

Google News Initiative. (2020, n.d.). *Impact Report 2020.* https://newsinitiative.withgoogle.com/impact/.

Google Support. (n.d.). "*Google News* in Spain." https://support.google.com/news/publisher-center/answer/9609687?hl=en.

Gonzalez-Tosat, Clara and Sadaba-Chalezquer, Charo. (2021). "DNI's DNA: Where is Google's money in European media?." *Sustainability*, 2021:13, p. 11457. https://doi.org/10.3390/su132011457.

Graham, Megan. (2020, May 17). "To show how easy it is for plagiarized news sites to get revenue, I made my own." CNBC. https://www.cnbc.com/2020/05/17/broken-internet-ad-system-makes-it-easy-to-earn-money-with-plagiarism.html.

Grant, D. and Fritsch, M. (2020, 3 December). "How Local French journalists used a Facebook Messenger bot to engage readers on COVID-19, elections." Meta Journalism Project. https://www.facebook.com/journalismproject/programs/accelerator/facebook-messenger-chatbot-groupe-centre-france.

Greenstein, Shane. (2020, October 18). "The fox and the shepherd problem." Truth on the Market. https://truthonthemarket.com/2020/10/18/the-fox-and-the-shepherd-problem/.

Greenwald, Glenn, MacAskill, Ewen, and Poitras, Laura. (2013, June 11). "Edward Snowden: the whistleblower behind the NSA surveillance revelations." *The Guardian.* https://www.theguardian.com/world/2013/jun/09/edward-snowden-nsa-whistleblower-surveillance.

Guiliani-Hoffman, Francesca. (2019, August 16). "How the Washington Post has changed under Jeff Bezos." CNN. https://edition.cnn.com/2019/08/16/media/jeff-bezos-donald-graham/index.html.

Ha, Anthony. (2013, August 17). "Fox invests in Vice, a media company that makes money being terrible and brilliant." *TechCrunch.* https://techcrunch.com/2013/08/16/vice-fox/.

Ha, Anthony. (2014, August 30). "Vice Media confirms that it's selling a stake to A&E Networks at a $2.5B valuation." *TechCrunch.* https://techcrunch.com/2014/08/29/vice-media-confirms-that-its-selling-a-stake-to-ae-networks-at-a-2-5b-valuation/.

Ha, Anthony. (2018, March 1). "LittleThings blames its shutdown on Facebook algorithm change." *TechCrunch.* https://techcrunch.com/2018/02/28/littlethings-shutdown/.

Habermas, Jurgen. (1992). *The Structural Transformation of the Public Sphere.* Cambridge: Polity Press.

Hagey, Keach and Horwitz, Jeff. (2021, September 15). "Facebook tried to make its platform a healthier place. It got angrier instead." *The Wall Street Journal.* https://www.wsj.com/articles/facebook-algorithm-change-zuckerberg-11631654215.

Hagey, Keach, Cherney, Mike, and Horwitz, Jeff. (2022, May 5). "Facebook deliberately caused havoc in Australia to influence new law, whistleblowers say." *The Wall Street Journal.*

https://www.wsj.com/articles/facebook-deliberately-caused-havoc-in-australia-to-influence-new-law-whistleblowers-say-11651768302.

Haim, Mario, Graefe, Andreas, and Brosius, Hans-Bernd. (2018). "Burst of the filter bubble? Effects of personalization on the diversity of Google News." *Digital Journalism*, 6:3, pp. 330–43.

Hallin, Daniel C. (1992). "The passing of the 'high modernism' of American journalism." *Journal of Communication*, 42:3, pp. 14–25.

Hannam, Peter. (2022, February 26). "Reining in the digital giants: Rod Sims on the trials and triumphs of a decade as head of the consumer watchdog." *The Guardian*. https://www.theguardian.com/australia-news/2022/feb/26/reining-in-the-digital-giants-rod-sims-on-the-trials-and-triumphs-of-a-decade-as-head-of-the-consumer-watchdog.

Hanusch, Folker. (2017). "Web analytics and the functional differentiation of journalism cultures: Individual, organizational and platform-specific influences on newswork." *Information, Communication & Society*, 20:10, pp. 1571–86.

Harcup, Tony and O'Neill, Deirdre. (2017). "What is news? News values revisited (again)." *Journalism Studies*, 18:12, pp. 1470–88.

Hardy, Jonathan. (2017). "Money, (co)production and power: The contribution of critical political economy to digital journalism studies." *Digital Journalism*, 5:1, pp. 1–25.

Hayes, Alex. (2016, June 24). "Ooh Media buys Junkee Media in surprise move." *Mumbrella*. https://mumbrella.com.au/ooh-media-buys-junkee-media-surprise-move-376329.

Heath, Alex. (2021, October 25). "Facebook's lost generation." *The Verge*. https://www.theverge.com/22743744/facebook-teen-usage-decline-frances-haugen-leaks.

Helberger, Natali. (2012). "Exposure diversity as a policy goal." *Journal of Media Law*, 4:1, pp. 65–92.

Helberger, Natali. (2019). "On the democratic role of news recommenders." *Digital Journalism*, 7:8, pp. 993–1012.

Helberger, Natali, Karppinen, Kari, and D'acunto, Lucia. (2018). "Exposure diversity as a design principle for recommender systems." *Information, Communication & Society*, 21:2, pp. 191–207.

Helmore, Edward. (2019, January 27). "Future of digital journalism in question as *BuzzFeed* and *HuffPost* lay off 1,000." *The Guardian*. https://www.theguardian.com/media/2019/jan/26/huffpost-buzzfeed-layoffs-digital-journalism.

Herrman, John and Isaac, Mike. (2016, May 9). "Conservatives accuse Facebook of political bias." *New York Times*. https://www.nytimes.com/2016/05/10/technology/conservatives-accuse-facebook-of-political-bias.html.

Hess, Kristy and Waller, Lisa. (2020). "Charting the media innovations landscape for regional and rural newspapers." *Australian Journalism Review*, 42:1, pp. 59–75.

Hiller, Jennifer. (1998, February 24). "GoTo searches with a capitalist engine." *Wired*. https://www.wired.com/1998/02/goto-searches-with-a-capitalist-engine/.

Honan, Mat. (2016, April 6). "Why Facebook and Mark Zuckerberg went all in on live video." *Buzzfeed News*. https://www.buzzfeednews.com/article/mathonan/why-facebook-and-mark-zuckerberg-went-all-in-on-live-video.

Hurcombe, Edward. (2022). *Social News: How Born-Digital Outlets Transformed Journalism*. Switzerland: Palgrave Macmillan.

Hurcombe, Edward, Burgess, Jean and Harrington, Stephen. (2021). "What's newsworthy about 'social news'? Characteristics and potential of an emerging genre." *Journalism*, 22:2, pp. 378–94.

IAB. (2020). "Internet advertising and revenue report." *PWC*. https://www.iab.com/wp-content/uploads/2020/05/FY19-IAB-Internet-Ad-Revenue-Report_Final.pdf.

Ingram, Mathew. (2018, January 26). "Jonah Peretti: Everything is fine." *Columbia Journalism Review*. https://www.cjr.org/q_and_a/jonah-peretti-facebook.php.

ISBA. (2020, May 6). "Executive summary – Programmatic supply chain transparency study." *PWC*. https://www.isba.org.uk/knowledge/executive-summary-programmatic-supply-chain-transparency-study.

Israely, Jeff. (2019, January 31). "2009: The internet is killing (print) journalism. 2019: The internet is killing (internet) journalism." *NiemanLab*. https://www.niemanlab.org/2019/01/2009-the-internet-is-killing-print-journalism-2019-the-internet-is-killing-internet-journalism/.

James, Meg. (2020, April 17). "Coronavirus crisis hastens the collapse of local newspapers. Here's why it matters." *Los Angeles Times*. https://www.latimes.com/entertainment-arts/business/story/2020-04-17/coronavirus-local-newspapers-struggle.

Jarvey, Natalie. (2019, February 1). "Vice Media to reorganize, lay off 10 percent of staff (exclusive)." *The Hollywood Reporter*. https://www.hollywoodreporter.com/business/business-news/vice-media-reorganize-lay-10-percent-staff-1181785/.

Johnson, Bobbie. (2009, November 9). "Murdoch could block Google searches entirely." *The Guardian*. https://www.theguardian.com/media/2009/nov/09/murdoch-google.

Junkee. (2017, March 14). "If you fill out this super easy survey for us, we might give you $1,000." https://junkee.com/fill-super-easy-survey-us-might-give-1000/98345.

Junkee Media. (2021). *Treasury Laws Amendment (News Media and Digital Platforms Mandatory Bargaining Code) Bill 2020*. Submission 8. https://www.legislation.gov.au/Details/C2021A00021.

Kacholia, Varun and Ji, Minwen. (2013, December 2). "Helping you find more news to talk about." *Facebook Newsroom*. https://about.fb.com/news/2013/12/news-feed-fyi-helping-you-find-more-news-to-talk-about/.

O'Kane, Ciaran. (2009, September 18). "New DoubleClick ad exchange is open, neutral and allows real-time bidding." *ExchangeWire*. https://www.exchangewire.com/blog/2009/09/18/new-doubleclick-ad-exchange-is-open-neutral-and-allows-real-time-bidding/.

Karppinen, Kari. (2013). *Rethinking Media Pluralism*. New York: Fordham University Press.

Katzenbach, Christian. (2012). "Technologies as institutions: Rethinking the role of technology in media governance constellations." In N. Just and M. Puppis (eds), *Trends in Communication Policy Research: New Theories, Methods and Subjects*. Bristol: Intellect Books.

Kawamoto, Dawn. (2008, March 21). "FTC allows Google-DoubleClick merger to proceed." *CNET*. https://www.cnet.com/news/ftc-allows-google-doubleclick-merger-to-proceed-1/.

Kayali, Laura. (2021, June 7). "Google agrees to advertising changes after €220M French antitrust fine." *Politico*. https://www.politico.eu/article/france-competition-google-advertising-antitrust-fine/.

Kayali, Laura and Larger, Thibault. (2020, October 8). "French court sides with press publishers in Google license fee stand-off." *Politico*. https://www.politico.eu/article/french-court-sides-with-press-publishers-amid-breakthrough-with-google-over-payment/.

Kelly, Martin. (2017, July 13). "The birth of real time bidding." Infectious Media. https://blog.infectiousmedia.com/birth-real-time-bidding.

Kenyon, Andrew. (2021). *Democracy of Expression: Positive Free Speech and Law*. Cambridge: Cambridge University Press.

Kim, Eugene. (2014, November 7). "Mark Zuckerberg wants to build the 'perfect personalised newspaper' for every person in the world." *Business Insider*. https://www.businessinsider.com.au/mark-zuckerberg-wants-to-build-a-perfect-personalized-newspaper-2014-11.

Koch, Tommaso. (2014, October 31). "La Ley de Propiedad Intelectual, aprobada solo con los votos del PP." *El Pais*. https://elpais.com/cultura/2014/10/30/actualidad/1414657007_768641.html.

Koetsier, John. (2020, August 29). "Facebook's news subscription challenges Apple News+, threatens Flipboard and Google's coming news product." *Forbes*. https://www.forbes.com/sites/johnkoetsier/2020/08/29/facebooks-news-subscription-challenges-apple-news-threatens-flipboard-and-googles-coming-news-product/?sh=7e7d4ecd2283.

Kosterich, Allie and Weber, Matthew. (2018). "Starting up the news: The impact of venture capital on the digital news media ecosystem." *International Journal on Media Management*, 20:4, pp. 239–62.

Kyriakopoulos, Arthur. (2022). "Free-to-air television broadcasting in Australia." *IBISWorld*. Report J5621.

L.A.T. Guild. (2020, May 1). "L.A. Times Guild strikes deal to avoid newsroom layoffs." *Los Angeles Times Guild*. https://latguild.com/news/2020/5/1/la-times-guild-strikes-deal-to-avoid-newsroom-layoffs.

LaFrance, Adrienne. (2014, March 12). "Why venture capitalists are suddenly investing in news." *Quartz*. https://qz.com/186492/why-venture-capitalists-are-suddenly-investing-in-news/.

Leaver, Tama. (2021). "Going dark: How Google and Facebook fought the Australian news media and digital platforms mandatory bargaining code." *M/C Journal*. https://journal.media-culture.org.au/index.php/mcjournal/article/view/2774.

Leaver, Tama, Highfield, im and Abidin, Crystal. (2020). *Instagram: Visual Social Media Cultures*. London: Polity.

Ledlin, Chris. (2018, January 18). "The forgotten players in the great Facebook NewsFeed purge." *Medium*. https://medium.com/@chrisledlin/the-forgotten-players-in-the-great-facebook-newsfeed-purge-3772463a0130.

Lee, Dave. (2017, September 7). "Facebook uncovers 'Russian-funded' misinformation campaign." BBC News. https://www.bbc.com/news/technology-41182519.

Lee, Eun Jeong. (2019). "Traditional and new media: A comparative analysis of news outlets' news feeds on Snapchat." *International Journal of Interactive Communication Systems and Technologies (IJICST)*, 9:1, pp. 32–47.

Lee, Karen and Molitorisz, Sacha. (2021). "The Australian News Media Bargaining Code: Lessons for the UK, EU and beyond." *Journal of Media Law*, 13:1, pp. 36–53.

Lewis, Adam. (2019, June 26). "Vice, BuzzFeed become latest cautionary tale for digital media investors." *Pitchbook*. https://pitchbook.com/news/articles/vice-buzzfeed-become-latest-cautionary-tale-for-digital-media-investors.

Lewis, Seth C. and Molyneux, Lewis. (2018). "A decade of research on social media and journalism: Assumptions, blind spots, and a way forward." *Media and Communication*, 6:4, pp. 11–23.

Lincoln, Kevin. (2012, January 4). "The free hipster's bible Vice Media had revenues of $100+ million in 2011." *Business Insider*. https://www.businessinsider.com.au/the-free-hipsters-bible-vice-media-had-revenues-of-100-million-in-2011-2012-1.

Lindskow, Kasper. (2020, 6 January). "2020: The year publishers regain control of their platforms." International News Media Association. https://www.inma.org/blogs/digital-strategies/post.cfm/2020-the-year-publishers-regain-control-of-their-platforms.

Ljunggren, David. (2021, February 19). "Canada vows to be next country to go after Facebook to pay for news." *Reuters*. https://www.reuters.com/business/media-telecom/canada-vows-be-next-country-go-after-facebook-pay-news-2021-02-18/.

Logsdon, Brie. (2021, February 18). "The Guardian, Aftenposten bring newsrooms into their reader revenue strategies." INMA. https://www.inma.org/blogs/conference/post.cfm/the-guardian-aftenposten-bring-newsrooms-into-their-reader-revenue-strategies.

Lomas, Natasha. (2020, July 25). "Data from Dutch public broadcaster shows the value of ditching creepy ads." *TechCrunch*. https://techcrunch.com/2020/07/24/data-from-dutch-public-broadcaster-shows-the-value-of-ditching-creepy-ads/.

Lopezosa, Carlos, Codina, Luis and Pérez-Montoro, Mario. (2019). "SEO and digital media news media: Visibility of cultural information in Spain's leading newspapers." *Trípodos*, 44, pp. 41–61.

Lotz, Amanda. (2021). *Media Disrupted*. Cambridge: The MIT Press.

Lu, Donna. (2021, 18 February). "Facebook's Australian news ban is a fight the whole world should watch." *New Scientist*. https://www.newscientist.com/article/2268431-facebooks-australian-news-ban-is-a-fight-the-whole-world-should-watch/.

Lyons, Kim. (2020, August 29). "Facebook pilot program linking its users' news subscriptions could cut down on password fatigue." *The Verge*. https://www.theverge.com/2020/8/29/21406664/facebook-pilot-news-algorithm-publishers-subscriptions.

Mansell, Robin and Steinmueller, W. Edward. (2020). *Advanced Introduction to Platform Economics*. Cheltenham: Edward Elgar Publishing.

Marshall, Josh. (2018, June 29). "How Facebook punked and then gut punched the news biz." *TPM*. https://talkingpointsmemo.com/edblog/how-facebook-punked-and-then-gut-punched-the-news-biz.

Martin, Fiona and Dwyer, Tim. (2019). *Sharing News Online: Commendary Cultures and Social Media News Ecologies*. London: Palgrave Macmillan.

Marvin, Ginny. (2020, June 15). "Black Lives Matter content: Latest unintended brand safety consequences." *Search Engine Land*. https://searchengineland.com/black-lives-matter-and-brand-safety-its-more-complicated-than-keywords-335881.

Mason, Max. (2020, June 16). "The number of Australians paying for news doubles." *Australian Financial Review*. https://www.afr.com/companies/media-and-marketing/the-number-of-australians-paying-for-news-doubles-20200616-p5534h.

Marchive, Valéry. (2013, February 4). "Google seals 'link tax' deal with French publishers with €60m fund." ZDNet. https://www.zdnet.com/article/google-seals-link-tax-deal-with-french-publishers-with-eur60m-fund/.

Masnick, Mike. (2014, October 23). "German Publishers grant Google a 'Free License' Google never needed to post news snippets." Techdirt. https://www.techdirt.com/2014/10/23/german-publishers-grant-google-free-license-google-never-needed-to-post-news-snippets/.

Masnick, Mike. (2015, July 29). "Study of Spain's 'Google Tax' on news shows how much damage it has done." Techdirt. https://www.techdirt.com/2015/07/29/study-spains-google-tax-news-shows-how-much-damage-it-has-done/.

Mayhew, Freddy. (2020, September 14). "Report predicts five years of steep global decline for newspaper industry revenue (print and online)." *Press Gazette*. https://www.pressgazette.co.uk/report-predicts-five-years-of-steep-global-decline-for-newspaper-industry-revenu-print-and-online/.

Mayhew, Freddy. (2021). "Google and Facebook's deals with publishers: What we know so far." *Press Gazette*. https://pressgazette.co.uk/google-and-facebooks-deals-with-publishers-what-we-know-so-far/.

Mayhew, Freddy and Tobitt, Charlotte. (2020, August 14). "Covid-19 crisis leads to more than 2,000 job cuts across UK news organisations." https://www.pressgazette.co.uk/covid-19-crisis-leads-to-more-than-2000-job-cuts-across-uk-news-organisations/.

McCabe, David and Wakabayashi, Daisuke. (2020, December 16). "10 states accuse Google of abusing monopoly in online ads." *New York Times*. https://www.nytimes.com/2020/12/16/technology/google-monopoly-antitrust.html.

McChesney, Robert. (2008). *The Political Economy of Media: Enduring Issues, Emerging Dilemmas*. New York: NYU Press.

McChesney, Robert. (2013). *Digital Disconnect: How Capitalism Is Turning the Internet Against Democracy*. New York: The New Press.

McCormick, Rich. (2015, January 27). "Snapchat's new Discover feature puts news and entertainment a swipe away from your stories." *The Verge*. https://www.theverge.com/2015/1/27/7919809/snapchat-launches-discover-feature-ad-support.

McLaughlin, Matt. (2020, March 17). "Brand suitability series part 2: Demystifying DV's keyword blocklist service." *DoubleVerify*. https://doubleverify.com/brand-suitability-series-part-2-demystifying-dvs-keyword-blocklist-service/.

McQuail, Denis and Van Cuilenburg, Jan J. (1983). "Diversity as a media policy goal." *Gazette*, 31:3, pp. 145–62.

Meade, Amanda. (2019, January 29). "BuzzFeed loses 11 staff in Australia amid global job cuts." *Guardian Australia*. https://www.theguardian.com/media/2019/jan/29/buzzfeed-loses-11-staff-in-australia-amid-global-job-cuts.

Meade, Amanda. (2020, April 14). "Dozens of Australian newspapers stop printing as coronavirus crisis hits advertising." *The Guardian*. https://www.theguardian.com/media/2020/apr/14/dozens-of-australian-newspapers-stop-printing-as-coronavirus-crisis-hits-advertising.

Meade, Amanda and Hanna, Conal. (2022, March 3). "NSW flood-affected towns turn to Facebook and WhatsApp after local news sources disappear." *The Guardian*. https://www.theguardian.com/media/2022/mar/03/nsw-flood-affected-towns-turn-to-facebook-and-whatsapp-after-local-news-sources-disappear.

Media, Entertainment & Arts Alliance. (2010). *Life in the Clickstream: The Future of Journalism*. Sydney: The Media Alliance.

Meta Journalism Project (MJP). (2020, August 4). "The Atlantic sells nearly 8,000 subscriptions in 4 months via instant articles." Meta Journalism Project. https://www.facebook.com/journalismproject/instant-articles-the-atlantic.

PA Mediapoint. (2018, January 11). "News publishers told to reduce reliance on Facebook amid steep drop in user engagement with content from top news sites." *Press Gazette*. https://www.pressgazette.co.uk/news-publishers-told-to-reduce-reliance-on-facebook-amid-steep-drop-in-user-engagement-with-content-from-top-news-sites/.

Meese, James. (2021). "Journalism policy across the commonwealth: Partial answers to public problems." *Digital Journalism*, 9:3, pp. 255–75.

Meese, James and Hurcombe, Edward. (2021). "Facebook, news media and platform dependency: The institutional impacts of news distribution on social platforms." *New Media & Society*, 23:8, pp. 2367–84.

Meese, James and Hurcombe, Edward. (2022). "Global platforms and local networks: An institutional account of the Australian News Media Bargaining Code." In T. Flew and F. Martin (eds), *Digital Platform Regulation: Global Perspectives on Internet Governance*. London: Palgrave Macmillan, pp. 151–72.

Musil, Steven. (2012, December 13). "Google settles copyright dispute with Belgium newspapers." *CNET*. https://www.cnet.com/tech/services-and-software/google-settles-copyright-dispute-with-belgium-newspapers/.

Meyer, Robinson. (2013, December 9). "Why are UpWorthy headlines suddenly everywhere?." *The Atlantic*. https://www.theatlantic.com/technology/archive/2013/12/why-are-upworthy-headlines-suddenly-everywhere/282048/.

Molla, Rani. (2017, December 11). "Google is sending more traffic than Facebook to publishers – again." *Vox*. https://www.vox.com/2017/12/11/16748026/google-facebook-publisher-traffic-2017-increase.

Molla, Rani. (2018, February 15). "Google is replacing Facebook's traffic to publishers." *Vox*. https://www.vox.com/2018/2/15/17013618/google-facebook-traffic-publishers-amp-chartbeat.

Möller, Judith, Trilling, Damien, Helberger, Natali and van Es, Bram. (2018). "Do not blame it on the algorithm: An empirical assessment of multiple recommender systems and their impact on content diversity." *Information Communication & Society*, 21:7, pp. 959–77.

Moore, Martin and Tambini, Damien. (eds). (2018). *Digital Dominance: The Power of Google, Amazon, Facebook, and Apple*. Oxford: Oxford University Press.

Morton, Fiona and Dinielli, David. (2020, June 1). "Roadmap for a digital advertising monopolization case against Google". *Omidyar Network*. https://omidyar.com/wp-content/uploads/2020/09/Roadmap-for-a-Case-Against-Google.pdf.

Moses, Lucia. (2017a, September 29). "Facebook loses attention as publishers shift focus to other platforms." *Digiday*. https://digiday.com/media/facebook-loses-attention-publishers-shift-focus-platforms/.

Moses, Lucia. (2017b, November 20). "The pivot to reality for digital media." *Digiday*. https://digiday.com/media/pivot-reality-digital-media/.

Moses, Lucia. (2017c, July 14). "Publishers are switching affections from Snapchat to Instagram." *Digiday*. https://digiday.com/media/publishers-switching-affections-snapchat-instagram/.

Moses, Lucia. (2018, January 18). "As Facebook retreats from publishers, Snapchat is rolling out a publisher charm offensive." *Digiday*. https://digiday.com/media/snapchat-rolling-publisher-charm-offensive/.

Moses, Lucia. (2020, April 8). "The nation's top ad agencies are calling on advertisers to support news outlets as publishers struggle to monetise their coronavirus content." *Insider*. https://www.businessinsider.com/ad-agencies-call-on-advertisers-to-ease-coronavirus-news-blocking-2020-4.

Mosseri, Adam. (2018, January 11). "Bringing people closer together." *Facebook Newsroom*. https://about.fb.com/news/2018/01/news-feed-fyi-bringing-people-closer-together/.

Moyo, Dumisani, Mare, Admire and Matsilele, Trust. (2019). "Analytics-driven journalism? Editorial metrics and the reconfiguration of online news production practices in African newsrooms." *Digital Journalism*, 7:4, pp. 490–506.

Moz. (n.d.). "Meta description." *Moz*. https://moz.com/learn/seo/meta-description.

Mullin, Benjamin. (2018, February 27). "Digital publisher LittleThings shuts down, citing Facebook news feed change." *The Wall Street Journal*. https://www.wsj.com/articles/digital-publisher-littlethings-shuts-down-citing-facebook-news-feed-change-1519787564.

Mullin, Benjamin and Patel. Sahil. (2019, August 8). "Facebook offers news outlets millions of dollars a year to license content." *The Wall Street Journal*. https://www.wsj.com/articles/facebook-offers-news-outlets-millions-of-dollars-a-year-to-license-content-11565294575.

Myllylahti, Merja. (2014). "Newspaper paywalls—The hype and the reality: A study of how paid news content impacts on media corporation revenues." *Digital Journalism*, 2:2, pp. 179–94.

Myllylahti, Merja. (2016). "Newspaper paywalls and corporate revenues: A comparative study." In B. Franklin and S. Eldridge II (eds), *The Routledge Companion to Digital Journalism Studies*. London: Routledge, pp. 166–75.

Myllylahti, Merja. (2017). "What content is worth locking behind a paywall? Digital news commodification in leading Australasian financial newspapers." *Digital Journalism*, 5:4, pp. 460–71.

Myllylahti, Merja. (2020) "Paying attention to attention: A conceptual framework for studying news reader revenue models related to platforms." *Digital Journalism*, 8:5, pp. 567–75.

Myllylahti, Merja. (2021). "It's a Dalliance! A glance to the first decade of the digital reader revenue market and how the Google's and Facebook's payments are starting to shape it." *Digital Journalism*. https://doi-org.ezproxy.lib.rmit.edu.au/10.1080/21670811.2021.1965487

Napoli, Lisa. (1999, July 14). "DoubleClick buys NetGravity." *New York Times*. https://archive.nytimes.com/www.nytimes.com/library/tech/99/07/cyber/articles/14advertising.html.

Napoli, Philip. (1999). "Deconstructing the diversity principle." *Journal of Communication*, 49:4, pp. 7–34.

Napoli, Philip. (2003). *Audience Economics: Media Institutions and the Audience Marketplace*. New York: Columbia University Press.

Napoli, Philip. (2010). *Audience Evolution: New Technologies and the Transformation of Media Audiences*. New York: Columbia University Press.

Napoli, Philip. (2015). "Social media and the public interest: Governance of news platforms in the realm of individual and algorithmic gatekeepers." *Telecommunications Policy*, 39:9, pp. 751–60.

Napoli, Philip. (2019). *Social Media and the Public Interest*. New York: Columbia University Press.

Napoli, Philip. (2020). "Connecting journalism and public policy: New concerns and continuing challenges." *Digital Journalism*, 8:6, pp. 691–703.

Napoli, Philip and Caplan, Robyn. (2017). "Why media companies insist they're not media companies, why they're wrong, and why it matters." *First Monday*, 22:5. https://doi.org/10.5210/fm.v22i5.7051.

Nechushtai, Efrat. (2018). "Could digital platforms capture the media through infrastructure?." *Journalism*, 19:8, pp. 1043–58.

Nechushtai, Efrat and Lewis, Seth C. (2019). "What kind of news gatekeepers do we want machines to be? Filter bubbles, fragmentation, and the normative dimensions of algorithmic recommendations." *Computers in Human Behavior*, 90, pp. 298–307.

Neheli, Nicole B. (2018). "News by numbers: The evolution of analytics in journalism." *Digital Journalism*, 6:8, pp. 1041–51.

Nelson, Jennifer. (2017, October 17). "How four media organisations are using events to raise revenue, engage audiences." *SNPA*. https://snpa.org/stories/events,4136380.

Newman, Nic, Fletcher, Richard, Kalogeropoulos, Antonis, Levy, David and Nielsen, Rasmus Kleis. (2018, n.d.). *Digital News Report 2018*. Oxford: Reuters Institute for the Study of Journalism. http://media.digitalnewsreport.org/wp-content/uploads/2018/06/digital-news-report-2018.pdf.

Newman, Nic, Fletcher, Richard, Kalogeropoulos, Antonis and Nielsen, Rasmus Kleis. (2019, n.d.). *Digital News Report 2019*. Oxford: Reuters Institute for the Study of Journalism. https://reutersinstitute.politics.ox.ac.uk/sites/default/files/2019-06/DNR_2019_FINAL_0.pdf.

Newman, Nic, Fletcher, Richard, Schulz, Anne, Andi, Simge and Nielsen, Rasmus Kleis. (2020a, n.d.). *Digital News Report 2020*. Oxford: https://reutersinstitute.politics.ox.ac.uk/sites/default/files/2020-06/DNR_2020_FINAL.pdf.

Newman, Nic, Fletcher, Richard, Schulz, Anne, Andi, Simge, Robertson, Craig. and Nielsen, Rasmus Kleis. (2021, n.d.). *Digital News Report 2021*. Oxford: Reuters Institute for the Study of Journalism. https://reutersinstitute.politics.ox.ac.uk/sites/default/files/2021-06/Digital_News_Report_2021_FINAL.pdf

News Corp. (2021, March 15). *News Corp and Facebook Reach Agreement in Australia.* https://newscorp.com/2021/03/15/news-corp-and-facebook-reach-agreement-in-australia/.

News Revenue Hub. (2020, March 30). "The future is audience-first, and other takeaways from the GNI Audience Lab." *Hub Reports.* https://fundjournalism.org/news/the-future-is-audience-first-and-other-takeaways-from-the-gni-audience-lab/.

Newton, Casey. (2014, April 22). "You might also like this story about weaponized clickbait." *The Verge.* https://www.theverge.com/2014/4/22/5639892/how-weaponized-clickbait-took-over-the-web.

Newton, Casey. (2016, November 10). "Zuckerberg: The idea that fake news on Facebook influenced the election is 'crazy.'" *The Verge.* https://www.theverge.com/2016/11/10/13594558/mark-zuckerberg-election-fake-news-trump.

Ng, C. and Yeo, K. (2021, October 31). "How New Media Group grew Instant Articles and programmatic revenue." Meta Journalism Project. https://www.facebook.com/journalism-project/New-Media-Group-grew-revenue-both-Instant-Articles-and-programmatic-web.

Nicas, Jack. (2018, October 25). "Apples News' radical approach: Humans over machines." *New York Times.* https://www.nytimes.com/2018/10/25/technology/apple-news-humans-algorithms.html.

Nielsen, Rasmus Kleis. (2018, May 25). "What is journalism studies studying? (ICA 2018 edition)." *Rasmuskleisnielsen.net.* https://rasmuskleisnielsen.net/2018/05/25/what-is-journalism-studies-studying-ica-2018-edition/.

Nielsen, R. Rasmus Kleis. (2019). "Economic contexts of journalism." In K. Wahl-Jorgensen and T. Hanitzsch (eds), *The Handbook of Journalism Studies*. New York: Routledge, pp. 324–40.

Nielsen, R. Rasmus Kleis and Ganter, Sarah Anne. (2018). "Dealing with digital intermediaries: A case study of the relations between publishers and platforms." *New Media & Society*, 20:4, pp. 1600–17.

Nielsen, Rasmus Kleis and Ganter, Sarah Anne. (2022). *The Power of Platforms: Shaping Media and Society*. Oxford: Oxford University Press.

Nine Entertainment. (2021). *FY21 Final Results*. https://www.nineforbrands.com.au/investors/financial-reports/.

New York Times (NYT). (2014, March 24). "Innovation." https://sriramk.com/memos/nytimes-innovation-report.pdf.

Official Journal of the European Union (2022, 19 October). "Regulations." https://eur-lex.europa.eu/legal-content/EN/TXT/PDF/?uri=CELEX:32022R2065.

O'Hara, Kieron and Stevens, David. (2015). "Echo chambers and online radicalism: Assessing the Internet's complicity in violent extremism." *Policy & Internet*, 7:4, pp. 401–22.

O'Regan, Tom, Balnaves, Mark and Sternberg, Jason (eds). (2002). *Mobilising the Audience*. Brisbane: University of Queensland Press.

O'Reilly, Lara. (2017, March 22). "The real motivations behind the growing YouTube advertiser boycott." *Business Insider*. https://www.businessinsider.com.au/why-advertisers-are-pulling-spend-from-youtube-2017-3.

Ofcom. (2021, November 17). "Statement: The future of media plurality in the UK." Ofcom. https://www.ofcom.org.uk/consultations-and-statements/category-2/future-media-plurality-uk.

Ogbebor, Binakuromo. (2020). *British Media Coverage of the Press Reform Debate*. London: Palgrave Macmillan.

Olsen, Stefanie. (2008, July 22). "Facebook's Sandberg: Growth before monetisation." *CNET*. https://www.cnet.com/tech/services-and-software/facebooks-sandberg-growth-before-monetization/.

Ong, Jonathan Corpus and Cabañes, Jason Vincent. (2019). *Politics and Profit in the Fake News Factory: Four Work Models of Political Trolling in the Philippines*. Latvia: NATO Strategic Communications Centre of Excellence.

Oremus, Will. (2013, October 13). "Google's Big Break." *Slate*. https://slate.com/business/2013/10/googles-big-break-how-bill-gross-goto-com-inspired-the-adwords-business-model.html.

Oremus, Will. (2018a, June 27). "The great Facebook crash." *Slate*. https://slate.com/technology/2018/06/facebooks-retreat-from-the-news-has-painful-for-publishers-including-slate.html.

Oremus, Will. (2018b, October 18). "The Big Lie Behind the 'Pivot to Video'." *Slate*. https://slate.com/technology/2018/10/facebook-online-video-pivot-metrics-false.html.

Osmani, Addy and Grigorik, Ilya. (2018, July 26). "Seed is now a landing page factor for Google Search and Ads." *Google Developers*. https://developers.google.com/web/updates/2018/07/search-ads-speed.

Osofsky, Justin. (2021, May 6). "More ways to drive traffic to news and publishing sites." *Facebook Media*. https://www.facebook.com/notes/2680958112120337/.

Ots, Mart and Robert, G. Picard. (2018). "Press subsidies." In J. Nussbaum (ed.), *Oxford Research Encyclopedia of Communication*. Oxford: Oxford University Press.

Outdoor Media Association. (2019, June 13). "Junkee and oOh!media release in-depth research into young Australians." *Outdoor Media Association*. https://www.oma.org.au/news/junkee-and-oohmedia-release-indepth-research-young-australians.

Owen, Laura H. (2019a, August 13). "Tighten up that paywall! (And some other lessons from a study of 500 newspaper publishers." *NiemanLab*. https://www.niemanlab.org/2019/08/tighten-up-that-paywall-and-some-other-lessons-from-a-study-of-500-newspaper-publishers/.

Owen, Laura H. (2019b, March 15). "One year in, Facebook's big algorithm change has spurred an angry, Fox News-dominated—And very engaged!—News Feed." *NiemanLab*. https://www.niemanlab.org/2019/03/one-year-in-facebooks-big-algorithm-change-has-spurred-an-angry-fox-news-dominated-and-very-engaged-news-feed/.

Owen, Laura H. (2019c, August 7). "The *New York Times* and *The Guardian* are celebrating good digital revenue news today." *NiemanLab*. https://www.niemanlab.org/2019/08/the-new-york-times-and-the-guardian-are-celebrating-good-digital-revenue-news-today/.

Owen, Laura H. (2022, June 22). "After 8 years, Google News returns to Spain." *NiemanLab*. https://www.niemanlab.org/2022/06/after-8-years-google-news-returns-to-spain/.

Owens, Simon. (2018a, November 20). "Every publisher is launching a subscription model. Is there a ceiling?." *WNI*. https://whatsnewinpublishing.com/every-publisher-is-launching-a-subscription-model-is-there-a-ceiling/.

Owens, Simon. (2018b, December 18). "Verizon made a $9 billion bet on digital media. Here's why it failed." *New York Magazine*. https://nymag.com/intelligencer/2018/12/why-verizons-usd9-billion-bet-on-digital-content-failed.html.

Pallotta, Frank. (2017, November 29). "BuzzFeed to cut staff as it reorganizes business side." *CNN Business*. https://money.cnn.com/2017/11/29/media/buzzfeed-layoffs/index.html.

Pariser, Eli. (2011). *The Filter Bubble: What the Internet is Hiding from You*. London: Penguin.

Parliament of Australia. (2021, March 2). Treasury Laws Amendment (News Media and Digital Platforms Mandatory Bargaining Code) Bill 2021. https://parlinfo.aph.gov.au/parlInfo/search/display/display.w3p;query=Id%3A%22legislation%2Fbillhome%2Fr6652%22.

Parse.ly. (n.d.). "The Parse.ly Dashboard." *Parse.ly*. https://www.parse.ly/resources/data-studies/referrer-dashboard.

Part, Tim. (2020, October 12). "Financial Times aligns virtual newsroom, culture to new reality." *INMA*. https://www.inma.org/blogs/value-content/post.cfm/financial-times-aligns-virtual-newsroom-culture-to-new-reality.

Patel, Sahil. (2017, December 13). "Facebook plans to stop paying publishers to make news feed videos." *Digiday*. https://digiday.com/media/facebook-plans-to-stop-paying-publishers-to-make-news-feed-videos/.

Pathak, Shareen. (2019, December 27). "DigiDay research: The changing business model for publishers, in five charts." *DigiDay*. https://digiday.com/media/digiday-research-changing-business-model-publishers-five-charts/.

Paul, Kari. (2020, October 22). "Google is facing the biggest antitrust case in a generation. What could happen?." *The Guardian*. https://www.theguardian.com/technology/2020/oct/21/google-antitrust-charges-what-is-next.

Peiser, Jaclyn. (2019, January 25). "BuzzFeed's first round of layoffs puts an end to its national news desk." *New York Times*. https://www.nytimes.com/2019/01/25/business/media/buzz-feed-layoffs.html.

Pengue, Maria. (2021, March 14). "25 insightful *New York Times* readership statistics." *Letter.ly*. https://letter.ly/new-york-times-readership-statistics/.

Perlberg, Steven and Seetharaman, Deepa. (2016, June 22). "Facebook signs deals with media companies, celebrities for Facebook live." *The Wall Street Journal*. https://www.wsj.com/articles/facebook-signs-deals-with-media-companies-celebrities-for-facebook-live-1466533472.

Perlberg, Steven and Marshall, Jack. (2015, December 31). "How Gawker brings in millions selling headphones, chargers and flashlights." *The Wall Street Journal*. https://www.wsj.com/articles/how-gawker-brings-in-millions-selling-headphones-chargers-and-flash-lights-1451579813.

Petre, Caitlin. (2015). *The Traffic Factories: Metrics at Chartbeat, Gawker Media, and the* New York Times. New York: Tow Center for Digital Journalism.

Petre, Caitlin. (2021). *All the News That's Fit to Click: How Metrics Are Transforming the Work of Journalists*. Princeton: Princeton University Press.

Picard, Robert G. (1982). "State intervention in U.S. press economics." *Gazette*, 30:1, pp. 3–11.

Pickard, Victor. (2011). "Can government support the press? Historicizing and internationalizing a policy approach to the journalism crisis." *The Communication Review*, 14:2, pp. 73–95.

Pickard, Victor and Williams, Alex T. (2014). "Salvation or folly? The promises and perils of digital paywalls." *Digital Journalism*, 2:2, pp. 195–213.

Pickard, Victor. (2019). *Democracy Without Journalism? Confronting the Misinformation Society*. Oxford: Oxford University Press.

Pickard, Victor. (2020). "Restructuring democratic infrastructures: A policy approach to the journalism crisis." *Digital Journalism*, 8:6, pp. 704–19.

Piechota, Grzegorz. (2016, n.d.). "Evaluating distributed content in the news media ecosystem." International News Media Association. https://www.inma.org/report/evaluating-distributed-content-in-the-news-media-ecosystem.

Poell, Thomas, David, B. Nieborg, and Brooke, Erin Duffy. (2022). *Platforms and Cultural Production*. Cambridge: Polity Press.

Popiel, Pawel. (2020). "Addressing platform power: The politics of competition policy." *Journal of Digital Media & Policy*, 3:1, pp. 341–60.

Quinn, Ben. (2013, August 17). "Rupert Murdoch firm dips into hipsters' bible with $70m stake in Vice. *The Guardian*. https://www.theguardian.com/media/2013/aug/17/rupert-murdoch-vice-magazine-stake.

Radcliffe, Damian. (2020, October 12). *The Publisher's Guide to Navigating Covid-19*. Oregon: University of Oregon. https://www.scribd.com/document/488780455/The-Publishers-Guide-to-Navigating-COVID-19.

Rahman, K. Sabeel. (2018a). "Infrastructural regulation and the new utilities." *Yale Journal on Regulation*, 35:2, 911–40.

Rahman, K. Sabeel. (2018b). "The new utilities: Private power, social infrastructure, and the revival of the public utility concept." *Cardozo Law Review*, 39:5, 1621–89.

Rceves, Matthew. (2022, March 31). "Newspaper publishing in Australia." IBISWorld. Report J5411. https://www.ibisworld.com/au/industry/newspaper-publishing/169/.

Reisinger, Don. (2011, July 18). "Google scrubs Belgian newspapers from search." *CNET*. https://www.cnet.com/home/smart-home/google-scrubs-belgian-newspapers-from-search/.

Reuters Staff. (2013, February 2). "Google to pay 60 million euros into French media fund." *Reuters*. https://www.reuters.com/article/us-france-google-idUSBRE91011Z20130201.

Richter, Felix. (2022, February 8). "Amazon Leads $180-Billion Cloud Market." *Statista*. https://www.statista.com/chart/18819/worldwide-market-share-of-leading-cloud-infrastructure-service-providers/.

Rieder, Bernhard and Hofmann, Jeanette. (2020). "Towards platform observability." *Internet Policy Review*, 9:4. https://doi.org/10.14763/2020.4.1535.

Rosemain, Mathieu. (2021, February 13). "Exclusive: Google's $76 million deal with French publishers leaves many outlets infuriated." *Reuters*. https://www.reuters.com/article/us-google-france-copyright-exclusive-idUSKBN2AC27N.

Rusli, Evelyn. (2021, April 9). "Facebook buys Instagram for $1 billion." *New York Times*. https://dealbook.nytimes.com/2012/04/09/facebook-buys-instagram-for-1-billion.

Ryan, Colleen. (2013). *Fairfax: The Rise and Fall*. Melbourne: The Miegunyah Press.

Salari, S. (2019, June 4). "Facebook expands Instant Articles support for subscriptions-based news publishers." *Meta Journalism Project*. https://www.facebook.com/journalismproject/facebook-expands-instant-articles-support-subscriptions.

Samios, Zoe. (2018, May 17). "Four months on: How Facebook's algorithm change has affected publishers." *Mumbrella*. https://mumbrella.com.au/four-months-on-are-facebooks-algorithm-changes-a-win-for-publishers-518040.

Samios, Zoe. (2020, May 14). "BuzzFeed to close Australian, UK news operations." *The Sydney Morning Herald*. https://www.smh.com.au/business/companies/buzzfeed-to-close-australia-uk-news-operations-20200514-p54srs.html.

Samios, Zoe. (2021a, January 20). "'There's no other law like this in Australia': Facebook hits out at digital media code." *The Sydney Morning Herald*. https://www.smh.com.au/business/companies/there-s-no-other-law-like-this-in-australia-facebook-hits-out-at-digital-media-code-20210120-p56vkk.html.

Samios, Zoe. (2021b, February 17). "Google, Nine agree commercial terms for news content." *The Sydney Morning Herald*. https://www.smh.com.au/business/companies/google-nine-agree-commercial-terms-for-news-content-20210217-p5736c.html.

Saroff, John. (2018, February 14). "Google referrals are up: Why that's good and how to make the most of it." Digital Content Next. https://digitalcontentnext.org/blog/2018/02/14/google-referrals-thats-good-make/.

Schindler, Philipp. (2018, March 20). "The Google News Initiative: Building a stronger future for news." Google News Initiative. https://blog.google/outreach-initiatives/google-news-initiative/announcing-google-news-initiative/.

Scire, Sarah. (2022, November 14). "Meta's layoffs make it official: Facebook is ready to part ways with the news." Nieman Lab. https://www.niemanlab.org/2022/11/metas-layoffs-make-it-official-facebook-is-ready-to-part-ways-with-the-news/.

Seale, Shelley. (2020a, n.d.). "The 'New Abnormal' of media advertising." *INMA*. https://www.inma.org/report/the-new-abnormal-of-media-advertising.

Seale, Shelley. (2020b, September 23). "The Guardian shares its programmatic strategy as third-party data disappears." *INMA*. https://www.inma.org/blogs/conference/post.cfm/the-guardian-shares-its-programmatic-strategy-as-third-party-data-disappears.

Seaver, Nick. (2019). "Knowing algorithms." In J. Vertisi and D. Ribes (eds), *digitalSTS*. New York: Princeton University Press, pp. 412–22.

Shakil, Ismail. (2022, April 6). "Canada introduces legislation to compel Facebook, Google to pay for news." *Reuters*. https://www.reuters.com/world/americas/canada-lays-out-details-proposed-law-compel-facebook-google-pay-news-2022-04-05/.

Sharma, Amol and Alpert, Lukas. (2017, November 16). "BuzzFeed, Vice to miss revenue targets; Mashable sells at huge discount." *MarketWatch*. https://www.marketwatch.com/story/buzzfeed-vice-to-miss-revenue-targets-mashable-sells-at-huge-discount-2017-11-16.

Shaw, Lucas. (2017, June 27). "Fox Sports cuts web writing staff to invest more in online video." *Bloomberg*. https://www.bloomberg.com/news/articles/2017-06-26/fox-sports-cuts-web-writing-staff-to-invest-more-in-online-video.

Shepherd, Emma. (2021, August 2). "Google and News Corp partner to provide training to local and regional news professionals." *Mumbrella*. https://mumbrella.com.au/google-and-news-corp-partner-to-provide-training-to-local-and-regional-news-professionals-696299.

Shelanski, Howard. (2013). "Information, innovation, and competition policy for the Internet." *University of Pennsylvania Law Review*, 161:6, pp. 1676–705.

Sherman, Alex. (2019, November 14). "Apple News+ has struggled to add subscribers since first week of launch in March, sources say." *CNBC*. https://www.cnbc.com/2019/11/14/apple-news-has-struggled-to-add-subscribers-since-march-launch.html.

Shields, Mike. (2017a, January 26). "Vice encroaches on ad agency business with creation of Virtue Worldwide." *The Wall Street Journal*. https://www.wsj.com/articles/vice-encroaches-on-ad-agency-business-with-creation-of-virtue-worldwide-1485428401.

Shields, Mike. (2017b, April 2017). "Digital publisher Mic raises $21 million in Series C round." *The Wall Street Journal*. https://www.wsj.com/articles/digital-publisher-mic-raises-21-million-in-series-c-round-1491559201.

Shields, Ronan. (2020, October 23). "Inside Google's targeting plans for a post-cookie world." *Adweek*. https://www.adweek.com/programmatic/inside-googles-targeting-plans-for-a-post-cookie-world/.

Silverman, Craig. (2020, April 2). "These fake local news sites have confused people for years. We found out who created them." *BuzzFeed News*. https://www.buzzfeednews.com/article/craigsilverman/these-fake-local-news-sites-have-confused-people-for-years.

Singer, Jesse. (2017, May 1). "Snapchat? No thanks; I'm an old millenial." *CNN*. https://edition.cnn.com/2017/05/01/health/young-old-millennial-partner/index.html.

Slefo, George. (2020, March 20). "Publishers complain about media buyers blacklisting coronavirus content." *AdAge*. https://adage.com/article/media/publishers-complain-about-media-buyers-blacklisting-coronavirus-content/2245406.

Sluis, Sarah. (2019, September 18). "Can the Washington Post take ad dollars from Facebook? It hopes to, with Zeus Prime." *Ad Exchanger*. https://www.adexchanger.com/platforms/can-the-washington-post-take-ad-dollars-from-facebook-it-hopes-to-with-zeus-prime/.

Smith, Gerry. (2016, April 1). "How a small tech site found a new way for publishers to get paid." *Bloomberg*. https://www.bloomberg.com/news/articles/2016-04-01/how-a-small-tech-site-found-a-new-way-for-publishers-to-get-paid.

Solon, Olivia. (2017, March 25). "Google's bad week: YouTube loses millions as advertising row reaches US." *The Guardian*. https://www.theguardian.com/technology/2017/mar/25/google-youtube-advertising-extremist-content-att-verizon.

Solon, Olivia. (2018, August 14). "Facebook exec: Media firms that don't work with us will end up in 'hospice.'" *The Guardian*. https://www.theguardian.com/technology/2018/aug/13/facebook-news-media-campbell-brown-hospice.

Southern, Lucinda. (2019, May 20). "How Swedish newspaper Dagens Nyheter halved subscriber churn in 2 years." *Digiday*. https://digiday.com/media/how-swedish-newspaper-dagens-nyheter-halved-churn-to-8-in-2-years/.

Southern, Lucinda. (2019, November 22). "Keyword block lists still cause headaches for publishers." *Digiday*. https://digiday.com/media/keyword-block-lists-still-cause-headaches-publishers/.

Spangler, Todd. (2018, November 29). "Bustle Digital Group acquires Mic following Mic's massive layoff." *Variety*. https://variety.com/2018/digital/news/bustle-acquires-mic-1203051696/.

Spangler, Todd. (2019a, January 23). "Verizon Media laying off 800 employees, or 7% of staff in AOL and Yahoo group.' *Variety*. https://variety.com/2019/digital/news/verizon-media-layoffs-800-employees-aol-yahoo-1203115993/.

Spangler, Todd. (2019b, February 1). "Vice Media to axe 10% of staff, laying off about 250 employees, amid revenue slowdown." *Variety*. https://variety.com/2019/digital/news/vice-media-layoffs-250-employees-1203125890/.

Spangler, Todd. (2020, June 24). "Vice urges advertisers to stop blocking 'Black Lives Matter' and related keywords." *Variety*. https://variety.com/2020/digital/news/vice-advertiser-block-black-lives-matter-keywords-1234648046/.

Spurgeon, Christina. (2008). *Advertising and New Media*. London: Routledge.

Srinivasan, Dina. (2020). "Why Google dominates advertising markets." *Stanford Law Review*, 24:1, 55–175.

Statista. (2021a). "Market share of leading web analytics technologies worldwide in 2021." https://www.statista.com/statistics/1258557/web-analytics-market-share-technology-worldwide/.

Statista. (2021b, March 17). "Market share of major office suites technologies in the United States as of October 2020." https://www.statista.com/statistics/961105/japan-market-share-of-office-suites-technologies/.

Statista. (2021c, January 27). "Google: Revenue distribution 2001–2018, by source." https://www.statista.com/statistics/266471/distribution-of-googles-revenues-by-source/.

Statt, Nick. (2020, June 9). "Facebook's revamped news section launches in the US with a focus on local sources." *The Verge*. https://www.theverge.com/2020/6/9/21285656/facebook-news-tab-section-launch-us-local-publishers-partnership.

Stearns, Josh. (2017, n.d.). "Journalism live: How news events foster engagement and expand revenue." Local News Lab. https://localnewslab.org/wp-content/uploads/2018/02/LNL-Guide_NewsEvents_2017FEB.pdf.

Stein, Gabriel. (2016, February 24). "The viral publishing game is over and we all lost." *Medium*. https://gabestein.medium.com/the-viral-publishing-game-is-over-and-we-all-lost-f789b43498ca.

Steiner, Linda. (2017). "Gender and journalism." In J. Nussbaum (ed.), *Oxford Research Encyclopedia of Communication*. Oxford: Oxford University Press.

Stewart, Rebecca. (2020, April 30). "Covid-19 heats up the race to combat advertising's keyword blocking problem." *The Drum*. https://www.thedrum.com/news/2020/04/30/covid-19-heats-up-the-race-combat-advertising-s-keyword-blocking-problem.

Story, Louise and Helft, Miguel. (2007, April 14). "Google buys DoubleClick for $3.1 billion." *New York Times*. https://www.nytimes.com/2007/04/14/technology/14DoubleClick.html.

Strachan, Maxwell. (2019, July 23). "The fall of Mic was a warning." *HuffPost*. https://www.huffpost.com/entry/mic-layoffs-millennial-digital-news-site-warning_n_5c8c144fe4b03e83bdc0e0bc.

Stringer, Paul. (2020). "Viral media: Audience engagement and editorial autonomy at *BuzzFeed* and *Vice*." *Westminster Papers in Communication and Culture*, 15:1, 5–18.

Submission to Senate Economics Legislation Commission. (2020, 18 January). "Submission 50-Facebook." https://www.aph.gov.au/Parliamentary_Business/Committees/Senate/Economics/TLABNewsMedia/Submissions.

Summerfield, Patti. (2020, March 11). "How blacklisting 'coronavirus' could affect programmatic." *Media in Canada*. https://mediaincanada.com/2020/03/11/blacklisting-coronavirus-the-programmatic-effect/.

Sweney, Mark. (2015, 23 October). "Google launches €150m fund for publishers' digital news projects." *The Guardian*. https://www.theguardian.com/media/2015/oct/22/google-fund-publishers-digital-news-projects.

Sweney, Mark. (2018, May 24). "Mail Online's falling traffic blamed on Facebook's newsfeed overhaul." *The Guardian*. https://www.theguardian.com/media/2018/may/24/mail-onlines-falling-traffic-blamed-on-facebooks-newsfeed-overhaul.

Tambini, Damien. (2021). *Media Freedom*. Cambridge: Polity Press.

Tandoc Jr., Edson. (2014). "Journalism is twerking? How web analytics is changing the process of gatekeeping." *New Media & Society*, 16:4, 559–75. https://doi.org/10.1177/1461444814530541.

Tandoc Jr., Edson. (2015). "Why web analytics click: Factors affecting the ways journalists use audience metrics." *Journalism Studies*, 16:6, pp. 782–99.

Tandoc Jr., Edson. (2018). "Five ways BuzzFeed is preserving (or transforming) the journalistic field." *Journalism*, 19:2, pp. 200–16.

Tandoc Jr., Edson. (2019). *Analyzing Analytics: Disrupting Journalism One Click at a Time*. New York: Routledge.

Tandoc Jr., Edson. and Maitra, Julian. (2018). "News organisations' use of native vidoes on Facebook: Tweaking the journalistic field one algorithmic change at a time." *New Media & Society*, 20:5, pp. 1679–96.

Taylor, Josh. (2020, 20 April). "Facebook and Google to be forced to share advertising revenue with Australian media companies." *The Guardian*. https://www.theguardian.com/media/2020/apr/19/facebook-and-google-to-be-forced-to-share-advertising-revenue-with-australian-media-companies.

TechXplore. (2019, September 17). "Washington Post ad tech platform aims at Google-Facebook duopoly." *TechXplore*. https://techxplore.com/news/2019-09-washington-ad-tech-platform-aims.html.

The Oaklandside. (2022, n.d.). "About us." https://oaklandside.org/about/.

Thomas, Julian. (2018). "Programming, filtering, adblocking: Advertising and media automation." *Media International Australia*, 166:1, pp. 34–43. https://doi.org/10.1177/1329878X17738787.

Thorpe, Esther. (2020, August 6). "How three media companies are approaching virtual events and monetization." *Digital Content Next*. https://digitalcontentnext.org/blog/2020/08/06/how-three-media-companies-are-approaching-virtual-events-and-monetization/.

Thorson, Kjerstin, Medeiros, Mel, Cotter, Kelley Chen, Yingying, Rodgers, Kourtnie, Bae, Arram and Baykaldi, Sevgi. (2020). "Platform Civics: Facebook in the local information infrastructure." *Digital Journalism*, 8:10, pp. 1231–57.

Tobitt, Charlotte. (2019, September 2). "FT puts massive profit growth down to digital subscription success." *PressGazette*. https://www.pressgazette.co.uk/ft-financial-times-two-thirds-profit-growth-digital-subscription-success/.

Tobitt, Charlotte. (2021, January 26). "Facebook's cash-for-content News scheme launches in the UK with most publishers on board." *Press Gazette*. https://pressgazette.co.uk/facebook-news-launches-uk/.

Tracy, Marc. (2020a, April 14). "Furloughs and paycuts hit the Los Angeles Times." *New York Times*. https://www.nytimes.com/2020/04/14/business/los-angeles-times-furloughs-cuts.html.

Tracy, Marc. (2020b, May 5). "The *New York Times* tops 6 million subscribers as ad revenue plummets." *New York Times*. https://www.nytimes.com/2020/05/06/business/media/new-york-times-earnings-subscriptions-coronavirus.html.

Tracy, Marc. (2020c, August 5). "Digital revenue exceeds print for 1st time for New York Times Company." *New York Times*. https://www.nytimes.com/2020/08/05/business/media/nyt-earnings-q2.html.

Tracy, Marc. (2021, February 4). "The *New York Times* tops 7.5 million subscriptions as ads decline." *New York Times*. https://www.nytimes.com/2021/02/04/business/media/new-york-times-earnings.html.

Trielli, Daniel. and Diakopoulos, Nicholas. (2019). "Search as news curator: The role of Google in shaping attention to news information." In *Proceedings of the 2019 CHI Conference on Human Factors in Computing Systems*, Glasgow, Scotland, pp. 1–15.

Tucker, Catherine. (2020, November 19). "Competition in the digital advertising market." *The Global Antitrust Institute Report on the Digital Economy*, pp. 679–706. https://papers.ssrn.com/sol3/papers.cfm?abstract_id=3733720.

Turner, Jerome. (2021). "'Someone Should Do Something': Exploring public sphere ideals in the audiences of UK hyperlocal media Facebook pages." *Journalism Studies*, 22:16, pp. 2236–55.

Turvill, William. (2020a, December 15). "Facebook News: US publishers happy with cash for content – But say project is a 'PR move'." *Press Gazette*. https://pressgazette.co.uk/facebook-news-us-publishers-happy-with-cash-for-content-but-say-project-is-a-pr-move/.

Turvill, William. (2020b, December 17). "Interview: How Wall Street Journal used subscriptions 'science' to sign up 350,000 new online subscribers this year." *Press Gazette*. https://www.pressgazette.co.uk/interview-how-wall-street-journal-used-subscriptions-science-to-sign-up-350000-new-online-subscribers-this-year/.

Turvill, William (2020c, December 22). "The 100k club: Most popular subscription news websites in the world revealed." *Press Gazette*. https://www.pressgazette.co.uk/news-publishers-surpassed-100000-digital-subscriptions.

Turvill, William. (2021, September 30). "Google News Shh-owcase: Publishers break silence over secret deals behind $1bn scheme." *Press Gazette*. https://pressgazette.co.uk/google-news-showcase/.

Tworek, Heidi and Buschow, Christopher. (2016). "Changing the rules of the game: Strategic institutionalization and legacy companies' resistance to new media." *International Journal of Communication*, 10, pp. 2119–39.

Uberti, David. (2019, 30 April). "How Fox News dominates Facebook in the Trump era." *Vice News*. https://www.vice.com/en/article/wjvdem/how-fox-news-dominates-facebook-in-the-trump-era.

US DoJ. (2020, October 20). "Justice Department sues monopolist Google for violating anti-trust laws: Google complaint." United States District Court, pp. 1–64. https://www.justice.gov/opa/press-release/file/1328941/download.

Usher, Nikki. (2013). "Al-Jazeera English online: Understanding web metrics and news production when a quantified audience is not a commodified audience." *Digital Journalism*, 1:3, pp. 335–51.

Usher, Nikki. (2014). *Making News at the* New York Times. Ann Arbor: The University of Michigan Press.

Usher, Nikki and Kammer, Aaske. (2019). "News startups." In Jon Nussbaum (ed.), *Oxford Research Encyclopedia of Communication*. Oxford: Oxford University Press.

Usher, Nikki. (2021). *News for the Rich, White and Blue: How Place and Power Distort American Journalism*. New York: Colombia University Press.

Usher, Nikki and Poepsel, Mark. (2021). "The business of journalism and studying the journalism business." In N. Usher and V. Bélair-Gagnon (eds), *Journalism Research that Matters*. Oxford: Oxford University Press.

US Securities and Exchange Commission (USSEC). (2019, n.d.). "Alphabet Inc. Form 10-K." https://www.sec.gov/Archives/edgar/data/1652044/000165204420000008/goog10-k2019.htm.

Van Dijck, José, Nieborg, David and Poell, Thomas. (2019). "Reframing platform power." *Internet Policy Review*, 8:2, pp. 1–18. https://doi.org/10.14763/2019.2.1414.

Van Dijck, José, Poell, Thomas and De Waal, Martijn. (2018). *The Platform Society: Public Values in a Connective World*. New York: Oxford University Press.

Vázquez-Herrero, Jorge, Direito-Rebollal, Sabela and López-García, Xosé. (2019). "Ephemeral journalism: News distribution through Instagram stories." *Social Media + Society*, 5:4, pp. 1–13.

Vázquez-Herrero, Jorge, Negreira-Rey, María-Cruz and López-García, Xosé. (2020). "Let's dance the news! How the news media are adapting to the logic of TikTok." *Journalism,* 23:8. https://doi.org/10.1177/1464884920969092.

Vogelstein, Fred. (2007, February 1). "How Yahoo blew it." *Wired*. https://www.wired.com/2007/02/yahoo-3/.

Voight, Joan. (1996, December 1). "Beyond the banner." *Wired*. https://www.wired.com/1996/12/esadvertising/.

Vos, Tim and Russell, Frank Michael. (2019). "Theorizing journalism's institutional relationships: An elaboration of gatekeeping theory." *Journalism Studies*, 20:16, pp. 2331–48.

Vrijenhoek, Sanne, Kaya, Mesut, Metoui, Nadia, Möller, Judith, Odijk, Daan and Helberger, Natali. (2021, March 14). "Recommenders with a mission: assessing diversity in news recommendations." In *Proceedings of the 2021 Conference on Human Information Interaction and Retrieval*, Canberra, Australia, pp. 173–83.

Vu, Hong Tien. (2014). "The online audience as gatekeeper: The influence of reader metrics on news editorial selection." *Journalism*, 15:8, pp. 1094–110.

Waldman, Steven. (2011). *The Information Needs of Communities: The Changing Media Landscape in a Broadband Age*. Washington, DC: Federal Communications Commission. https://www.fcc.gov/sites/default/files/the-information-needs-of-communities-report-july-2011.pdf.

Wagner, Kurt. (2016, June 29). "Facebook is cutting traffic to publishers in favour of user-generated content." *Vox*. https://www.vox.com/2016/6/29/12053800/facebook-news-feed-algorithm-change-publisher-traffic.

WAN. (2019, November 5). *World Press Trends 2019: The Balancing Act of Publishers*. Frankfurt: World Association of News Publishers. https://wan-ifra.org/2019/11/world-press-trends-2019-the-balancing-act-of-publishers/.

Wang, Shan. (2017, September 15). "BuzzFeed's strategy for getting content to do well on all platforms? Adaption and a lot of A/B testing." *NiemanLab*. https://www.niemanlab.org/2017/09/buzzfeeds-strategy-for-getting-content-to-do-well-on-all-platforms-adaptation-and-a-lot-of-ab-testing/.

Wang, Qun. (2020). "Differentiation and de-differentiation: The evolving power dynamics between news industry and tech industry." *Journalism & Mass Communication Quarterly*, 97:2, pp. 509–27.

Ward, Miranda. (2021, July 8). "oOh!Media puts Junkee Media on the market." *Australian Financial Review*. https://www.afr.com/companies/media-and-marketing/ooh-media-to-sell-off-junkee-media-20210708-p58821/.

Warrell, Helen, Ghazan, Guy and Peel, Michael. (2020, February 16). "Mark Zuckerberg admits Facebook was slow on Russian disinformation." *Financial Times*. https://www.ft.com/content/5b42ef72-501e-11ea-8841-482eed0038b1.

Warren, Elizabeth. (2019, March 8). "Here's how we can break up Big Tech." *Medium*. https://medium.com/@teamwarren/heres-how-we-can-break-up-big-tech-9ad9e0da324c.

Waterson, Jim. (2019, May 1). "Guardian breaks even helped by success of supporter strategy." *The Guardian*. https://www.theguardian.com/media/2019/may/01/guardian-breaks-even-helped-by-success-of-supporter-strategy.

Waterson, Jim. (2020, December 1). "Facebook to pay UK media millions to license news stories." *The Guardian*. https://www.theguardian.com/technology/2020/dec/01/facebook-to-pay-uk-media-millions-to-licence-news-stories.

Watson, Imogen. (2020, March 5). "Tackling LGBT+ blocklists: Publishers and agencies rally against digital censorship." *The Drum*. https://www.thedrum.com/news/2020/03/05/tackling-lgbt-blocklists-publishers-and-agencies-rally-against-digital-censorship.

WebWise. (2012). "What are cookies?." *BBC*. http://www.bbc.co.uk/webwise/guides/about-cookies [link no longer available].

Weinberger, Matt. (2016, November 11). "Mark Zuckerberg says the idea that fake news on Facebook swung the election is 'pretty crazy'." *Business Insider Australia*. https://www.businessinsider.com.au/mark-zuckerberg-facebook-donald-trump-2016-11.

Weiss, Brennan. (2017, November 2). "From 'crazy' to 'regret' – Here's how Facebook's positions on Russian interference evolved over time." *Business Insider*. https://www.businessinsider.com/facebook-changing-statements-russian-meddling-2016-election-2017-11?r=AU&IR=T#november-10-2016-mark-zuckerberg-dismisses-russias-influence-1.

Welch, Chris. (2018, October 17). "Facebook may have knowingly inflated its video metrics for over a year." *The Verge*. https://www.theverge.com/2018/10/17/17989712/facebook-inaccurate-video-metrics-inflation-lawsuit.

Whitehead, Robert. (2019). "How to decode the publisher-platform relationship." International News Media Association. https://www.inma.org/report/how-to-decode-the-publisher-platform-relationship.

Whitehead, Robert. (2021, 16 March). "What Facebook's big deals in Australia tell us." International News Media Association. https://www.inma.org/blogs/Digital-Platform-Initiative/post.cfm/what-facebook-s-big-deals-in-australia-tell-us.

Wilding, Derek. (2021). "Regulating news and disinformation on digital platforms: Self-regulation or prevarication?." *Journal of Telecommunications and the Digital Economy*, 9:2, pp. 11–46.

Wilkinson, Earl. (2016, n.d.). "News Media Outlook 2016: The dimension behind the façade." International News Media Association. https://www.inma.org/report/news-media-outlook-the-dimension-behind-the-fa-ade.

Willard, Laura. (2015, July 7). "Semicolon tattoo: Here's what it means and why it matters." *Up Worthy*. https://www.upworthy.com/have-you-seen-anyone-with-a-semicolon-tattoo-heres-what-its-about.

Willens, Max. (2018a, November 30). "Pivoting to nowhere: How Mic ran out of radical makeovers." *Digiday*. https://digiday.com/media/mic-transformations-pivoting-nowhere/.

Willens, Max. (2018b, December 3). "Why 'news for millennials' media plays never panned out." *Digiday*. https://digiday.com/media/mic-news-millennials-media-plays/.

Willens, Max. (2019, February 25). "'Hard to back out': Publishers grow frustrated by the lack of revenue from Apple News." *Digiday*. https://digiday.com/media/hard-to-back-out-publishers-remain-frustrated-by-apple-news-monetization/.

Willens, Max. (2020a, January 9). "As publishers pivot to paid, newsrooms focus more on sales." *DigiDay*. https://digiday.com/media/publishers-pivot-paid-newsrooms-focus-sales/.

Willens, Max. (2020b, March 9). "Coronavirus climbs up keyword block lists, squeezing news publishers' programmatic revenues." *DigiDay*. https://digiday.com/media/coronavirus-climbs-keyword-block-lists-squeezing-news-publishers-programmatic-revenues/.

Wilson, Cameron. (2020, November 6). "'In digital, the right-wing material is 24/7': How Sky News quietly became Australia's biggest news channel on social media." *Business Insider Australia*. https://www.businessinsider.com.au/sky-news-australia-biggest-social-media-channel-culture-wars-2020-11.

Wilson, Cameron. (2022, December 7). "'Complete chaos': how an ex-Fox exec and investor buying Junkee became a shambles." https://www.crikey.com.au/2022/12/07/junkee-racat-group-piers-grove-david-haslingden/

Winseck, Dwayne. (2020). "Vampire squids, 'the broken internet' and platform regulation." *Journal of Digital Media & Policy*, 11:3, pp. 241–82.

Wolde, Harro Ten and Auchard, Eric. (2014, November 6). "Germany's top publisher bows to Google in news licensing row." *Reuters*. https://www.reuters.com/article/us-google-axel-sprngr-idUSKBN0IP1YT20141105.

Wolfe, Natalie. (2019, January 29). "BuzzFeed gives entire news team redundancy letters in international effort to cut costs." *News.com.au*. https://www.news.com.au/finance/business/media/buzzfeed-gives-entire-news-team-redundancy-letters-in-international-effort-to-cut-costs/news-story/3e0834f4b7ff027beadcf80eb810bb9f.

The Wall Street Journal. (2020, n.d.). "The content review: A guide to great journalism." *The Wall Street Journal.* https://www.documentcloud.org/documents/7275714-Wsj-Report.html.

Wu, Ethan and Winicov, Rachel. (2020, June 16). "Advertisers now have a new keyword concern: 'Protest.'" *Adweek.* https://www.adweek.com/programmatic/advertisers-keyword-blocking-protest/.

Zamith, Rodrigo. (2018). "Quantified audiences in news production: A synthesis and research agenda." *Digital Journalism*, 6:4, pp. 418–35.

Zenith. (2019, n.d.). "Global intelligence: Data & insights for the new age of communication." https://www.zenithmedia.com/wp-content/uploads/2019/12/Global-Intelligence-10.pdf.

Index

Milton Keynes UK
Ingram Content Group UK Ltd.
UKHW052138200923
429073UK00004B/24